When We Were Rangers

Frances Reneau

Thank you to:
David Sanguinetti
Cindy Roessler
Loro Paterson
Stan Hooper
Dennis Danielson
Alice Cummings
Annette Coleman
Mark Casaretto
Kerry Carlson
For their stories

Thank you to:
Deane Little
For the cover photograph

Thank you to:
Becky Bach
Stacy Fredericksen
Emma Shelton
Rosi Weller
For editing, proofreading, and formatting

Thank you to:
Carol and Henk Pechler
For getting me started, keeping me going, and seeing me through

Table of Contents

Introduction

"Guess what; I can't believe it, but I got the job!" I exalted to my friends and family. I'd paused only briefly to bask in the glorious glow of success before phoning everyone to share in my excitement. The long-delayed silver platter of security and happiness had finally landed in my lap. The telephone call from the Midpeninsula Regional Open Space District offering me the full-time, permanent, benefitted ranger position was one of the most memorable and life-changing events of my life. The transformation it presaged ranks right up there with opening the envelope to find I'd been admitted to my first-choice college, or the phone call telling me that I was indeed expecting a child. No longer would I be floundering around working temporary, part-time, and volunteer jobs, and trying to figure out what to do with myself. Quite suddenly I was whisked off to ranger training academy and committed to mastering a new job and a new way of life.

All that was 16 way-too-short years ago, wonderful years of exploration and adventure, but also sad years of loss and change, 16 years of working a job with no idea of what crazy incident might happen next. A golden haze of nostalgia is already settling over the earliest days, gilding the good times and glossing over the bad. The stories I've told and retold are already feeling distant and dated, as though from the life of a familiar but younger woman. My "short-timer" career wasn't nearly long enough, but when is there ever enough of a good thing? Doesn't one always want more? I left this job with one huge regret, not that I didn't stay longer, but that I didn't start sooner. Why couldn't my "silver-platter job" have arrived when I was 28 instead of 43? I regret missing out on 15 years of early District life that I would happily have been a full part of. At least I was a part-time seasonal OST (Open Space Technician) for five of those earlier years. I was also one of the first volunteers for the nascent outdoor education program working with school kids at the Daniels Nature Center in Skyline Ridge Open Space Preserve. I'm sure it was these volunteer and part-time jobs that helped me wedge my foot in the door when applying for the full-time ranger position. They were fun jobs and interesting in their own ways, but only as a District ranger did I finally find my calling. I envy those fortunate men and women who spent their entire working lives nestled in that sweet spot, safely ensconced in District employment.

~~~

No sooner had the words, "I'm retiring at the end of the year," exited my mouth, than I wished them back in. What was I thinking? Why was I doing this? Whenever I looked out over the wide, green, San Mateo Coast toward the Pacific Ocean or stood in the sultry, silent darkness under the stars on Skyline Ridge, a little wave of sadness would well up inside me. It swelled bigger and bigger over the next several weeks as the realization sunk in that I would never again be out here doing this. The big, sad wave crested and broke over me: how could I possibly give this up forever?   Slowly it receded, leaving behind an ephemeral gleam of anticipation.   Another big life change was upon me, another search for sanctuary, for meaning and belonging.

Perhaps to make myself feel better, to provide justification for leaving, I started to make a mental tally of all the ludicrous, tedious, frustrating, and boring ranger tasks that I would no longer have to put up with: the time-sucking weekly hand delivery of citations to the courts, the "weekly update" summary of citations, warnings, and note-worthy incidents, the quarterly vehicle inspections, the bi-weekly electronic timecards, the mandatory PowerPoint trainings, and the inane video conference meetings all made my list.   Yes, I'd miss being a ranger, but a lot of what I'd miss was already missing from the job. The old time ranger job had left with the old time rangers. It was a new age in ranger-dom, and I had come to feel like an old has-been.

~~~

In 2022, the Midpeninsula Regional Open Space District will be 50 years old. We will proudly celebrate our founding, our successful growth, and our truly amazing land conservation achievements. In terms of acreage acquired, the District has not just caught up with but far surpassed the San Mateo, Santa Clara, and Santa Cruz County Park systems, an especially impressive achievement given our comparative youth.   At 63,500 acres, Midpen is currently the largest landowner in the Santa Cruz Mountains, and still growing. At the very time that the federal government is trying to jettison and un-protect many national monuments, and the county and state systems are loathe to take on any additional acreage, Midpen's dedication to land preservation powers on, as strong as the day our original mission statement was adopted in 1972.

Mission Statement of The Midpeninsula Regional Open Space District: To acquire and preserve a regional greenbelt of open space land in perpetuity, protect and restore the natural environment, and provide opportunities for ecologically sensitive enjoyment and education.

Midpen might just be the biggest, wealthiest, most powerful land management agency that no-one has ever heard of. As a ranger I was constantly being asked, "So, do you work for the state parks?" No, and not for any of the three local county park systems, nor for the feds, nor was I a "rent-a-ranger," working for the local private ranger contractor. Midpen is a unique, local public agency on the San Francisco Peninsula, supported by local property taxes, and governed by a seven-member Board of Directors. As of 2018, there are about 70 field employees—rangers, OSTs (Open Space Technicians), seasonals, supervisors, and resource management folks—and an equal number of planners, analysts, administrative assistants, IT people, lawyers, and managers. The Board meets on the second and fourth Wednesdays of every month and oversees an annual budget of about $70 million. Their decisions affect the experience of thousands of visitors and District neighbors, and the disposition of millions of dollars in contracts, salaries, and land acquisitions. If your property is within the District boundaries, you have been paying to help support all of this and you probably didn't even know it. The preserves are open to all, for free, 365 days a year.

As a mere 50-year-old, Midpen is now passing through adolescence and is still figuring out what kind of an agency it wants to be. Its founders were ardent purists working in the heat of the environmental movement of the 60's and 70's, with the federal Wilderness Act of 1964 still ringing in their ears. They believed that undeveloped land had greatest value in its most raw, wild, "virgin" state, and not just in its potential for human exploitation, be it recreation or agriculture.

The founders' focus on purity came to an end in 2004, with the inception of the Coastal Protection Program. A compromise of our original mission was needed in order to save the verdant coastal hillsides south of Half Moon Bay from real estate development. Agriculture, mostly in the form of cattle grazing, had to be accommodated under the umbrella of District protection. Perhaps in an effort to shield our original "virgin" lands from the political power of the newly admitted grazing advocates, the District created a separate Coastal Mission Statement.

Coastal Mission Statement: To acquire and preserve in perpetuity open space land and agricultural land of regional significance, protect and restore the natural environment, preserve rural character, encourage viable agricultural use of land resources, and provide opportunities for ecologically sensitive public enjoyment and education.

The other big impetus for change in District land management practices came from the other side of the hill. Crowds of nature-starved visitors swarmed into the Santa Cruz Mountains from the urban metropolis of Silicon Valley every weekend and prompted reconsideration of what services, amenities, and regulations were needed to keep pace with population growth and new technology. The Americans with Disabilities Act forced the District to install gates and stiles that would admit wheelchairs, but would also impede motorcycle access, and the District had to modify office entrances and public restrooms. Ubiquitous new inventions such as cell phones, satellite-driven GPS devices, Google maps, E-bikes, drones, automatic parking lot gates, and motion-activated cameras have greatly impacted the preserves, and the jobs of District field employees. These new devices have relentlessly chipped away at the remote character of District lands. Radios now reach deep valleys once out of range; satellites map preserve boundaries to within a few inches; pedal-assist bicycles (still prohibited in Midpen, but for how long?) allow even physically unfit folks access far from their vehicles. Drones fly overhead and hidden cameras silently monitor both wildlife and scofflaws. There are no blank spots left on the map, so what good are those wonderful old thousand freedoms?

As we District retirees look back on our working lives, nostalgia surfaces, especially for those devoted employees who stood by the agency for 20 or 30 years. We remember the excitement of being hired into this young and forming agency, the satisfaction of seeing lands protected and trails built, the security of camaraderie, taking part in the building and shaping of something special and different. Of course, we are also looking back at our own younger selves, our personal aspirations and passions. It is hard to let go, to trust that the rangers, OSTs, equipment operators, supervisors, and resource specialists of the future will be equally dedicated to the District's mission and that our little agency, to which we have given the best parts of our lives, will continue to thrive. Our far-sighted District founders can end their days knowing that their life work has succeeded beyond their wildest dreams. District retirees can rest assured that our beloved lands will be cared for and cherished by generations to come.

~~~

Until the mid-1980's the Operations Department was just the rangers, as there was no such thing as an OST (Open Space Technician.) Rangers were responsible for all fieldwork, from firefighting, medical response and law enforcement to weed abatement, trail construction and restroom cleaning. The OSTs, or "crew," gradually evolved to take on the burgeoning task of trail building demanded by the growing land bank. With the additional funding from the passage of Measure AA in 2014, the number of field employees mushroomed and Operations was finally split into two departments. The two new departments, Visitor Services and Land and Facilities, represent the final parting of the ways between maintenance and patrol. The 70-some field employees, the rangers and OSTs, now barely all fit into the District's largest meeting room at the Foothills Annex at Rancho San Antonio. Their jobs have diversified and specialized to the point that one group's particular problems and concerns are of no great interest to the other. OSTs now have even less contact with visitors and volunteers, and rangers do even less maintenance. Rangers and OSTs nowadays rarely work together, and they certainly have little occasion to work cooperatively with employees from one of the other departments in the main office.

I hardly even got to know the newest crop of rangers hired just before I retired. I barely saw them once they finished their training rotation through the SFO (Skyline Field Office), and disappeared down to either FFO (Foothills Field Office) or SAO (South Area Outpost.) By contrast, the field employees of yesteryear all knew each other well. They worked together on projects and incidents; they saw each other every day. Fewer people at meetings meant that everybody had a better seat at the table, a chance to be heard and to feel like their opinions counted. Those lucky first rangers built this agency together; they also built a shared culture.

That intimate culture is long gone, a casualty of the District's tremendous success. That tiny upstart agency is long gone, too. Some of the original rangers even watched it happen right under their noses. The many, little, seemingly insignificant changes slowly piled up. Brown uniform pants changed to green ones. The original "dope leaf" logo changed, and then changed again. Dispatch went from "Control 12" (Santa Clara County Parks) to "Mt. View" (City of Mountain View Police and Fire.)

Computers appeared, first in the offices and then in the patrol trucks. Volunteer programs were created to do interpretive hikes and environmental education and to assist with resource management and trail patrol. With a view to the eventual opening of the summit of Mt Umunhum (in 2017), the South Area Outpost was created, operating out of an old house off Hicks Road. The radio system was upgraded from analog to digital around 2010, and crew acquired their own frequencies, separate from those used by patrol. The AO (Administrative Office, also called the main office) moved from Distal Circle in Los Altos to the Old Mill Shopping Center on San Antonio Road, and then moved back again, expanding every time. By 2020 there will be yet another new AO, an enormous three-story building fronting on El Camino Real in Los Altos. All this growth and change must have felt exciting and satisfying to the founders and early employees, until the day it dawned on them that they were anachronisms, and that no one else remembered how things used to be. They must have wondered, "What happened to my little agency? Where did it go?"

I mostly missed out on those early days, arriving just a bit too late. I only got to hear little snippets about how great things used to be. Those longtime early field employees, now mostly retired or moved on to supervisory or administrative positions, reminiscing about "the good old days," seemed always to be describing a much wilder and woolier place than the policy-bound office or the sanitized, carefully planned and managed preserves where I recently patrolled. I'm envious of the freedom they had to explore, investigate, and get to know both the wild land and some of the wild and crazy characters who still lived out there.

~~~

My purpose in conducting and transcribing these interviews with my former co-workers was simply to record a little slice of life, a glimpse of the culture of the District in its earlier years. I was curious about how the working lives of previous field employees compared to my own experience. Maybe 30 years from now some future ranger will come knocking on my door, seeking my reminiscences.

In the pages that follow, transcribed interviews with retirees alternate with my own short tales and essays. Italicized text in my pieces is writing taken directly from my old work journals. In order to honor the working lives of these real people--the rangers, supervisors, technicians, biologists and others whose names appear in the transcriptions--I have kept their real names, except for a few pseudonyms and obfuscations. Although many of those interviewed talked about some of their frustrations with various restrictive policies, they all clearly valued their jobs and were proud to have been part of District history. They didn't want the District's image or reputation sullied, and were at times reluctant to discuss controversial topics. At the same time, these conflicts of opinion about land use (Should the District protect agricultural land?) and trail use (Should we allow bikes or even e-bikes?) and amenities (Should we provide garbage cans?) often resulted in changes to District policy and thus changed the course of District history. Conflicts also make for good stories. Certainly not all of my ex-workmates agree with my personal opinions, as expressed in the short vignettes between interviews. I didn't always agree with everything they had to say either. Most of all, it was clear that we all cared very much about the District's future and the future of the land it protects. Long live the District!

Photo by Carolyn Caddes. Used by permission of MROSD

David Sanguinetti
Ranger, Supervising Ranger, Area
Superintendent, and Operations Manager

I was born in Stockton, CA, where my family lived until I was twelve, but we spent all our summers, vacations and holidays at our cottage in Capitola, because my Dad didn't like Stockton. My mother's side of the family came to Stockton from Ohio by wagon train in the 1860's and my father's side came from Genoa, Italy. My parents eventually bought a restaurant in

Soquel, CA, and we moved permanently to the Live Oak Area of Santa Cruz County, where I attended middle school through junior college.

Growing up, I was always attracted to the outdoors, primarily the mountains. My parents had no interest in in hiking, camping, or exploring, so I only got outdoors by going off on my own. We seldom vacationed anywhere other than our cottage, initially because we couldn't afford it, and then, as restaurant owners, because they didn't have the time. Essentially, they were married to the restaurant. I ended up working there from between ages 13 and 18, and always considered it forced labor, but it did give me a strong work ethic, and money to buy nice cars. Unfortunately, my Dad passed away unexpectedly when I was 21 and suddenly my brother and I were in a position to take over the restaurant, but we had no interest in it.

My passions in high school were fast cars, motorcycles, and exploring the mountains. Soquel High School is right at the base of the Santa Cruz Mountains, and after school I would drive up Old San Jose Road and explore all the back roads. They were like magnets for me. When I was 15 1/2, my father helped me buy a motorcycle, even though it was a bone of contention between my parents. My dad shared my love of vehicles, and lived vicariously through me. I promised my mother I wouldn't ride my motorcycle on the city streets, only on mountain fire roads. In those days, it was more acceptable to drive private mountain roads, which usually weren't locked, as long as you were respectful. To avoid problems, I would hide my motorcycle in the bushes and walk, sometimes having to hide myself. I met all kinds of interesting characters. After the Summer of '67, the Santa Cruz Mountains were full of hippie communes and makeshift homes. I looked out of place, with the conservative clothes and short hair my mother insisted on. In reality, I was more of an adventurer and risk taker. I liked meeting these different people, hiking to remote locations, and meditating in the beauty of the mountains. I also liked exploring historical sites, both European and Native.

On one trip, I came across this house made of tree branches and logs. It had a front porch with some chairs made with branches. The house itself was made of logs, with clear sheets of plastic for windows. Sitting on the porch was this old bearded guy with his dog. He looked like Rumplestiltskin. He had no shoes, and the bottoms of his feet were like leather. He welcomed me like he had been expecting me and we talked for about an hour. He told me he had been living there for over 30 years. He only went into town every six months for supplies, surviving by hunting, gathering, and gardening, and would go bivouac with his dog for a couple weeks at a time. I took this all with a grain of salt. Some of it was probably true, but embellished, or even made up, like his stories of running across bears. Bears haven't been seen in the Santa Cruz Mountains since the 1930's. As a 16-year old high school student, I found him fascinating. He told me about some beautiful spots, and encouraged me to research and visit abandoned historic communities.

One day I rode up Old San Jose Road and over into what is now Nisene Marks State Park. I found a commune called Buzzard Lagoon. These three school buses were half-buried into a hillside with a clan of hippies living in them. They found my clothes and hair very interesting too. They, of course, wore long hair and very little else, or nothing!

One time when I went searching for an abandoned railroad and Chinese labor camp that were associated with an old limekiln, I was pulled over by an old-timer state park ranger who had started his career in the early 1950's. He was initially not happy because I was on a motorcycle on a closed state park road. He told me to get out. Then, a few weeks later, he pulled in to fill up his patrol truck at the service station where I was working! I reminded him of our previous contact, profusely pleaded my ignorance, and apologized. I told him I had gone in there to find the Chinese labor camp and the abandoned narrow gauge railroad. From then on, he was a regular customer, and he shared the history of the area that would become Nisene Marks State Park. His most provocative claim was that a steam engine was buried in a side canyon above the old limekilns. He let me explore the Chinese camp as well as follow the old rail route up the canyons above the kilns, as long as I did not bring my motorcycle into the parkland. I was never able to locate the buried steam engine, but did found several wooden trestles, lots of abandoned ties, and some sections of rail.

I started going to the Bookshop Santa Cruz, and spent many hours in the Santa Cruz Mountain history section, reading about abandoned railway tunnels and resorts like Wrights Station. Bookshop Santa Cruz allowed you to read books without buying them, in the hopes you would buy their drinks and snacks. They still operate pretty much that way today. I found all the old railway tunnel entrances I learned about. They were all blown up during World War II to prevent the Japanese from using them as part of an invasion. Originally, the tracks serviced a tourist connection all the way from San Francisco, through Los Gatos, to Santa Cruz. Wrights Station was near the summit of the route, and San Franciscans would come spend the weekend at a fancy mountain resort. All that remains today is the rail path, a concrete trestle, a tunnel opening, and an abandoned swimming pool. I also found another old Chinese labor camp along Fall Creek in Felton. These places were removed in the late 1960's as public nuisances, and even back then they were closed to the public, but while exploring I listened for vehicles and hid in the bushes, sweating, worried that the rangers would catch me.

I had trouble staying focused in school. As seniors we took aptitude tests that showed I should work in business, so I entered Cabrillo Junior College as a business major. I quit working at my parents' restaurant and became a full-time service station attendant. I loved cars and wanted to learn how to work on them myself. Service station work turned into an eight-year profession. After three semesters in business administration, I ended up on academic probation, and left college. Then a couple of life-changing experiences helped redirect me. First, I spent the summer after high school on a college course traveling through Europe studying its history. Second, my friend Bill Walker and I went camping in Yosemite for a weekend, my first camping experience. I remember when we came out of the Wawona Tunnel and saw the valley for the first time. I was stunned, and just sat on the wall in the pullout for the longest time.

A funny story from our Yosemite trip was my being run over by a bear! We were sleeping on the ground around the fire, in our sleeping bags. All of a sudden, in the middle of the night, I woke up to a woman in the next site screaming, "George, there's a bear!" I looked over to my friend Bill, who had already jumped up, still in his sleeping bag, and was sitting on the top of his car. I saw a big black shape barreling toward me, and I curled up in my bag just in time for a full-grown black bear to run me over! The ranger chewed out our neighbors for leaving out their cooler, which now had its lid ripped off. It was at that moment, and that night at a campfire talk, that I realized I could be a ranger too. This became my new career goal.

I dropped out of Cabrillo just in time to avoid suspension from the California Junior College System for three years. I went back to work fulltime at the service station. Eighteen months later, the owner sold the service station. The timing was perfect. I spent the summer of 1973 again traveling through Europe, now with a friend, by car, staying in campgrounds. We saw it as a rite of passage, spending time with young people from all around the world. It is a tradition for European youth to take time off to learn about their rich history and culture. Very few American youth were able to do this.

After my summer in Europe, I got serious about college, and I re-enrolled in Cabrillo College as a science major, with my new goal of becoming a park ranger. I had to take three semesters of high school math and science before qualifying to transfer to a four-year university. I really didn't understand much about the ranger job or how to get there. I just started applying to forestry schools and was accepted into Oregon State. In the summer 1976, I traveled to Oregon State for their orientation and immediately became concerned about their focus on timber production. My passion was for interacting with people and getting them excited about visiting and protecting nature.

Just a couple weeks before the start of the fall semester, a friend talked me into going with him to look at Chico State University. He still needed to find an apartment for the upcoming school year. I immediately applied and so we spent the day looking for an apartment. I was accepted as a biology major with a minor in history.

At the end of my first semester there, I explained to the dean my goal of become a ranger. For that reason I wanted to transfer into the natural science major. He suggested their park management major, but I figured I would learn park management on the job. He explained that my future options would be much greater if I got my BA in biology, but begrudgingly agreed to add me to the natural science program. He also specified that my senior thesis topic would be a justification for keeping the (to the dean's mind) useless BA in natural science at Chico State!

In the spring of 1978, I finished my eight-year college career and graduated. I immediately applied for a job with the California State Parks at the Pajaro Coast District office in Aptos. Ranger Bob Culbertson told me that even though I was qualified for a seasonal park aide job, due to affirmative action and military service preferences, no positions were now open to me.

He did encourage me to check back in case someone else did not work out. After a couple of weeks, he told me that a temporary position for a radio dispatcher had become available. At that time, professional dispatchers just kept track of the patrol rangers during the busy summer months and spring break. It just so happened that I had worked evenings as a dispatcher for the Aptos Fire Department in addition to my service station job while at Cabrillo. I'd spent three or four nights a week studying or sleeping on a cot next to the fire radio, dispatching evening fire and first aid calls. With that prior experience, Ranger Culbertson was able to justify hiring me over the normal restrictions. It wasn't my ideal placement, considering I would work in a windowless bunker at the back of the State Parks main office, but I wasn't complaining. I'd got my foot in the door.

Seasonal employees got only six months. Three of them were taken up by the dispatch job. The remaining three I could work in the field. I came on dispatch every weekday evening from 5:00 to 11:00 PM, and again, on weekends and holidays, from 7:00 to 12:00 AM. The admin assistants dispatched during normal business hours. The tracking system was pretty primitive. We had a big pegboard with cardboard key rings with the rangers' call numbers on them. I'd move the rings around to monitor their whereabouts. I also relayed mutual aid requests by telephone from our rangers to other agencies because radio communications between agency personnel was allowed only on our own licensed frequency. And, of course, when an outside agency needed our rangers to respond, they would have to phone me, and I'd radio to our field rangers. I could scan other agencies' radio traffic and did so to insure accurate information was being relayed.

After my first season at dispatch, I got out into the field, working the entrance stations at Seacliff and New Brighton State Beaches. On weekends, I would volunteer after my regular work shift to ride along with different rangers on night patrol. It was not unusual for me to be in uniform 16 hours a day on Fridays, Saturdays, and Sundays, learning the challenges of being a full time ranger.

During my second summer in dispatch, I was assigned to Natural Bridges State Park, where Ranger Darryl Geroy became my mentor. We'd made friends my previous season during those evening ride-alongs. He was a true generalist ranger of the bygone days, as park management was by then already moving toward specialization. Rangers were already armed and were becoming more like park police, while park maintenance was handled more and more exclusively by maintenance employees. But Darryl's passions were visitor education, park maintenance, and construction. He did also have a good feel for what was necessary in enforcement situations. During the week, he would put his service belt and firearm in a locker, load his truck with supplies, and take on maintenance projects that otherwise were neglected. I spent very little time sitting in the kiosk that fall! Darryl and I would identify a project and drive into the New Brighton maintenance yard with a big box of doughnuts. They would let us take on projects not normally entrusted to rangers. Not everyone appreciated this. The rule of thumb was, rangers did not go to the maintenance yard, and maintenance workers did not go into the ranger office. Darryl taught me the way to overcome these stereotypes, to be accepted and comfortable in both places.

This served me well when I eventually became a supervisor and manager with the District. While working on projects and going on patrol, I had numerous discussions with Darryl about the parks' cultural differences and communication problems. He argued that we were all important and necessary to the success of the park. I agreed with him, and carried this forward in my career. I always expected my teams to cooperate with every department in our agency, and I fought to keep maintenance and patrol together in the same office, insisting they interact and work togeher. It was my idea to call them "field offices," not ranger offices or maintenance offices.

I continued to volunteer in the evenings at Natural Bridges, almost exclusively with Darryl. I was allowed to make contacts and participate in campground confrontations, definitely pushing the limits of risk management! I was just happy for the experience. He taught me not to take visitor reactions personally, to be self-deprecating, and respectful, escalating authority only in response to resistance. Again, this philosophy has stayed with me throughout my career. I always favored interpersonal trainings and tried to practice those skills as a manager. I became ever more confident about becoming a park ranger, preferably as a "lifer" for California State Parks.

I took the tests, went to the interviews in San Francisco and Sacramento, but could never score high enough on the hiring list. State Parks used the "rule of three." When there was an opening, current employees could apply for transfer. If not filled internally, only the top three external candidates were an interview. And the list, with over 300 applicants, would only last for a year, before applicants would have to start all over again. The top 30 candidates on the list were sent to the "Ranger Peace Officer Standards and Training Class," to become badged peace officers. Try as I might, I was never able to score high enough.

I was getting discouraged and thought, "how can I improve my odds?" So I applied for a State Parks intermittent ranger position. These positions weren't as hard to get because they were part time, plus applicants had to pay for their own training. Then you could transfer to a full time position later. I enrolled, on my own dime, in the POST (Peace Officer Standards and Training) Police Academy at Gavilan Junior College in Gilroy. I was one of the first two park ranger candidates ever to attend the academy. This turned out to be a great adventure and as close as I ever got to being in the military. They taught teamwork by breaking down your sense of individuality, then building everyone back up as a team. Two weeks into my ten-week training, I had gone from stress and dread to total comfort and commitment, and I learned a lot about myself.

There were three personality types there: the "Puritans," people who had never knowingly done anything illegal and believe everyone they contacted had done something wrong; the "Wannabes," who had insecurities and used the badge to pump up their self confidence; and the "Envelope Pushers," the folks who had done things they knew were wrong, and had learned from them. I related best with the third group. Empathy for the violator, and the trouble they'd gotten themselves into, is important because this contact may end up affecting the rest of this violator's life. I could easily have become a police officer or sheriff deputy. Fortunately, the one police job I applied for took six months before an offer came, and a ranger job offer intervened.

I returned to Natural Bridges State Park after the academy and continued my work with Darryl. I had taken the State Parks maintenance worker test the previous summer and had ranked well up on that list. After two years of work for the state, I could apply for a lateral to the ranger job. So then San Simeon State Park contacted me and invited me for a maintenance worker interview and a behind-the-scenes tour of Hearst Castle! And then the Capitola Police Department contacted me to ask if I was still interested in becoming a police officer! Just a few days after that, I was contacted by this little-known agency, the Midpeninsula Regional Open Space District (MROSD). Six months earlier, I had lost out to Bob McKibben for the first MROSD ranger job. Now I had gone from famine to feast in a matter of days, and I suddenly had to make the biggest decision of my life. I decided I wanted to stick to my dream of becoming a ranger, not a police officer, and that the MROSD job in the Santa Cruz Mountains would likely get me to a State Parks job more quickly.

Photo by Carolyn Caddes. Used by permission of MROSD
Operations Supervisor Eric Mart

On March 30, 1980, both new ranger David Topley and I
reported for work at the District office for orientation. Our new
boss was Operations Supervisor Eric Mart, who had come from
the National Park Service. The District had created the ranger
position in 1975. Eric Mart's vision of the District was heavily
influenced by his experience with the National Parks. I always
appreciated his insistence on professional-looking uniforms and
vehicles. We wore khaki-colored peace officer shirts with a
District patch on the left shoulder, and brown (later green)
pants, Wesco work boots, and basketweave campaign hats. There
were no collar emblems or sleeve stripes to designate rank. Our
nametag included our title, with our full names, and our badge
was gold with the District logo in the center. Our belt and
equipment pouches were all polished basketweave brown

leather. All of this simulated the National Park and California State Park ranger uniforms.

Photo used by permission of MROSD
Rangers Warren Phillips and Matt Ken with new (1992) logo (left) and old logo (right) on patrol trucks.

Each ranger was assigned a white, 4-wheel-drive, 3/4 ton pickup with the District logo on each door and the back lift gate. Equipment storage was standardized so any ranger could find things easily. I took particular pride in the appearance of my truck, often spending the afternoon in a District parking lot greeting visitors while washing, waxing, and organizing it. We were trained and certified in law enforcement, fire suppression, CPR, first aid, and park maintenance. During the fire season, each vehicle carried a 100-gallon pumper with hose reel. I deeply embraced these high levels of professional appearance and standardized equipment.

Originally, per Eric's plan, there would be nine rangers, in three teams of three. The teams rotated every three months, two teams on patrol, and one on maintenance. Each team had one lead ranger and two line rangers. Of the two teams assigned to patrol, one would have Monday-Tuesdays off, and the other Wednesday-Thursdays off. The third team, assigned to maintenance, had Saturday-Sunday off. This plan required a generalist ranger, such as historically had been the case with State and National Parks.

Unfortunately, before this program was completely established, Eric left, in late 1981, to start a private ranger service business we all called "rent a ranger." We, the rangers Eric hired, always called ourselves the "original 8."-- Jim Boland, John Escobar, Dave Camp, Wendy Lieber, Dennis Danielson, Bob McKibben, David Topley, and myself. Joan Ferguson was hired to replace Wendy Lieber, who left to join State Parks. This group developed a bond that I had never experienced before or since. Most of us still remain in contact. We pioneered the District ranger position. It was a special time for all of us. The idea of creating a special, single-purpose district has proven to be a very successful means of public park management.

My legendary nickname, Sango, actually dates back to my high school years when Sanguinetti seemed way too long to my friends. When I joined the District, there were a few too many Davids, and Eric Mart asked me for something better than David S. to use on the schedule. I proudly embrace Sango to this day, and have always considered it a term of endearment.

I worked as a field ranger for my first seven years. This was all before the maintenance worker position was created. Rotating to maintenance was special, because then we got weekends off, and we worked on many amazing projects, such as building trails, retaining walls, and bridges, as well as operating heavy equipment. I was involved in the construction of all the bridges in Wildcat Canyon at Rancho. The original culverts were destroyed in the winter storms of 1982; they all ended up in a pile down near Deer Hollow Farm. There was a picture of me in *Open Space Magazine* standing in water up to my waist dressed in yellow rain gear and holding a bent shovel.

About five years after I started, The District began hiring ranger aides, which allowed us to work on more projects at once. With the departure of Eric, Jim Boland became operations supervisor, which opened up a lead ranger position. I had been a ranger for a year and a half and I saw this as an incredible opportunity. Of course, several of the other rangers had the same idea, and more experience, and David Topley got the job. Initially, I took this very hard, especially as I was now transferred to David Topley's team. So on top of losing out to the person I was hired with, I now had to leave my established work group and help David in his new position. I decided I would concentrate on helping him be a success, to focus on the positive, not the negative. I ended up developing an enduring friendship with David. Eventually I appreciated the additional five and a half years I was able to spend as a ranger. As a supervisor and manager, your role changes from working in the field to mostly working in the office.

Photo used by permission of Carolyn Caddes
Ranger David Topley

We had some work jargon such as "driving the bus" (driving the long stretches of public road between preserves), "making the loop" (driving Hwy. 280, Page Mill Road, Skyline Boulevard, and Hwy. 9, which together described a loop), and "going to the barn" (returning to the office). You had to enjoy spending time alone, and doing a job that was difficult to define by what you had accomplished for the day. Most of us enjoyed patrol, but looked forward to the three-month period when we got weekends off.

I have Eric to thank for introducing me to my wife, Michele. Eric would send me over to Foothills Park on various errands. The District had a good relationship with Palo Alto, and Eric had a good relationship with their Parks Supervisor, Jerry Lawrence. We shared purchases, like a log splitter, since it was an expensive item that was used just once a year to split wood for employee residences. The first time Eric assigned me to pick stuff up over there, he told me to ask for Michele. I then started stopping at the entrance station, which was convenient to pull through on the way up Page Mill Road, while driving the loop. After a while, we developed a friendship. At the end of August, Eric announced he was holding the annual End of the Season party, and asked if I could go by Foothills Park and invite Michele, since she knew all the MROSD rangers. Eric was trying to get us together! During our event around Eric's pool (since demolished) at his Rancho ranger residence, I asked Michele out for our first date.

The Skyline Field Office opened in 1984, which led to splitting the Ops Department into two areas, Foothills and Skyline. Staff was split, with each half to work exclusively in one or the other area. Most of us felt this was a sad loss. We all really enjoyed working throughout the District and knew we would miss the other half. So, John Escobar and his team went to the Skyline Area, and Dave Camp and David Topley's teams went to the Foothills Area. Then the rotation of lead rangers onto crew stopped, and instead, promoted them to supervising rangers. Then David Topley became Maintenance Supervising Ranger, District-wide, and the other two supervising rangers were put in charge of the two new areas--Dave Camp over Foothills and John Escobar over Skyline. Next came a brand new position, crew coordinating ranger, which would let David Topley spend more time in the office meeting with the planning department while working on more complex projects. I took on the crew-coordinating ranger position temporarily even though this wasn't a direction I ultimately wanted to head, as it would evolve into a non-badged maintenance supervisor. I saw it as an opportunity to develop my leadership and project management skills.

Rangers continued to rotate individually onto crew for three-month periods, even as their numbers gradually increased. As crew-coordinating ranger, I assigned projects and supervised the permanent ranger aides, now called Open Space Technicians (OSTs). I would frequently take on the more complex projects myself. I found the position both challenging and rewarding, stressing my leadership and organizing abilities. I credit this job, with the wonderful maintenance and construction training the District provided, with giving me the knowledge and confidence to take on many other sorts of projects. This certainly helped me when, in 1987, Supervising Ranger Dave Camp left to start his own business, and I got the supervising ranger job in the Foothills area.

Photo used by permission of Patrick Congdon
**Top Row: Patrick Congdon, David Topley, Lisa
Varney, John Escobar, Jim Boland, David Sanguinetti
Bottom Row: Bob McKibbin, Dave Camp, Joan
Ferguson, Dennis Danielson.**

Photo used by permission of Eric Mart
**From left to right: David Topley, Dennis Danielson,
Dave Camp, Jim Boland, Eric Mart, Bob McKibbin, and
Dave Sanguinetti. In front are John Escobar and Joan
Ferguson. Having a good time dressed as old time
rangers**

As the District grew, and added layers of leadership, it was difficult to maintain cohesiveness. And too, the days of learning on the job gave way to specialization and certification. No more jumping on a piece of equipment and practicing in the yard before heading out on a project. In 1987, just when I became a supervising ranger, the field staff voted to form a union, something the "original 8" had managed to avoid. It was a factor in why Eric Mart left. Although I did not support it, I realized it was inevitable. The general manger at the time felt the operations department was too much of a drain on acquisition, and too police-like. The result was below average pay and staffing, and slow property improvement. Field staff saw a union as a way to increase their power within the District, but there were both positive and negative results. It protected poor-performing employees and decreased the trust between line staff and management. But it resulted in fair pay and benefits that probably wouldn't have happened otherwise.

At the start of 1990, Jim Boland departed and John Escobar promoted to Operations Supervisor, opening up the Skyline supervising ranger position. I had dreamed of going to Skyline as it was an easier commute, and was reminiscent of the lands I had explored in my youth. However, I had become comfortable and established as Foothills supervising ranger. Going to Skyline would be a challenge. Some of the rangers on Skyline were apprehensive about my leadership style, and worried I would be too controlling; however, I decided to take the job. The Skyline team was more independent, perhaps due to the remoteness of the area compared to Foothills. I started to learn that I did not need to know everything; I just needed to utilize the expertise and knowledge all around me. My 18 years on Skyline were the most fun and rewarding of my career.

What I enjoyed most during my time with the District was sharing my passion for open space and wilderness with the public. It was my policy to never pass a trail user without acknowledging them. I loved promoting the District. I was blessed to be a part of it.

During the last seven years of my career, I served in upper management, reporting directly to the GM as the operations manager. I was in charge of 20 rangers, 20 maintenance workers, three resource specialists, a management analyst, a support services supervisor, and an administrative assistant, as well as 24 Open Space preserves, and 64,000 acres of property. When I finally decided to take it, I knew this job would require upwards of ten hours a day and include many weekend and evenings. Had I promoted to Ops Manager seven years earlier when I had the chance, I might have had the experience to replace the GM, Craig Britton, when he retired a year after I became Ops Manager. I have no regrets. If conditions had been different, I would have continued with the District until I was 65 years old, rather than retiring at 61

After about five years as a supervisor, I started to notice the struggle between staff and supervisors, union and management, rangers and maintenance workers, staff and neighbors, etc. Park management requires a lot of skills in how to deal with difficult relationships. I had wanted to work in parks because I loved the wild outdoors, but after some interpersonal trainings, my new passion became mastering effective communication. Ops Manager John Escobar agreed to send me to an annual management training given by the California Parks and Recreation Society at Lake Arrowhead. The seminar called Influencing Skills had a huge impact on me. It called for setting team agreements, and taught respectful confrontation techniques. With the support of GM Craig Britton, we were able to require the program District-wide. This lasted from 1996 until Craig's retirement in 2008. I saw an amazing change in District relationships and morale. Refreshers were scheduled every couple of years. I enthusiastically embraced influencing skills as a life-changing experience. The program thrived until Craig retired, and was not embraced by his successor, but survived in the Operations Department until the day I retired.

The Human Interaction training at the NTL Institute in Bethel, Maine had a similar impact on me. It allowed me to identify my demons and weaknesses and learn how to work with them. I learned that many of my fears about how others saw me were wrong. I tended to go into fight or flight mode over challenging interpersonal situations. I learned to not take things so personally, especially as a manager when I needed to correct a behavior or confront a mistake. I came back understanding that most people liked me, respected me, and valued my opinion. With this training, in combination with influencing skills, I learned to state what I needed and not take it personally if my listeners didn't like it.

I really enjoyed being part of the management team, where we set the course of the District. I looked forward to presenting to the Board of Directors on Wednesday evenings twice a month. I embraced the collaboration with other managers, was comfortable with myself, and calm under fire. It was exciting to work with other agencies during difficult emergency situations. I felt competent serving as the District's operations manager. However, the course of the District gradually changed directions. The last five years saw the sudden departure of almost all of our management team, and their replacements tended to be guarded. We no longer worked on issues together. By 2013, it was apparent that I would need to leave. Even though I felt I was still an asset to the District, I was advised to retire.

I like to say I grew up at the District. I started when we had eight preserves and about 8,000 acres, and we had reached 24 preserves and 64,000 acres by the time I retired. I started as a patrol ranger in an operations department consisting of nine employees, and left as the operations manager of a department of over 60 employees. I have no regrets, only tremendous appreciation for what the District gave me. I like to say that I would have done it for free. I saw myself working until at least 65, and volunteering until I was unable to go on. Unfortunately, life doesn't always work out the way you plan, and you have to adjust. All things considered, I am glad my forced retirement allowed me to be there for my family.

Significance Incidents

In 1979, I was working as an aide at Natural Bridges, driving a Jeep CJ, without doors, roof, or back seat. Just before closing I would drive through the picnic area parking lot, emptying garbage cans. I really had it down. I could pull up next to a garbage can, pull the lid off, pull the garbage bag up and tie it, toss it into the back, and put a fresh bag back in the can, all without getting out of the Jeep. One evening, I was hurrying along, running late, when I lifted the lid to the horrifying sight of the rear end of a skunk. Obviously the lid hadn't been on very tight, and the skunk was enjoying a smorgasbord of rib bones and corncobs. Before I could react, it sprayed me good. Unfortunately, I had to spend the rest of the shift enduring my reeking uniform. I never could wash it out of my shirt and pants and had to throw them away. It was an expensive, smelly lesson, as aides did not get a uniform allowance. From then on, I carried a broom handle to bang the can before going into my routine.

During my last season at Natural Bridges, I had the dubious honor of reporting the collapse of one of the scenic bridge formations. There's a famous picture of it with a Model T on top back in the 1920's. It was a stormy night, when I last saw it intact as I was closing up. When I returned at 7:00 AM to open the park, it was still windy and wet. When I went out onto the beach, I saw that the large bridge closest to the parking lot had collapsed into the ocean. I got on the radio and let the on-duty ranger know. We all spent the day dealing with the media and public who wanted to see the collapsed bridge. It was a sad day, thinking about the time Daryl and I had taken our chances walking out to install a sign closing the dangerous path over the bridge a year earlier.

When I came to the District, we had just added to a new property: Monte Bello Open Space Preserve. It had come with a hippy commune, "The Land." The property had belonged to an absentee landowner, who had allowed a group of squatters to take over a barn, and a spring water basin they called the "Sacred Cistern." They built platforms in the trees to sleep, to stay off the ground. They were afraid rattlesnakes would crawl into their sleeping bags. By the time I started, they had all been evicted, but they were still angry about it. Field staff had built a t-post and wire fence, "wildland fence," along the frontage of Page Mill Road, which these angry former squatters had cut down at least three times already, most recently about six months before. Some of the lingering squatters moved to a property near Long Ridge Preserve owned by Pacific Schools, a property later bought by Jikoji. Others moved to Struggle Mountain, a commune famous for its association with Joan Baez. My new coworkers had, of course, told me all about the trouble with the ex-residents tearing out the fence. We all knew who these guys were, but were unable to catch them in the act. We tried not to not to piss them off, to save ourselves more laborious fence-fixing. One evening, I contacted Bret, one of their leaders, out in Long Ridge Preserve after hours. Knowing it was Bret, and hoping to avoid retaliation, I let him off easy and just gave him a written warning, even though he had driven his truck onto District land, and was using a chainsaw to cut up a down tree for firewood!

Because I lived about an hour away from work, I would sleep at the office when I had back-to-back shifts. The next day I headed up Page Mill Road to start my early shift. As I came around the bend where The Land barn use to be, I felt my stomach drop. Every t-post was bent over and every strand of wire cut along the whole half-mile-long frontage! I became the least popular ranger on staff for the next couple of weeks—the amount of time it took to replace the fence. I was criticized for pissing off Bret and pulled from patrol to join maintenance and share the joy of replacing the fence. At least that was last time the fence came down.

Some time later, when Dave Camp and I were on our maintenance rotation, we filled in the Sacred Cistern with riprap so no one would fall in there and drown. We got more bad press for destroying their sacred water source. For many years, former The Land people continued to gather at Lone Oak Hill, even though the oak had fallen some time ago. It's about a half-mile down the Canyon Trail from the old barn site.

Photo by Frances Reneau
The Land's old bread oven in Monte Bello

A couple years later, Jikoji took over the Pacific School site and turned it into a Buddhist meditation center. The District agreed to a land swap, which gave Jikoji the stock pond in trade for the main access road, and also created a bypass road into Long Ridge Preserve. People used to park along Skyline in sneak in to swim in the pond, and our patrol trucks made a lot of dust driving through their compound, so the swap was to everyone's benefit. Many of us young guys had enjoyed driving through there though because Bret's girlfriend frequently walked around topless carrying a laundry basket on her head! The main access road, which we were to acquire, was lined with squatter structures occupied by former The Land people. We, however, had learned our lesson when clearing squatters out of Monte Bello, and required Jikoji to remove all occupants and structures before we would take possession. We made an arrangement with CDF (now CalFire) for a joint fire training, which eliminated the squatter dwellings.

One of my most traumatic and sobering incidents was finding a young man who had committed suicide at the Rancho entrance gate at the end of St. Joseph Avenue. I was driving to work at 7:15 AM and found a Mercedes Benz parked and blocking the gate into the preserve. I investigated, and found the car was idling. Then I noticed a hose running from the tailpipe in through the rear passenger window. In the driver's seat was a man laying back with his head and neck at a contorted angle, and I realized this was an attempted suicide. I went to the driver's side door, opened it, and tried to pull the man out onto the ground to start CPR, but he was completely stiff. Rigor mortis had set in. I was too late. I had to run approximately a half-mile to the office, to request a sheriff response for a suicide. I spent the rest of the morning waiting for the coroner before I drove to the office to begin my regular patrol shift. To this day, when I smell carbon monoxide, I see the face of that young man, and wonder what led him to take his life, and what his family felt when they were notified.

My next suicide was at Fremont Older Preserve in the parking lot. When I pulled in, I saw a vehicle parked in the far corner. I stopped and filled the map box, then noticed a man was leaning back in the driver's seat in this car. I walked over to contact him, thinking he must be asleep. As I walked up to the driver's door, I noticed a strange marble-sized bulge in the roof. I looked inside and saw a handgun in the man's lap. The man was dead. I realized he had put the gun in his mouth and the bullet had traveled up through his head and lodged in the headliner, pushing up the roof. I called for a sheriff response, and my boss Dave Camp came down from the Fremont Older ranger residence. We both stood by until the sheriff arrived.

Another memorable suicide, again during my time as Skyline Area Superintendent, we received a report from someone who's son had left a message he was going to commit suicide at "his favorite place." But where was that? We started by driving Skyline Boulevard looking for the subject's vehicle, and one of our units found it parked in the Purisima Creek parking lot. Rangers made a hasty search, checking around the parking lot and surrounding sections of trail, while other agencies responded. The sheriff broke into the vehicle looking for a note, but found nothing. County search and rescue arrived and a search ensued that would last a couple of days. Shifts of searchers reported to a search and rescue bus stationed in the parking lot. Some spent the night in their vehicles. Finally, after every corner of the preserve and the San Francisco Water District property across Skyline were searched, it was called off. Then, approximately a week later, after the vehicle had been towed away, we were in the parking lot, and happened to look up into the trees where we saw something swinging about 100 feet up on a branch. Our victim had been found. He had climbed up to a high branch and hung himself.

While working in my office as Skyline Superintendent, I heard a BOL (be on the lookout) for a vehicle belonging to a suicidal woman. I found the vehicle parked at the CalTrans vista point. District rangers and San Mateo County Search and Rescue set up an incident command there, and began searching Coal Creek and Russian Ridge Preserves. The sheriff in charge called it for the evening without having found any sign of her. They would return the following morning at 8:00 AM. Maintenance Supervisor Patrick Congdon and I were pretty bothered by their decision and kept District staff searching until dark.

I was up at 5:00 AM ready to go, when Patrick called me. We were both thinking the same thing, and met at 6:00 at the Skyline office. It was a very cold fall morning, and we worried about her being out all night. I said I wanted to go down the Mindego Trail because during the night I had started thinking about this deer track out there. I had always wondered where the track went. At the spot where it left the Mindego Trail there was a great view. I parked my vehicle there and took off on foot down this very narrow deer trail. I walked for about a half mile, until it came out on a small knoll where there was a view of the canyon below. I checked around the knoll and saw a purse. Opening the purse, I found empty prescription bottles with the woman's name. I radioed Pat Congdon with the best description I could of where I was, and he started my way. San Mateo County Sheriff and a Life Flight helicopter were also responding.

I saw some empty whisky bottles and was kneeling down looking at them when suddenly this person sat up from under the leaf litter, bowling me over onto my back. She looked like "The Creature from the Black Lagoon!" I scrambled to my feet and she lay back down, mumbling something like, "save me." I tried to take a pulse, but couldn't find it. I radioed that I had found the victim, and she was alive, but in poor shape. The woman was now moaning that she was freezing, so I took off my wool coat and covered her. Because she was breathing, talking, and shivering uncontrollably, but I was unable to find a carotid pulse, I thought she was going into shock. Finally I heard a helicopter overhead. While I dealt with the victim, Patrick directed Life Flight. The pilot landed in a flat meadow nearby. Two paramedics checked the victim and they loaded her on a stretcher. I don't think I ever saw a faster packaging of a victim; before I knew it, they were back up in the air. Between finding the purse, the pills, and the booze bottles, having the shit scared out of me, as well as finding the victim alive, I was tingling with excitement. Unfortunately, I heard only that she had survived, but not what became of her, which I wonder about to this day. However, I will always cherish the fact I found her and got her out alive. It all went down as it was supposed to.

One day while working as Skyline Area Superintendent, I heard a report of a man down on the Spring Ridge Trail at Windy Hill. Being the closest unit, I responded Code 3. Driving down the trail from Skyline, I found a man lying on the side of the road with a dog at his feet. I didn't see anyone else around, so I thought maybe the report came from someone looking down from the summit of Windy Hill. The victim was unresponsive, and I couldn't find a pulse. Within in a few minutes, CDF arrived and took over. It was soon clear the subject had been down for a while. Paramedics discontinued CPR and called for the coroner. Through all of this, the victim's dog remained at his feet, never taking its eyes off its owner. Eventually, CDF left, leaving me to wait. When a person dies this way, you cannot just assume it's due to natural causes. Once pronounced dead, no one can touch the victim or move anything that might be evidence. So waiting was my job for the next hour. As I waited, I had a lot of time to think, and I wept as I watched his faithful dog, waiting patiently for him to get up and continue their walk. I thought about the guy, who looked like he could be in his 70's. He looked fit. I wondered what he did, how he had been feeling, and who was waiting for him to return. His next of kin had been notified and were responding to retrieve his dog. Eventually, the coroner arrived and began packaging up the victim for transport. One of our rangers took the dog to the victim's family, waiting in the lower lot. Occasionally the thought of this incident comes back to me when I walk my dog, whom I hope never has to experience what this guy's dog did.

One day on patrol in Sierra Azul, I parked on the ridge across the canyon from Mt. Umunhum. The top of the mountain had an abandoned Air Force Station, which at that time still belonged to the federal government. These bases were built all up and down the west coast to cover any incoming Soviet attack. They had all become obsolete in the 1970's, and this one had been abandoned since 1980. On my topo map there was an old fire road that went up to the base of the mountain. The District property seemed to end where this trail started climbing the mountain. I decided I'd hike over and locate the property line, and check if this trail was being used. I had heard that the caretaker at the abandoned airbase was hostile to deal with, "a real piece of work." Just to make it really obvious from afar that I was a District ranger, I wore my campaign hat. Right when I got to where I thought the property line was, he jumped out of the bushes and put a double-barreled shotgun in my face! After I checked my drawers, I confronted him about pointing a gun at a peace officer. He told me he worked for the feds and this was how he was instructed to deal with trespassers. I begged to differ with him about the trespassing, as my map showed I was still several feet from the property line. He told me I "didn't know shit," and that we rangers had better stay off federal property, as we had no jurisdiction. I thanked him for his information, told him he better get used to seeing me, then turned and walked back to my truck. He and I were destined for some more run-ins in the future!

I was on patrol driving down the Limekiln Trail in Sierra Azul on a really warm Sunday in August 1985. I'd reached the flat halfway down to the gate at Alma Bridge Road, when I saw a column of smoke coming up from northeast of me. I stopped and used my binoculars to check exactly where it was coming from. I assumed we had the beginnings of a wildfire, and reported it to dispatch, then stood by on the flat, monitoring and reporting the rate of spread to the responding CDF units. Within a half hour the smoke column had expanded substantially, and I started worrying about the potential size of this fire, as the Sierra Azul Mountains are mostly chaparral and had last burned in back in 1962. About an hour after my initial report, CDF directed me to drive back up the ridge and continue south from there all the way to Mt. Umunhum Road advising everybody to evacuate. They were unable to get this fast-moving fire under control, and it was threatening everything to the south. At that time, the District owned only about half the land I would traverse getting to Mt. Umunhum Road, so I was going to have to use my "master key" (bolt cutters) to get through. I was headed into a reputed "No Man's Land" of gun-toting drug dealers, and pig hunters, an area I'd long been curious about.

I reached the private gate and cut my way through the chain of locks. I left the gate open and continued, going through an extremely steep, narrow section with a scary slip out. When I came to the first driveway, I pulled in and used the truck's PA to tell everyone to evacuate. I didn't see anyone, so I moved on to repeat my performance at about four more properties before I reached the gate at Mt. Umunhum Road and cut my way out. I did talk to a couple residents, who responded positively and were ready to evacuate. I continued notifying residents all the way up Mt. Umunhum Road to the station gate, which had a lock system designed so you couldn't cut your way in. Too bad. I would have liked cutting the base caretaker's chain!

At that point, I turned around and retraced my route back out the fire road, re-checking all the residences. When I reached the steep section with the slip out, I realized it was going to be a tricky climb. I got out and walked it first. If I lost traction or stopped, I'd be in danger of going over the edge, into the drainage. Not pretty. I just hugged the inside and went for it, fortunately climbing steadily through. From the top of the Limekiln, I saw that my route out that way was no longer an option. Helicopters and air tankers were on scene, dumping water and retardant. I waited at the flat and was released about 10 PM, after CDF started gettting a handle on the fire. I drove out Kennedy Road.

I was off for the next two days, but from my home in Scotts Valley, when I looked toward Sierra Azul, I couldn't believe my eyes! It was the largest column of smoke I'd ever seen, like an atomic bomb had gone off. The fire had jumped the line, and taken off. The whole preserve was at risk, including Summit Road, Mt. Umunhum, and possibly all the way to Watsonville. MROSD was not being called in, as it had gone way past our capacity to help. Michele and I drove up to her parents' house in Skyland Hill off Old San Jose Road. We loaded the cars with their belongings and spent the night on their deck, where we watched the mountains burn. Other than being scary, it was a beautiful sight. It was an incredibly warm night; we slept on mattresses with nothing over us. They evacuated to our house the next day.

By the time I returned to work on Wednesday, they were finally containing the fire. By Friday, I was driving up Mt. Umunhum Road to the air base. I found all the gates open and the whole area burned. CDF dozers had cut a big firebreak all around the airbase, sparing it, and I drove in for the first time. It was the size of a small town with apartments for enlisted men, houses for officers, a bar, motor pool, and the "monolith," the base of the old radar tower. Of course, I ran into my old buddy the caretaker. He just drove by and we exchanged glares.

Until recently this, the Lexington Fire of 1985, was the largest-ever fire in the Santa Cruz Mountains. It was started by an arsonist, who was captured and prosecuted. I had the honor of being the person who discovered and reported it.

After the District purchased Mt. Umunhum, I was assigned to oversee it, including making repairs for the new District caretaker, Chris Sanger. He also worked for Pac Bell maintaining telephone service on the ridgeop. The former caretaker was dismissed and moved to the McQueen property next door. My first job was to repair the sewer lines, which had been damaged by bulldozer operations during the fire. I also needed to re-establish water service, and move Chris into the base commander's old home. I started to meet all the locals, whom Chris knew through his job. Most of them were antisocial and cranky, and totally distrusted the District. One was known as "Crazy Jerry." The first time I met Jerry was on Mt. Umunhum Road where I was cleaning out the culvert basins. He pulled up in a panel truck that said "Jerry's TV Repair" on the side. I walked over to his passenger window to introduce myself. Jerry reached over, opened the glove box, and pulled out a handgun. He told me I should watch out, because there were lots of crazy people who didn't like the District or the people who worked there. Then he put his gun away and told me to have a nice day.

Photo by Frances Reneau
Old swimming pool at Umunhum Air Station

Another guy I met was Rick Estrada, who lived at the top of the mountain, just before the base gate. He was known for holding people at gunpoint, especially trespassing bicyclists who rode up the road. He eventually got himself in trouble with the sheriffs department for doing this. Through my work at the base, I learned a lot about how to deal with a hostile neighborhood. Every year, Rick would hold a "Porky Pig Roast" for all the neighbors. They would cook a wild pig and a domesticated pig, both in the ground like at a luau. I made it a point to attend, along with Chris Sanger, even though it was difficult. I figured it was the best way to gain their respect, and to show them that they couldn't intimidate me. After a few years, most of them respected me, but they didn't like the District.

Every Fourth of July, the District allowed "after hours" access for fireworks watching to several vista points in the preserves overlooking the peninsula. One Fourth, I was assigned to Hunters Point, in Fremont Older. At about 6:30 that evening I saw a dog running loose which I recognized as a neighbor's, who was not present. I brought the dog back to my truck and leashed it in the back bed. About then Michele arrived to join me for the evening. We were on the hilltop when a man came running up to us very panicked. "A dog is hanging by its collar over the side of your truck!" I took off at a full sprint back to my truck to find a struggling dog hanging by the leash and collar. I grabbed it and put it back in the bed of my truck. Needless to say, I was totally shaken up and embarrassed. All these folks, who had come up to watch the fireworks, got to watch a District Ranger hang a neighbor's dog! Worse yet, I knew this neighbor well, and she could be very difficult. I told Michele to keep an eye on the visitors, as I needed to handle this immediately, before word got back to her. I drove the dog home. At the house, I could see she was hosting a pool party. She saw me approaching with her dog, and, as she rushed toward me, I could tell she'd had plenty to drink. I apologized profusely, as I explained the whole incident to her. When I finished, I braced myself for what was coming. Instead, she grabbed me and kissed me on the lips, crying and thanking me. As I stumbled back to my truck, I made a commitment to never again leave a dog tied up in a truck.

One afternoon when I was a ranger, I met Michele at Deer Hollow Farm and she joined me on foot patrol up Wildcat Canyon. Two boys came running up to us saying that one of them had just been bit by a rattlesnake. He raised his finger to me showing me two fang marks. They had been daring each other to pick up a baby rattlesnake. After he was bit, they had run down the trail as fast as they could until they found us. Baby rattlesnakes don't control the amount of venom they release, usually giving the victim a full dose. Running is also not a good idea as it spreads the venom more quickly. Policy dictated I should call for paramedics, however I decided to get him to the hospital as soon as possible. Michele stayed with his friend, while I drove the victim code 3 (lights and siren) to El Camino Hospital and arrived within 15 minutes. I didn't hear anything further until a week later when a Los Altos Town Crier reporter contacted me for an article about the incident. She set up a meeting with the family for a picture. The article praised me, saying that my fast action saved the boy from any permanent damage.

About a year after that, I was again patrolling Deer Hollow Farm when a middle-aged man came over and said that he was mad at himself for getting bit by a rattlesnake. He had seen the snake some 20 minutes before and had thoughtlessly bent over to pick it up. It was just a stupid reaction. He showed me the fang marks on the side of his palm. I checked his vitals and told him he needed to go to the hospital. He declined. I shared the incident about the boy I had rescued a year earlier and he still declined. I explained what could happen to the soft tissues near the bite, and potentially systemically. Then he said he'd drive himself to the hospital. I explained that I could get him to the hospital faster, which could make a critical difference. He finally agreed, and I transported him code 3 to El Camino Hospital, where they were ready with the antivenin. Three months later, while driving through Deer Hollow Farm, I recognized and greeted my snakebite victim. He cursed me angrily for talking him into going to the hospital. He said he had had an allergic reaction to the antivenin, and had spent weeks in the hospital. He stomped off yelling at me "not to do him any more favors."

When Tom Lausten was hired as a ranger, I was assigned to help with his orientation. Tom had worked as a seasonal ranger for Santa Clara County Parks. There are differences in enforcement practice between agencies, and I wanted to help Tom adapt successfully. On patrol together at El Sereno Preserve, we came upon a man and woman with an off-leash dog. Furthermore, no dogs are allowed in El Sereno. The guy claimed to have entered where there were no signs, which was possible due to the many "volunteer trails" coming in off Bohlman Road. I had just been telling Tom that District rangers should issue a citation only if the visitor was willfully in violation; otherwise they received a written warning. I wanted to give this guy the benefit of the doubt, so I asked him to show us where he came in. After about 20 minutes of him searching around for where he supposedly entered, I suspected he was playing us, and issued a citation.

The next day, Operations Supervisor Jim Boland told me he had spent a half hour on the phone with this guy, who said he was a lawyer, and had been on his first date with the young woman. He said I had violated his civil rights by detaining him longer than was reasonable, before deciding to issue him a citation. A peace officer cannot detain a suspect longer than is necessary to determine if a violation has been committed and issue the citation. Technically, I had detained him longer than was reasonable. Jim was sympathetic, but considering that the guy was obviously an asshole and a lawyer, he recommended that I void the ticket. Given the low level of the violation, I concurred. I felt embarrassed about the example I had set for Tom, but I learned a valuable lesson. I never again allowed anything to influence my citation decisions, beyond the initial explanation by the suspect. And I often used this incident as an example in training other new rangers. Tom and I would both chuckle whenever that incident came up. I always wondered if that woman ever went on another date with that guy. I can't imagine acting like he did in front of a first date, just to get out of a citation he knew he deserved. What an ego!

I often drove up to check Hunters Point at the end of evening patrols. This vista point always attracted lots of after-hours use because of the magnificent view. It was routine to find teens and young adults there, frequently with alcohol or marijuana. After-hours violators usually received either a citation or written warning, depending their behavior, and our judgment of their intent. We usually had parents come pick up juveniles found drinking. To avoid detection, I would drive up blacked out, to a turnaround at the base of the hill in the old apricot orchard. I tried to sneak up and observe people before making contact. If it didn't look safe, which was rare, I would wait for backup from the sheriff, or another District ranger.

However, on this evening I heard a motorcycle on the other side of the hill, down toward Rainbow Drive. It sounded like it was coming toward the hilltop at full throttle. I went into "stupid mode"-- acting without thinking, and, in total violation of District policy, broke into a run up the hill. It was probably my frustration with motorcycle contacts: usually the motorcyclist got away. When I reached the crest of the hill, I met the motorcyclist, grabbed his handlebars, took the bike away from him, and put both him and the motorcycle on the ground. This is when I realized I should not be doing this! Too late, it was done.

I kept him on the ground and handcuffed him. He turned out to be very cooperative and completely shocked by what had just happened. I acted like this was just a routine contact for illegal motorcycle operation. He apologized, saying realized he could have injured someone (or a rabid ranger!) by his actions. I issued him a citation, took off the handcuffs, and followed him as he walked his motorcycle down to the Regnart Road gate, the closest preserve exit. Other than completely soiling my uniform, I suffered no ill effects. I decided to write up a "light" version. I said I got him to come to a stop before I grabbed the handlebars. After writing this incident report, I never said anything more about it to my co-workers, or knowingly broke another District policy again in my career.

As Foothills Area Superintendent on a Friday evening well after dark, I was checking the end of Jones Road in Los Gatos where a trail accesses St. Joseph's Hill Preserve. Several vehicles were parked along the road, the usual sign that an after-hours party might be found up on the old wooden flume. The flume (now dismantled) had a metal chute, with a boardwalk covering it. Before the Lexington dam was built, it brought water down to Los Gatos along the steep side slope overlooking Hwy. 17. It made for a spectacular walkway, especially at night, through the oak trees, and along cliffs. Ranger Tom Lausten joined me, and we hiked up the trail and climbed up onto the flume. After walking almost the full length of the flume, we found some juveniles just sitting and enjoying the lights below. They were very compliant, so we didn't issue citations. We were walking the group back to their cars, and were back on the trail, when we surprised another group heading in. One of the guys pulled a knife! Tom and I were taken by surprise. We deployed our batons (District rangers do not carry firearms) and I started ordering him to put down the knife. He did not comply, and maintained his aggressive stance, holding the knife out in front of himself. After multiple commands, he suddenly put down the knife. I ordered him to back up, and I took possession of the knife and we handcuffed him. We requested Los Gatos police meet us at the end of Jones Road. While walking the whole group out, it became clear that they all knew each other. They had planned to meet up on the flume. The knife-wielding suspect now apologized and said he didn't realize we were rangers; he thought we were part of their group, and that's why he pulled his knife, as a joke, to scare them. We met Los Gatos police at the trailhead and he took the guy away. After all the juveniles had left, Tom and I looked at each other with relief. This was definitely one of those contacts where you hope you didn't soil your shorts.

As Skyline Area Superintendent and Operations Manger I tried to reach out to the mountain bikers. We needed to have dialog, to explain the reasons for our regulations, answer their questions, and see if we could find some middle ground. I asked to attend some monthly meetings of ROMP (Responsible Organized Mountain Pedalers) held at various bike shops, and they scheduled me into several meetings a year. I would set up a stool in the middle of the room at the start of the meeting, and they would vent their frustrations at me. I practiced not losing my cool. I sympathized, even though I did not completely agree with them. I reminded them that the District provided more mountain bike trails than any other local public agency. Mostly we agreed to disagree, but I hope the District and I gained respect for coming into their den. Believe it or not, I am still Facebook friends with some of those bikers.

The District had a difficult relationship with ROMP because we didn't allow mountain bicycle use on all our properties. Even though they could ride most preserves, they felt they should be able to ride all preserves, just like the hikers. The Board developed a process to set standards for whether mountain bicycling would or would not be allowed in a preserve. They wanted visitors who didn't like bicycles coming up and surprising them to have bike-free preserves. They scheduled Board meetings at venues that could handle the large crowds, mostly of very contentious mountain bicyclists. As Skyline Area superintendent, I was in charge of security. During a meeting at the Elks Club in Palo Alto, some of the audience began threatening Board members. I called Palo Alto police, and while waiting for them to arrive, waded into the audience and explained to some of the troublemakers that they had a choice. They could participate respectfully, or I would have them removed, and possibly arrested. By the time the police arrived, I had the audience calmed down. They continued to stand by, but nobody had to be removed, or arrested.

My infamous patrol truck freeway rollover: February 22, 2003, a day of infamy in my life! I was at the main office in Los Altos and needed to get to a meeting at Thornewood Preserve. (I was forever going to meetings someplace!) Driving my assigned 1992 Blazer. I was merging onto Highway 280 at Page Mill Road going north. I pulled onto 280 right behind a minivan. As I came up to the 65 mph speed limit, the minivan driver suddenly slammed on her brakes. I hit my brakes, but started sliding across two empty traffic lanes toward the center divider. I turned the steering wheel into the slide, and the Blazer immediately rolled over onto its roof! I felt the pavement on the side of my cheek through my open side window as I rolled. Next, the Blazer slid back across the road on its roof, finally coming to rest on the shoulder, now rolled back to its passenger side facing backwards into oncoming traffic. I was bucked into my seat, hanging up in the air. I unbuckled the seat belt and fell down onto the passenger door. I stood up, stuck my head out and looked back across the freeway. Three lanes of cars had come to a dead stop. My equipment was spread all over the freeway.

A man came up and asked if I was all right, and offered his cell phone, with my boss, Operations Manager John Maciel, on the other end. The man told me he'd found my business cards on the roadway and had made the call. I now noticed my left middle finger was piled up behind my third knuckle and told John, "I really did it this time: you better tell them I won't make the meeting." When the paramedics arrived, I heard, "Sango! What the hell happened?" Great. Having destroyed my vehicle, shut down Hwy 280, and smashed up my hand, the fire fighters all knew me from other incidents! They used the "Jaws of Life" to cut me out. They shot me up with morphine and took me to Stanford Hospital. John Maciel and John Escobar came and told me not to worry about anything. Then the staff took a blood sample, per District policy. They just covered up my messed up finger until I could come back the next day and see the hand specialist. Michele showed up and took me home.

The next day I met with Dr. Amy Ladd, a world authority in hand surgery. We scheduled surgery for the following day, and she said I would probably lose my middle finger, but she would do her best to save it. During surgery, she aligned all my bones and installed an external fixator to take the place of my knuckle while it healed. She also repaired a grade three shoulder separation by bolting my clavicle down. After six weeks of hand therapy I regained full function, with the exception that my middle finger is a little crooked. She was really bothered by this, but I assured her I was thrilled to still have a finger that could grasp a wrench. I returned to work.

One day, driving up Page Mill Road, I saw the back end of a small, white dog sticking out of a hollowed-out log near the Canyon Trail gate. I parked, and walked over, and the dog started to walk backward, dragging the log. I grabbed the log, which was probably 18 inches long and looked into the other end. I could see the dog's face, covered with termites; it was definitely in distress. I tried to ease him out, but he was really stuck. Ranger Loro Paterson responded to help me. I fetched a screwdriver and hammer from my truck to try to chisel the log away. Loro held the dog and log firmly on the ground, and I started chiseling and pounding on the log with the hammer, starting a crack. Finally I was able to pull the log apart. Loro grabbed the dog and held it while I read the address on of the tags. It was about a mile back down Page Mill Road. Loro took the dog home where the owner said it had been gone for a day or so. We had a good laugh for a long time over that hard-to-believe rescue.

During my first months as operations manager, the District was involved in a large wildland fire in Monte Bello Preserve that threatened a housing development above Stevens Canyon Road. I parked where I had a good overview of the fire and was joined by Supervising Ranger Dennis Danielson. District and CalFire units were already on scene. Helicopters were dropping water hauled from Stevens Creek Reservoir. It was touch and go; firefighters were working to prevent any structures from burning. Things were so serious that air tankers were brought in from Southern California. District units searched for spot fires around the perimeter, driving side roads and reporting their locations to me. When the air tankers arrived, they started circling above where Dennis and I had set up. One went into the canyon below us to start its run. The plane was the size of a Boeing 732, but fitted with tanks full of fire retardant. Suddenly the tanker reappeared and I realized they were going to drop retardant early, right on top of Dennis and me! Dennis hit the ground, covering his helmet with his hands. I ran and dove through the open door of my Jeep Cherokee. Just as I landed across the two front seats, my vehicle was completely smothered in retardant! When I climbed out of my vehicle, I couldn't even tell where Dennis was until he stood up, leaving a body-shaped outline on the red retardant ground. My vehicle had gone from white to completely red. Because the door was still open, the jambs, the seat, and my Nomex pants were red too. We just looked at each other and began laughing.

The Cherokee still had red retardant in the jambs to the day I
retired.

When I was Ops manager, Craig Britton called me into his
office to ask about an article exposing a CalTrans animal dump
on Hwy 9. Craig thought it looked like it might be on District
land, based on their map. I thought we should be careful, as the
article was full of negative press, saying that CalTrans had been
taking all the road kill found on Hwy. 9 to this spot, and throwing
the animals over the edge of the road down into the drainage.
The public was furious because some of the road kill might be
dogs and cats. They might also be polluting the creek. I told
Craig we didn't want to get sucked into this, especially since the
property was remote, and no one seemed to care who owned it. I
said I would drive up in my personal car, in my street clothes,
and check it out. When I got to the dump, I determined it was
District property. I climbed down the steep chute and found
hundreds of decaying animals. It was obvious this had been
going on for years. Most of the pile was just bare bones spread
around by scavengers, but with fresh and decaying carcasses on
top. I took pictures, climbed back up, and returned undetected.
We managed to keep the District out of the fray.

Used by permission of MROSD
Topley and Sango at their retirement party

I was hired on the same day as David Topley. We worked together as rangers; he supervised me as crew-coordinating ranger. When I became operations manager, David worked for me as support services supervisor. In the end, we retired on the same day, and we had our retirement party together. We still see each other, and occasionally kayak together. Thanks for the good times David!

Photo used by permission of MROSD
Operations Manager Sango

I thought I would share some "Sangoisms" that I became known for. These are mostly the result of my tolerance for risk taking. I believe the only person at the District with a higher tolerance for risk-taking was General Manager Craig Britton, whom I absolutely loved working for.

"Get'er Done." Drop everything else to make it happen.
"Run Silent, Run Deep." When a critical issue would face roadblocks if brought to the attention of management, other departments, or regulatory agencies.
"It's On Me." If something goes wrong, and we get into trouble, I'll take responsibility.

"Put a Fork in it." We have beaten this issue to death: let's move on.

"It's Time to Stifle it." What we just talked about is not for anyone else's ears.

"Even I Clean Bathrooms." I lived by this, and expected everyone else to, too. Staff even posted a picture in the office of me repairing a chemical toilet at the Black Mountain Campground when I was area superintendent.

"We are all equally important to our success." Every position at the District is as essential as the next for us all to be successful.

"It's not about me, but about what I can contribute." If I can make something or someone else successful, then I too am successful.

Some comments about Sango's interview:

I found my share of suicides, one off the Mora Trail at Rancho, one at the pool house at Hicks Creek Ranch, and one on the Razorback Ridge Trail in upper Windy Hill. I wrote about the first two in my book, "Rangerchick." They were both hangings, arousing in me feelings of futility, frustration and great sadness as I helped to cut down and carry out the bodies. The Razorback Trail suicide was different, as I never got on scene with the victim. I did spend several hours standing around with his parents on the side of Skyline Boulevard at the trailhead as they told me about their son's long struggle with depression. He had blown his head off with a shotgun probably about an hour before I found his car at the trailhead. The driver's door was hanging open and the gun store receipt was on the passenger seat.

Sango says rangers like conflict as compared to OSTs, and when hearing him tell about attending Porky Pig Roasts and ROMP meetings, I have to say that he certainly had a better stomach for conflict than I ever developed. I could put up with the abuse for short periods, hold my tongue, and listen to viewpoints opposed to my own, but not for the kind of hours-long ordeal Sango is talking about. Go Sango!

Photo by Ranger Jessica Lucas

Me having a good time replacing the Plexiglas in the signboard at the Mindego lot

Ranger Frances: The Whole Job

Sango and I sure do see eye to eye on this one: District rangers and OSTs should view each other and treat each other as equals. Unfortunately, their job descriptions have only continued to diverge since Sango's time, widening the fault lines between patrol and maintenance. Like Sango, I think that rangers should continue to perform minor maintenance tasks, including cleaning the field offices on Wednesday mornings side by side with the crew. Working together periodically on larger maintenance projects would also help to engender a cooperative and respectful work environment. Employees who never work together, never learn to recognize and respect each other's work.

I always wished I had stronger technical maintenance skills, and admired the know-how of the OSTs who did. Their genius for diagnosing and fixing engines, motors, pumps, and other machines was astonishing. Most amazing to me was that they actually enjoyed all this tinkering, fiddling, and testing. I just wanted to get the damn weedwhip fixed so I could get back to work. District OSTs, maintenance supervisors, and EMOs always treated my requests for help with the utmost patience, and graciously granted me hours of assistance and advice. How could I then think myself "better" than the OSTs? Quite the other way around: I thought my job was easier by comparison.

Was I treated so patiently because I was a woman? Possibly. I was also always quick and willing to ask for help rather than waste time trying to figure out how to fix something myself.

So where does the "rangers are better" attitude come from? Is it just the money? It is true that a baseline ranger does make about three bucks an hour more than a baseline OST, but seniority pay can overwhelm this disparity between any two given field employees. Why should a brand new ranger be making more than an OST who may have been there for several years already, and who has a lot more institutional knowledge? Could it be their ability to pass the ranger academy and get the certificate that makes them better and more valuable employees? Maybe. The only District employees who can issue citations are the rangers, so it is perhaps this one specialized aspect of the job, their power as a peace officer that allows rangers to look down on mere OSTs and breathe the rarified air of the superior position.

Maybe the prestige problem has at least a little to do with the job title ranger. Visitors know what a ranger is, or at least they think they do. They have contact with rangers in visitor centers and campgrounds, and think of rangers as those friendly and knowledgeable folks leading nature hikes and campfire programs, at least in national and state parks: the interpretive rangers. Parks maintenance workers, by contrast, often work hidden away from the public. The trails they are brushing and repairing are often closed for public safety. Visitors certainly have no opportunity to watch as the crew painstakingly constructs a new bridge or replaces an enormous washed-out culvert. Rangers don't witness much of this work either. All the work the District crew does to repair utility systems in District-owned houses also goes on out of pubic (and ranger) view. So, the public doesn't recognize the work of park maintenance, and they have no idea what an Open Space Technician is. Who dreamed up the idea of calling the District's maintenance crew workers OSTs? Was avoiding the word maintenance in the job title an effort to help with the prestige problem? I think the title OST is confusing to visitors. I might suggest calling OSTs maintenance rangers, and rangers patrol rangers. Historically only those District employees charged with performing law enforcement have had the job title ranger, but this is not true across the spectrum of land management agencies. Interpretive rangers in national parks get to be rangers, after all, even though they do no law enforcement. Why not let all District field staff enjoy the word ranger in their job title?

~~~

As Sango discussed, District rangers traditionally did all the maintenance. They were generalists and performed all field operations, from building trails and cleaning restrooms to rendering first aid, fighting fires and writing citations. Even long after the creation of the maintenance crews, a ranger's job continued to include a host of minor maintenance tasks such as installing and replacing signposts, fixing cut fence wires, and replacing broken rails. We sawed up fallen trees across the trail and weedwhipped around the signs, stiles, parking lots and LZs (helicopter landing zones.) We dug out the silted-in waterbars and cleared plugged-up culverts. All these were non-technical, on-going maintenance tasks, most of which were straightforward grunt work, easily done alone. Our partners in the Operations

Department, the OSTs also known as crew, did all the actual construction of trails, bridges, and stiles. They annually brushed all the roads and trails, repaired electrical systems and plumbing in District buildings, and used their heavy equipment and technical knowledge for a myriad of other tasks.

In 2016, the huge and ungainly Operations Department was split in half: the rangers and volunteers became the Visitor Services Department; crew became Land and Facilities. (I always disliked the name Visitor Services as it made it sound like the rangers were only there to serve the visitors, as though we had no part in protecting the plants, animals and physical features of the preserves.) In keeping with the new emphasis on specialization, the rangers were now supposed to be weaned away from our minor maintenance role, so some of those generalist ranger-performed tasks were re-assigned to crew. Rangers would no longer mow LZs, clean out culverts, remove large downed trees, or fix damaged splitrail fences, unless it was only a very short stretch of fence. We would simply report the needed maintenance rather than take responsibility for fixing these things ourselves.

Both crew and rangers cried, "Foul!" Most rangers liked driving the little Canycom ride-on mower around the LZs, and enjoyed the occasional opportunity to work together with another ranger or crewmember on a splitrail fence repair project. We looked forward to the chance to practice our sawyer skills to safely remove large downed trees using one of the heftier chain saws. We relished that sense of accomplishment upon completion of a trail clearing or fence building project. Meanwhile, crew was not happy to now get stuck taking on the additional mowing, fixing, and trail-clearing tasks. They had enough to do. Why couldn't the rangers, who were expected to patrol the trails anyway, just carry a bent shovel and take care of the plugged culvert or silted-in waterbar when they found it, rather than crew having to go back out there and fix it?

I understand that the two new department managers had quite a time deciding exactly how many damaged posts and rails counted as a "very short stretch of fence," finally agreeing on one smashed post and two broken rails. In the summer of 2017, I was involved in two stealth splitrail fence repairs. Both projects involved short stretches of fence hit by cars in parking lots, but both included two smashed posts and three rails, and thus fell clearly into the Land and Facilities purview. In one case my partner in policy-breaking crime was none other than my supervisor at the time, Brendan, who had gotten sick of waiting for crew to fix a highly visible stretch of smashed splitrail fence in the Russian Ridge parking lot. Don't tell anyone.

Under our new directive from the visitor services manager, we rangers were to become primarily law enforcement officers, keep our uniforms clean, our boots polished and our badges shiny. Interact with visitors, represent the District, enforce the regulations, patrol the roads and trails, but, for God's sake, don't get dirty.

~~~

As a young 30-something seasonal on crew I excelled at grunt work, and could easily spend all day running a weedwhip or wielding a bent shovel. My technical skills never went far beyond installing and fixing fences and cleaning chainsaws, but I took pride in doing a thorough, high-quality job. The maintenance aspect of the ranger job was right in my comfort zone: fixing fences, cleaning equipment, and taking care of trails.

But, just as the rangers' job description was changing with time, and with the growth of the District, so too was this ranger's body. The maintenance chores I had enjoyed slowly lost their appeal after I blew out my back, and, later discovered that the growing pain in my neck was degenerative disc disease. I felt betrayed by my body. I had worked hard to stay strong and fit, but all this neck, back, and arthritic knee pain had conspired to turn me into a pretty worthless ranger, at least in my own estimation. I had to ask for help every time I needed to dig a posthole, as using the rockbar had become way too jarring. I couldn't run a weedwhip for more than half an hour without my hands vibrating for the rest of the day. All those repetitive, vibrating, pounding, chopping, digging tasks, at which I'd once excelled, were now anathema to my wellbeing. I came to feel I was no longer up to the ranger job, the whole job, as I envisioned it, and as I wanted it to be.

Journal entry 7/12/17: Neck, upper back and left scapula area are killing me. Thinking of going home sick. Took some more pain meds. Bothering me at swimming this morning but stayed in trying not to make any sudden moves, very slow and careful. Foot patrol today using the same mantra: careful, slow, no sudden moves. What really hurt was driving through the cow-cupped dried mud on the road into the Blue Brush property of Purisima. I was inching the truck forward at a slow walking pace and felt my neck, back and shoulder spasm with every tiny jerk. I finally got out and just walked down to Lobitos Creek, which was much better.

Journal entry 9/2/17: Away the last two weeks. Week one was a backpacking trip with David in Mineral King. Had a great trip. I'd been so worried that my knees wouldn't hold up, but they did much better than I expected. What blew out was my back, but not until the morning after we got home. I was changing my shoes when the oh-so-very-familiar pain hit. Ended up calling in sick all last week. Being laid up, unable to do the least damn thing reminded me of how decrepit I've become. Then, just after I'd logged on today and was heading out to open gates, Mt. View Dispatch came up with a call to Purisima: big dead deer in the middle of the parking lot. My back was in no shape for this one, so passed it off to Dennis and Kristin, who ended up using the Tommy Lift truck to move the thing.

As illustrated by the above two journal entries, the need for a healthy, fit, body cropped up all the time, and not just in the obvious case of maintenance tasks. Loading boxes of preserve brochures, wrenching open the Land-Sea storage containers to get out the ATV, kneeling and squatting on the ground to access patients: I was losing my ability to carry out everyday ranger activities, even driving bumpy roads. Losing my capacity for maintenance tasks saddened me, but maybe I could rationalize continuing as the rangers were doing less and less maintenance anyway. I tried to tell myself that I could just stick to the minimal basics of the new visitor services ranger job—driving around in the truck and writing tickets—and I'd be all right. Right? Not in my book. Sitting on my behind in the truck had always been among my least favorite aspects of the job, certainly nothing that I wanted to do more of. I wanted to be a generalist ranger, an old-time ranger. But that old-time ranger job had disappeared along with the old-time rangers, like me.

Photo used by permission of MROSD

Alice Cummings, Resource Management Planner and Dennis Danielson, Supervising Ranger

(The 2017 Henry Coe Backcountry Weekend offered the opportunity to interview both Alice and Dennis. They both indicated that they would prefer to be interviewed together. A year later, on the 2018 Henry Coe Backcountry Weekend, Dennis agreed to a solo interview, the last interview in this book.)

Dennis: When I first started with the District in 1979, I was coming off a season at Sequoia National Park where the National Park Service rangers were generally well liked. I worked five months there, three months as a seasonal ranger and two months on the fire crew. The year before that, I had worked one year at Tilden for East Bay Regional Parks, and there again we got a friendly reception most of the time. I started at Midpeninsula and right off the bat, I'd be driving down the road and instead of getting the happy wave out the window, I'd get the finger. The community up there on Skyline Boulevard hated the Open Space District. They were all fearful that the District would come in and condemn their land and kick them out of their houses. This wasn't really true, but we were buying land and we were the new kids on the block.

Then the demographic changed when people sold to other private owners, and new people came in. They were coming in because they wanted to be near parks and trails. I can't say exactly when it happened, because there was "the list," and then the Russian nun's thing, which were both public relations fiascos. It took 20 years before it was more the friendly wave than the finger. Part of it was that the rangers would help out neighbors who had a broken-down car or maybe a flat tire. We'd give them a ride home. They came to...I'm not sure trust is the right word...they came to appreciate the services that were there.

The neighbors also saw that the District wasn't condemning small, individual residences and kicking people out. We did very little condemnation on Skyline except for the...well; they never passed the resolution...except for the Russian nun thing. Mostly it was down closer to the urban area, like the Perham's at Rancho San Antonio. People like Larry Hassett (a long-time District Board member) changed their tune and said, "Hey, this isn't bad. The District is a good thing. This is why I'm living here on Skyline." Part of it was that somebody built a house right next his and he was shocked.

~~~

I remember that you (Alice) wrote the first resource management policies. That's worth something. Also memorable were the hikes we did together. One was at Alma College, the Jesuit property, the first go-round when we didn't end up buying it, when I think we should have. I had a connection to the property because I'd gone to the local Jesuit high school, and I'd gone on retreats up to the Alma College property.

You and I walked around and found the dump and I pulled out a bunch of old bottles. The other hike I remember was at Purisima, kind of near Bald Knob. It was in the early morning and it was moist and dewy. There were lots of spider webs across the trail, all lit up with dew and spectacular. I took a million pictures.

Alice: I don't remember those specific hikes, but I always loved hiking at Purisima.

Dennis: Another time, we went walking down the PG&E access road at Black Mountain that goes down towards those remote towers, toward Hidden Villa. We may have been checking out the cutover trail down into Rancho. It's now a trail easement that's still not on District property, the connector from the end of the PG&E road at Rancho, through the quarry, up to the Black Mountain fire road.

Alice: What I most remember with you is my assignment as a mentor for Tom Williams. He was a volunteer with a photographic memory for terrain. The District wanted him to map out redwood groves at Purisima, to have them as memorial groves. Tom went all around Purisima, then he brought me out there to show me the groves and somehow we met up with you. The three of us had a good time discussing the groves and the local natural history.

Dennis: To save a redwood grove, you could make a donation to the Save the Redwoods League. I think it was like $20,000 per grove. It was a fundraising thing. You got the plaque. Tom laid them all out, and later on it became my assignment to know where all those groves were. I actually ordered little markers and pounded them in the ground. I can't tell you how much time I spent out there trying to figure out where the boundaries were using a measuring wheel. There was no GPS at the time. We just did the ones along Purisima Creek Road, but there were some groves higher up as well. If somebody was considering a grove, they would come out and we would drive up Purisima Creek Road together, and I'd show them the possibilities. I would meet with the donors, and would try to convince them to have the signs hidden away from the road, to not be so obtrusive.

There was one grove there that I fought for, which honored the woman who won the Nobel Peace Prize, Wangari Maathai. She was from Africa, from Nairobi, and she was a speaker at the Open Space Conference sometime in the 1980's. There was leftover funding from the conference, and either Herb Grench or Craig Britton eventually donated that money to the Save the Redwoods League to create the Wangari Maathai Memorial Grove.

Photo used by permission of MROSD
Wangari Maathai

Save the Redwoods League had contributed half the cost of that part of Purisima, about $2 million. The deal was that Save the Redwoods could then market these memorial groves and recoup some of their money. These groves are all over the state parks; you see them all the time. Elisa did some memorial grove work along Skyline Boulevard because there was a guy at Kings Mountain who wanted to have a grove for his wife. Elisa took over the groves project, but I mentored her. We actually went together to the annual meeting of the Save the Redwoods League up in San Francisco. Doug McConnell was the master of ceremonies. It was my project for many, many years, and I spent a lot of time on it. Then the mowing tractor whacked off half my markers, so I'm not sure how many are left out there anymore. The groves guy from Save the Redwoods once told me, "You guys have the best marked groves of any park. Some parks are a real hodgepodge."

Alice: I always knew I liked the outdoors and wanted to have an outdoor job. I was educated in biology; I was zoology major at Wellesley College and then got a master's degree in biology from Yale. I met my husband, also a biologist, while taking classes and doing research at a biological field station in Colorado.

After we moved to California with our two young daughters, I stayed home to care for them and didn't work for a while. But after I got divorced, I wanted to find an environmental job. First, though, I needed to learn the California flora and fauna, so I enrolled in graduate school at Cal State Hayward. I took all the field classes I possibly could and I went on extensive field trips throughout the western U.S. and Baja. I also had a part-time job helping to write environmental impact reports.

While I was still at Cal State Hayward, I saw an ad for a District job titled environmental analyst. They were looking for someone with a degree in biology, familiar with the local flora and fauna, and able to write and analyze proposals. I thought I was qualified for that, so I applied, and was absolutely overjoyed to get the job. I believe this was in 1981. I don't know how many others applied, how many others I was competing with, but I think my good education and being involved in doing biology right at the time maybe helped me.

When I started, the District office was still at the original 330 Distal Circle, before the time of the move to the Old Mill Shopping Center location. I actually had to share a desk with Joyce Nicholas, who was the volunteer coordinator.

I remember my first project. They were trying to build a golf course at Edgewood County Park, and I had to write a rebuttal saying why there should not be a golf course at Edgewood. I wrote a very thorough rebuttal. I remember I was proud of it.

Dennis: In the 1970's, the District had paid for half of the acquisition of Edgewood, which was state property being held in reserve to build a state college, like Hayward State. But the District had agreed to sort of step away about the future of the property. The golf course idea had been floating around for quite a while, but when it looked like it might go through, as a recreation site for San Mateo County Parks, several of the District Board members got worked up. Herb probably got them to have Alice look at it, because of all the flowers and maybe there were red-legged frogs.

Photo used by permission of MROSD
Alice Cummings

Alice: There were many rare or endangered plant species there. I consulted with a photographer, who took lots of pictures of the flowers at Edgewood including rare ones. I got a lot of good material for why it should not be developed.

~~~

When I started with the District, we didn't have computers. I would handwrite my reports on yellow lined paper and then hand them to a secretary, Jo Combes, who was the typist, and she would type it up. She would get really mad at me if I ever wanted to change anything after the fact. I took photographs, mostly slides, all through my time with the District. I would get prints made and include them in the reports. I wrote many grant proposals, and made an effort to include pictures of the unique features of the properties. I'd select the pictures that showed the land to its greatest advantage. I got a lot of grants, so they must have liked my reports.

Dennis: After we acquired a property, regardless of whether through a grant or just tax dollars, Alice would often write the use and management plan environmental assessment, and she would write the acquisition report. She would go out and evaluate the environmental elements of geology and biology and...

Alice: And since I was not an expert, I often hired people, like Toni Corelli, who's a rare plants person. I would ask, "Toni come out and see if there are any rare plants here." I hired Eric Remington to look for wildlife and he would stay out all night looking for bats or moths. He would do a very thorough job.

After my first year, as an environmental analyst, a full-time job as a resource planner came up, which I applied for and got, so I became a planner.

Dennis: Alice wrote a lot of grant proposals for land acquisition, through the Land and Water Conservation Fund. I think maybe it was administered through California State Parks. They would dole out the money. Later on, some of the grant requests were through what some people called the Mountain Lion Fund. There were five categories. At one point, Alice had written up a whole report to acquire some property, but it had focused more on the upland wildlife category, which included animals like deer, and she didn't get the grant. She went to Sacramento to find out why not, and how she could do better. She discovered that, of the five categories, the one she had applied in was the most popular. Land was also so much more expensive in the Bay Area, that it wasn't seen as the biggest bang for their bucks. But they told her that anadromous fish was the least popular category, so after that, Alice always tried to incorporate an anadromous fish element. She became highly successful at winning grants. To this day, she may have gotten more grant money for the District than anybody ever.

Alice: One of the biggest grants that I got was for Mt. Umunhum. I worked really hard on that one, because I believed that it could be the Mt. Tamalpais, the Mt. Diablo, for the District. It took so long. I mean they are just now getting it open after all these years. That was one of my earliest projects, in the early 80's, and here we are in 2017. I went up to Umunhum a lot. I remember going up there when all the buildings were still there, about 50 buildings. The Air Force had just left it recently so it was still pretty much intact. There was a bowling alley and a swimming pool; some of the housing was still in good shape, with refrigerators and some furniture. There was also a bomb shelter, a huge underground thing. Later, when they were thinking of tearing down the blockhouse, Craig Britton, the general manager, had the idea to hire The A Team, which was a TV show where they blew up buildings. He said we could let them blow up the blockhouse and then put the debris into the bomb shelter. That would get rid of it! That never came to pass.

I had to write a whole string of grant proposals. They were sort of fun to work on because I needed to find information about what made the properties unique and interesting. As part of my job I was able to hike, explore, and photograph the new acquisitions. I always thought the District should do more with that information when they were writing the preserve brochures, to publicize some of these interesting facts.

~~~

I explored Tunitas Creek Ranch a lot with Eric Remington. He found the most horrifying thing when he looked underneath an old barn there. He called to me, "Come look at this!" It was a mummified dog that had died with its mouth open in a snarl. It was the worst looking thing! We also found bats roosting inside a wall-mounted ironing board in the ranch house. They actually offered that house to Eric to live in, even though a big landslide had taken out the driveway. They thought Eric could deal with that, but he didn't want the house. Tina, his wife, didn't like it.

For all these trips, I used my own vehicle. There were no District office vehicles back then, and I often had to go alone. I would go to Ravenswood Open Space Preserve, just go out there all by myself, but I never had any problems.

Dennis: David Olson, the general manager, even drove his own car, which was a nice car, like a BMW. He had a District radio installed it, and would call when he'd see problems.

I want to say the Skyline Field Office probably didn't happen until maybe '82 or '83. We owned it for a while when the ranch manager was still living there in the house that I later lived in. John Escobar and I, and I think Lisa Varney were the three who first worked out of the Skyline Office. The office then was just the little shower room on the north side of the driveway.

There was a three-car barn where the Skyline office is now. Across from what is now the shop, there is that one small building where there's now a shower and a bathroom that the seasonals use: that was the whole office, the Skyline Ranger Office. Of course, we had the shop building, but the bays that are now enclosed were all open bays. When we expanded, we brought in a temporary office trailer that sat right next to where the pressure washer is now. We dragged the old chicken coop up the hill to where the historic farming implements are. Patrick Congdon was the one who got that done, because he wanted to save as much historic stuff as possible. The chicken coop used to be about where the gas pumps are now. They re-leveled everything because that old three-car garage had been on three levels.

Photo used by permission of MROSD
Pat Congdon posing with old farm equipment at SFO

The slaughterhouse for the pig farm was down in that lower pasture by the Ipiwa Trail. The hooks and the blood channel are still there. That was built by Mr. Rickey, of Rickey's Hyatt House. Blue was his big prize pig. They had hog sheds up in the big flat by the tennis court, but I never saw any of that.

~~~

Alice wrote the first resource management policies. They were a guiding light for District policy. She was the only biologist at the District, the go-to person. Nobody else had the knowledge or background in natural resources. There were all these Board members and staff members who wanted to save parks and open space, but Alice was the only one who had the academic background and knowledge.

Alice: I had never written a grant proposal before I got hired. Originally they called me an environmental analyst, and the job was sort of like that Edgewood report where I had to look at what others were trying to do and criticize it. Make a case. I was in graduate school, so I was used to analyzing and criticizing, and grant proposals are not that hard to write. They have specific questions and you just go through answering each one as completely as possible. I tried to hire the right people to look into things so my answers could be rock solid. They couldn't say, "Oh, you're just saying this property is great." No.

Dennis: For about the first 20 years or so, maybe even up until now, the thinking was, "Well, let's experiment with this type of a position. Let's hire somebody on a temporary basis, half time, and see how it goes." If it seemed like it was successful, which it always was because there was a big need pushing it, then that person would get hired full time. You had to get your foot in the door, to get the half time position approved by the Board and the general manager. All the effort and sacrifice people did in the early days of the organization was in the effort to buy land. The money spent then was so valuable. Instead of on salaries...

Alice: ...and instead of on resource management. I'd say, "You know, we have all these invasive plants coming in here." They never had money to do any resource management. It was always, "You spend your time writing grants." But I did get to write resource management policies for the District, and made an effort to put environmental protection and restoration to the forefront. Recreation had to be compatible with that.

Dennis: Personally I kind of agreed with the District Board on this. Some of this stuff could be fixed down the road. You gotta buy the land now. You can't make the garden the way it was. You can't buy a ten-acre piece and focus just on that. We were able to buy, what, 75,000 acres or whatever? I think the focus has changed a little bit now that the staff is getting bigger. Maybe that's just the natural progression. There were many positions that were part time or temporary, and then got converted. The people they hired, like Alice, were so dedicated that they probably went well beyond their paid part-time hours. The rangers didn't make a big stink about the low pay, and we went the extra mile.

Photo used by permission of MROSD

Alice Cummings

Alice: It was more like a big family, in some ways, in the earlier years. The planning department was small and we saw each other every day and interacted a lot, so you knew everybody. I knew all the rangers.

Dennis: The rangers participated in what were called use and management plans, about how the land and trails were going to be used. Alice and the other planners would either write them, or they would take environmental elements from her acquisition reports and pull them into the use and management plans.

Alice: Another thing they had me do, which was really weird, was to be the CEQA (California Environmental Quality Act) person. I did all the early CEQA compliance. CEQA was just getting started back then, and I knew very little about it. I quite often did only the most minimal of CEQA reports. Now much more detailed studies are required.

~~~

Del and I were assigned to go up Mt. Umunhum to investigate a property that Craig, the GM, was negotiating to buy. We were met by the owner, who lived in a pickle barrel, a house made out of a pickle barrel. He greeted us with a shotgun! I can't remember what happened, but we didn't stay. We didn't have negotiations with him. I think there had already been talk about getting this property, but when the guy saw us, he was antagonistic. I'm trying to remember how big this pickle barrel was; it was big enough to stand up in.

I remember another interesting trip with Eric on Mt. Umunhum, although I forget what we were looking for. We were up on the summit and we started down on the south side, down a talus slope below the blockhouse. There were some rare plants there, a rare clarkia, so that was interesting. Then we got down lower and found the ruins of a house where a woman hermit had lived below the summit, near a spring. Eric picked up a rusty, old watercolor set, which he found interesting because his mother had liked to watercolor. Then we found this long PVC pipe and we followed it for a long way, maybe miles, going around the mountainside to the north. It led to a little fenced plantation of marijuana plants. We reported it, but I don't know what happened after that. There was nobody there, just plants. I don't remember any signs of a camp. I found a lot of marijuana sites with Eric. He seemed to have an instinct for them.

Dennis: The rangers were given map books that were Xeroxed copies; that's all we had. The map book was paper-thin, only about ten pages, and it only showed District lands. It certainly didn't have any of the names of local property owners on it, so I wrote them in. Maybe there were acquisition maps, but those maps were nothing like what there is today. Our maps were made from the USGS topo maps and had only the District property boundaries, not the lines for the adjacent landowners' properties. They didn't want to include those in case the map book, "fell into the wrong hands," and got some neighboring property owner upset. It was like, "Okay, here you go. Go out and patrol." I finally convinced the powers that be (and I kind of pat myself on the back for this) to also put in the boundaries of the adjacent properties and their owners' names, because often times we would have contact with neighbors, and we never knew their names. I would try to keep notes on 3 X 5 cards, but I was told not to have 3 X 5 cards, because of "the list."

Alice: I worked 14, well, they wouldn't count the first year, so the official number was 13, years for the District. By then I was living with Powell. When he retired from Lockheed, I felt like this was our chance to go do things together, to go on trips. I didn't want to keep working full time and it didn't seem like I could work part time, so...I retired early.

Thank you, Alice and Dennis

Some comments about Alice and Dennis' interview:

See the solo interview with Dennis Danielson below for more on "the list."

In the late 1990's, nine elderly Russian nuns wanted to build a convent on land they owned along Skyline Boulevard in the Kings Mountain area. The District threatened to use eminent domain to acquire their property and prevent the development. Eventually some compromise was reached, but the brouhaha over the District's taking steps toward using eminent domain took a long time to die down.

The memorial groves at Purisima Creek Redwoods now all have nice new redwood signs with incised yellow lettering and there is a brand new interpretive sign at the Higgins-Purisima entrance explaining the District's land-saving connection with the Save the Redwoods League

Stan Hooper (see interview below) seems to have taken the words straight out of Alice's mouth. Thirty years later, the struggle to establish non-native invasive weed control as a District priority continues.

Alice must have had her camera along on her trip with Eric Remington down the south slope of Mt. Umunhum on the day they found the hermit's cabin because there is now a nice interpretive sign at the old cabin site, alongside the new Mount Umunhum Trail. The sign includes a photo of that rusty watercolor paint set.

Photo used by permission of MROSD

Interpretation was not part of the ranger job, unless we volunteered for special events like this.

Ranger Frances: Snake Board Guy

Part of me always wanted to be a botanist or a biologist, or maybe a paleontologist, or an archaeologist, one of those field scientists who get to go poking around looking for great stuff under leaves and rocks, to explore the hidden and overlooked realms of life. I greatly admired and envied the District's resource management folks whom I knew personally, including Alice Cummings and Cindy Roessler. They find natural history endlessly interesting and exciting. They want to know more, to investigate, and to keep on learning. I've certainly got some of that same enthusiasm, and often wonder if a job with a greater focus on natural history might have suited me better. I would have loved going out with Alice on those long-ago field trips to explore prospective properties for rare, endangered and endemic species. I loved going out with Cindy from her house on the Big Dipper Ranch to look for red-legged frogs by flashlight, or to collect the data from the wildlife cameras.

All rangers love the outdoors, but not all love natural history. I'm ashamed to say I've even known District rangers who were horrified by creepy-crawly critters and repulsed by my barehanded explorations of scat and dead animals. Although we were supposed to be generalist rangers, that never included much resource management except pulling weeds, and included no required training whatsoever in natural history. Visitors were genuinely surprised to learn that knowledge of local flora and fauna was not part of the ranger job requirement. Resource protection, however, is supposed to be part of the job. And unless you thoroughly know and appreciate the resource—all those horrid little creepy-crawly things—how are you going to do a good job protecting it?

When on patrol, I took advantage of the opportunity to do as much poking around under leaves and rocks as I could get away with, which never met with much approval from my supervisors. I remember Michael Newburn pointedly directing me to spend more time patrolling the trails in the popular preserves, "where the visitors are." I figured that those trails were already well patrolled by the visitors themselves. When the number of visitors reached a certain critical mass, the public shame of misbehavior kept most miscreants at bay. No, the real bad guys were to be found in the closed areas, and along the creeks and ridgelines far off trail. Marijuana gardeners, elicit trail builders, and, in the case that follows, wildlife poachers, hide their activities far from public discovery.

This is Ranger Andrew's incident report, the first evidence I saw of a snake poacher on Skyline:

Date: *4/10/2016*
Time: *1500*
Violation: *Infraction MROSD 700.4*

Incident: *Collecting Reptiles Prohibited*
Reporting Ranger: *Verbrugge*

Synopsis: *On April 10ᵗʰ 2016, 47 small plywood boards (cover boards) were found and removed from Monte Bello Open Space Preserve. The boards were placed around a meadow in a fashion used to collect reptiles. The boards were removed and thrown away.*
Statements: *None.*
Investigation:
Initial Observation: *I observed approximately ten boards in a meadow around a Douglas-fir tree.*
Crime Scene: *Monte Bello Preserve is located within the City of Palo Alto. I found the boards in a meadow along Skyline Boulevard approximately 1.5 miles south of Alpine Road, accessed from the first pullout south of Gate MB07. The cover boards were around the perimeter of the meadow against the tree line.*
Evidence Taken: *47 cover boards used for collecting reptiles were removed and disposed of.*
Action Taken: *Ranger Hapke, Ranger Chance and I searched the meadow for cover boards. All boards were transported to the Skyline Field Office for disposal*
Additional Information: *California Department of Fish and Game was notified by email of the incident.*

I don't know what led Andrew to go looking around this roadside meadow in the first place. The report doesn't say. Could he see the boards around the tree from his truck? Probably not. Subsequent personal experience showed that such cover boards were usually well concealed, and certainly not visible from the roadway. Maybe he found the boards incidental to heading to the far side of a tree for personal reasons. It's amazing what I've found when simply looking to see a man about a horse. This must have occurred on a Thursday or Friday, my days off, because I don't remember even hearing about the boards and their removal until a week or two later. I never saw this first-discovered board array or got in on the start of the story.

I was certainly familiar with the concept of reptile cover boards. Reptiles and amphibians, such as snakes, lizards, salamanders and newts are ectothermic and need to have ready access to both sun and shade for warming or cooling themselves. They are also prey species for birds and mammals and so want to stay hidden as much as possible. The ecotone between forest and meadow or between chaparral and meadow, therefore, makes great habitat. Go out in the meadow and warm yourself, then back into the bushes or trees to cool off. So much the better if there is a convenient pile of rocks or a nice, big rotten log right there on the meadow perimeter under which to hide. Critters searching this desirable real estate along the ecotone and finding the alluring underside of a chunk of plywood will likely set up housekeeping. Housing is scarce in this neighborhood and a single small (2 'X 3') board might house some unlikely roommates: snakes and mice under the same board, for example.

Richard, a herpetologist under contract with the District, had board arrays, as well as other capture devices, down at Big Springs Pond in the Mindego Hill part of Russian Ridge and I one day happened upon him and got to help him clear his traps and record his findings. That was really fun. Another long-time District wildlife research contractor, Eric Remington, had board arrays set up in five or six different spots around South Skyline, and I once went out with him to check a new array of some ten boards in Long Ridge. All of his boards were stenciled to show that they were authorized research boards and not to disturb them. There were no critters under his boards that day, but as Eric explained, it was a new array and the critters hadn't moved in yet. Additionally it was winter, and the boards would mostly be inhabited during the following summer.

I also don't know how Andrew figured out the significance of the 47 boards scattered around the edge of that meadow in Monte Bello. Did he just think it was strange and suspicious? Did someone authorize him to contact Fish and Game, or how did he know to do that? From Eric and Richard I knew about cover boards, but it hadn't occurred to me that they might easily be put to nefarious purposes. Fish and Game must either have suggested or confirmed Andrew's poaching suspicions. Having never sold anything online myself, it never occurred to me that unscrupulous reptile enthusiasts were making a living illegally selling rare and endangered wildlife on the Internet. Removing rare and endangered animals from their diminished wild population and thus contributing to species extinction seemed to me a deplorable crime. Once I knew what was going on, I was hot to get this guy.

Journal entry 1/2/2017: We continue to pursue the Reptile Board Guy. Yesterday I found a big array of about 30 boards in Castle Rock State Park. I had been down on foot inside Gate LR13, the Red Mountain area, checking on a report that the illegal bench hangout had been rebuilt. On my way back out, I ran into Andrew and his trainee, Kyle, who had come to check on the same thing. Andrew, however, had first thought to check the perimeter of the small meadow near the gate, and had found six boards. I went to look at those, and then noticed that there was a slightly larger meadow just across Highway 9, so went and walked around that. Bingo. Lots of boards there, about 40, I'd guess. Unfortunately, both sets of boards are on state parks property, so we can't do anything. Andrew says he will contact state parks as well as the F & G warden he's been working with. Turns out that F & G already knew about the South Skyline board guy even before Andrew contacted them following the Monte Bello incident. They faxed us his driver's license photo, and vehicle information. His Portola

Heights address means that our suspect has super-easy access to all the meadows of South Skyline.

The problem with trying to cite the reptile poacher was that you had to catch him red-handed, with a snake in his hand stuffing it into a bag. Just seeing the guy wandering around a board-laced meadow wouldn't prove anything. That's not illegal. Seeing him in the act of placing boards could count as littering, but good luck happening upon that, and anyway, I wanted to get him on a misdemeanor or even a felony, not just an infraction littering citation. We considered putting out camouflaged wildlife cameras trained on individual boards in the hopes of catching him in the act, but unless you were lucky enough to get a clear video of the guy's face and his stuffing the animal into the container, you'd still have nothing. Besides, the poacher would quite likely see and destroy the camera, so the camera never happened.

I think it was during this time, after we were all aware of the snake poacher that I almost got myself in trouble out at Mindego. I was in the area when A12, Cindy Roessler, came up on the radio reporting two suspicious males heading back toward the parking lot from Mindego Hill. They were reportedly dirty, wearing kneeling pads and gloves and carrying a big blue bag that looked heavy. Moreover--and the first thing to pop into my mind--they were exiting an area known to house one of the last remaining populations of endemic San Francisco Garter Snakes (SFGS).

I drove slowly down the Mindego Ridge Trail looking for the suspicious guys and thinking about how to manage this contact should they prove hostile. Poaching a SFGS is a felony. Might they be armed? Was I being stupid? When I laid eyes on them, and then made verbal contact, my fears were allayed. The men, both at least middle-aged, were immediately friendly and cooperative. They were looking to collect a small live redwood tree, but they hadn't been successful. They consented to a search of their blue bag (digging tools) and their one small backpack (remains of lunch) and I let them go with a warning that collecting anything from the preserve is illegal. End of story, I thought.

But this stop provoked a big discussion at the next patrol meeting. Many rangers, including my supervisor, seemed to feel that I had gone overboard in my enthusiasm to apprehend bad guys, and that I had unduly harassed the visitors. I had gone beyond the bar warranted by reasonable suspicion, and had entered the realm of probable cause. Everyone agreed that I had sufficient suspicious circumstances to stop them (dirty, knee pads, gloves), but nothing on which to base a search of their backpack or bag. There was clearly no tree sticking out of it. I argued that the additional circumstances of their having been in a SFGS area, and having been reported as suspicious by a District resource protection specialist, added to my case for searching the bags, but I guess they were right, darn it.

But what if these two really had been snake poachers, and were allowed to just waltz away under my very nose carrying a snake in their bag? Two guys who obviously had been scrambling around in the dirt in an endangered species area: what more evidence did I need before I had enough probable cause to search their bags? Did I have to see the bag wiggle, or the snake poke its head out? Trying to get this snake poacher was going to be impossible. We were never going to stop him collecting animals by trying to catch him in the act, or stopping him with a bag full of snakes, but maybe we could go at it from the other end. We could simply remove all his boards, and then just keep removing them.

I also realized that poacher-guy didn't even have to bother setting up his own board arrays, because he could simply use Eric's. Why not? Eric's boards just sat out there undefended. He could check under them just as easily as Eric could, just swiping the critters rather than studying them and recording the information. I brought this all up with the area superintendent and with the Resource Management Department and got permission to remove any and all of Eric's boards. He had been contacted and told to pull out his boards as his contract was up anyway. We had to endure a silly training about District protocol for how to check under boards, supposedly wearing gauntleted gloves, and 12" leather boots, and requiring two persons. It was all based on fear of rattlesnakes. No one ever checked to ensure my compliance, or even seemed to care. I think I just might have repeatedly violated protocol.

Photo by Kristin Perry
Rubber boa in my hands, found under cover board in Long Ridge

So, armed with maps showing Eric's cover boards with GPS points, I set out to pull them all. It was a ton of work. Most of these meadows are steep, with the road at the top end, so Eric, in setting the boards out, had only to pull the boards downhill. I, on the other hand, had to drag them back up the hill. Sometimes the boards were small, only 1' X 2,' but more often much larger, around 3' X 4,' just big enough that I couldn't quite fit one between my fingertips and my armpit for easy carrying, meaning that I had to either drag the board or balance it on my head, while struggling back up the steep hill. I had some help, but it was my project and I did a lot of it myself. The only truly fun part was finding all the animals. I didn't record my findings, just enjoyed them. Lots of rubber boas, ring neck snakes, and slender salamanders. Lots of mice. Plus arboreal salamanders, newts, a racer snake, and two or three rattlers. One of the rattlers I almost stepped on. Ranger Kyle, who was helping me that day, just said, "Frances, you need to take two big steps forward right now." Pretty good for a guy seeing his first rattlesnake. Toward the end of my board removal project, I gave up on actually hauling the boards back out to the truck and driving them back to the SFO dumpster. I admit I would instead just locate a nearby gully full of poison oak or French broom and launch them into it. Why not?

But then we got a big break:

Journal entry 3/25/2017: Finally laid eyes on the cover board snake poacher guy, about ten days ago now. His white BMW was parked on Skyline, in a turnout just north of the Jikoji driveway. I just knew it was him, but ran the plate anyway, and asked for a fill so someone could sit on his car while I went to see if I could catch him, reptile in hand. But, before anyone got there, he appeared, coming up through the trees from the meadow below. He was cooperative and talkative. He willingly opened his daypack to show it contained nothing but camera equipment. (Did I have probable cause? Ooo, I think not.) He said he was tired of District rangers hassling him, that he was "one of the good guys," and "an honest enthusiast," etc. Did I believe him? I'm leaning toward no, but why? Because I know he's been seen in association with other cover board arrays by L34 (Andrew), for one. California Fish and Game also have a record of his buying an alligator gar online; this is according to poacher-guy himself. I need to talk to Andrew to get the whole story. Anyway, I had exactly nothing, so I let him go, warning him that putting out cover board arrays and checking them was illegal.

Later that same day, Ranger Chris cited him for molesting wildlife. He saw the BMW at Waterman Gap and went looking for him after calling for a state park ranger to fill. Chris reportedly saw him turning over, or picking up rocks, and cited him for that, having first gotten supervisor permission to cite on state parks property. I guess State Park Ranger Knapp was on scene by then and signed as citing officer, while Chris signed as arresting officer.

I was incredulous when I heard they had cited him for turning over rocks. Does this mean visitors aren't allowed to pick up sticks, rocks or leaves, examine them and set them back down? Technically yes, because that is disturbing the habitat of thousands of microscopic creatures, but this seems way too extreme to me. Are we saying that only good people can turn over rocks, but bad people can't? Anyway, I hear that Ranger Knapp now wants to talk to me because snake guy said that I told him that looking under rocks was okay. Did I tell him that? I don't remember. I remember telling him that rangers have discretion and can cite or not cite depending on the totality of the circumstances. I told him that putting out boards was littering, and that if we could show that his intent in putting them out was to commit a further crime, we could ding him for that too. Rocks? I don't know. I think Chris was quite right to cite as far as intent, but how do you prove that?

I never heard how this case got resolved. I think it never went to trial, or hasn't yet. Our poacher is still out there, on the loose in the area. No doubt there are still boards out there, just not ones I've found yet. Until the day I retired I continued to walk the perimeters of meadows, ever vigilant. I still hope we will someday nail him, and prevent further kidnapping of innocent wild creatures.

Photo used by permission of MROSD

Annette Coleman
Area Superintendent

I grew up here in Palo Alto. When I went away to school, to University of California at Davis, my idea was to major in botany, but botany required taking a lot of chemistry, and my first experience in introductory chemistry class was not good. The course was very competitive because all the pre-med and vet students were required to pass it. I just didn't find chemistry interesting, so I switched my major to environmental planning and management with an emphasis on environmental interpretation. I took all these great natural science classes, like entomology, botany, geology and geography, which I really loved.

When I graduated from UCD, I worked for the USGS for a year and a half at their Menlo Park campus doing administration. I called myself a typewriter jockey. Then I got a six-month seasonal ranger job at Palo Alto Foothills Park. When one of the permanent rangers went on a leave of absence, I took her job as a provisional, and when she came back there was an opening that I got. I promoted to the senior ranger position after a while, but I didn't see much chance of moving up and doing anything different at Foothills Park, so I applied for jobs at other park agencies.

I actually had applied for the ranger job at the Open Space District at about the same time that I was hired at Foothills Park, but I didn't get it. For a long time the District had hired for more of a generalist ranger position, but by then they were looking for people to do more law enforcement. Ten years later, when I was hired as the District's Foothills area superintendent, I was the first female supervisor and the first supervisor hired from outside the organization. My son called me a Super Nintendo; he was three at the time. The Skyline superintendent then was David Sanguinetti, and John Escobar was our boss, the operations manager. I think John Escobar was Foothills area superintendent before me.

~~~

This man was out hunting, I'm not sure where--not on District land, obviously--and shot a mama pig, and then discovered she had three tiny babies. He brought the babies home with him to the San Jose area and he and his wife raised them for a while at their house, until they could no longer manage to keep them. These were the huge, wild boar kind of pigs, peccaries, with big, long tusks. They decided to release them back into the wild--at Rancho San Antonio. The pigs had names, Tom, Dory, and Olga, names the hunter and his wife had given them.

Before long, visitors were being pursued around Rancho by these three big pigs, because the pigs, of course, were friendly and used to people, having been hand-raised by humans. The rangers were dealing with all these aggressive pig calls because the visitors were terrified. I never saw the animals myself. We found out about their human parents because someone who knew them ratted them out, or maybe they ratted themselves out. This whole story even made the TV news, maybe Channel 5? I have no idea what happened to those pigs. We did make an effort to trap them ourselves with some pig traps we got from Santa Clara County Vector Control, but we were never able to trap them. I think some hunter must have shot them.

Then there was a second, completely different pig incident. This was not that long after the three wild pigs, so by this point all the regular visitors were on pig alert, because the three pigs had been so scary, with their tusks and chasing behavior. These neighbors to Rancho San Antonio in Los Altos near the St. Joseph's Avenue access, on the west side of Permanente Creek had two horses. Then one of the horses died, and the remaining horse was lonely, so they bought a pot-bellied pig to keep it company. Maybe they thought a pig would be easier to take care of than another horse. So, every now and then Lily the pot-bellied pig--who didn't have tusks, but was quite a stout creature, probably around 45 pounds--would get loose and follow people around. She liked jogging along behind people, and, of course, that's what Tom, Dory and Olga had also done. Lily would get out and start "terrorizing" all the hikers at Rancho. They were scared of her, even though she was only a pet pig out for a jog herself.

One day, one of our rangers, Tom Karnofel, caught Lily— Lily had to be tackled-- and he brought her to the ranger office and he was trying to get her up into his truck to transport her back home. He had her up in the bed of the truck and was trying to move her. He was hanging on to her hind legs and she was thrashing around. Tom's arms were going like pistons! It was crazy, so I yelled at him, "Hey, Tom, leave that poor pig alone," and he yelled back, "She's doing it to me!" That pig was just shaking Tom's arms back and forth trying to get loose. He finally was able to calm the pig down and take her home. She was funny. Lily the pig.

~~~

I don't know if the great horned owls are still using that one eucalyptus tree below the Parim house, now the Annex. When I was in charge there during a drought time, there was a real problem with the eucalyptus trees' self-pruning habit. When they don't have enough water, they just drop their big limbs, and these huge trees were planted all along the main corridor at Rancho. For $1,000 a tree, I had ten trees taken down through a contract with McClenahan's. I don't know how they did it so cheaply. They left the stumps, and girdled them, and put in some sort of herbicide. It worked really well; there was hardly any stump sprouting at all. I think they just put a big, heavy dose of Roundup in-between the bark and the living layer of the tree. They cut a groove, a trough, and they poured the Roundup directly in that trough. It worked great. They left the one tree that the owls nested in. The tree is still there, but I don't know if the owls use it anymore.

~~~

Shortly after I was hired we were nearing the end of the fiscal year and the rangers presented me with a request to upgrade the Stokes litter, which we used for carrying out injured people. They showed me an attachment to the litter they wanted; it had an all-terrain tire and an aluminum frame that clipped onto the litter. You could have rescuers in the front and back just guiding it along and keeping it on the trail, but nobody supporting the patient's weight. The tire attachment cost $400. I looked at that thing and I looked at my budget, and I didn't have any money left, but I went ahead and bought it anyway. I learned that, if you wanted to get as much or more money in your budget the next year, you overspent by a couple percent, and bought something critical, something beneficial to the staff or the organization.

This litter was something they'd been looking at for a long time, trying to get someone to authorize it. I didn't get in too much trouble. I mean, $400! People didn't even blink an eye at spending that kind of money in other organizations. It improved field staff safety, and visitor medical rescue. Our trails weren't wide enough to have rescuers on both sides of a litter. The wheel litter only needed a rescuer at either end, and maybe on one side, not on the outside edge of the trail where they could fall off. I felt good about that purchase. Later on the Skyline office got one too.

I also introduced cameras for the field staff, film cameras; there weren't digital cameras yet. We made photo albums of maintenance projects, and the rangers took pictures of wildlife. I think the albums are still around. It started out with just the supervisors having cameras, just two or three cheap cameras. I had to take the film in for processing, so it wasn't practical to use the pictures in incident reports. It was mostly about making the photo albums, documenting our work as an historical record. I just wanted there to be a record of what we'd done.

At the time I left, email was just starting and there were all these policies about it. They were really picky about how you couldn't use it as your private email. Of course, everybody now has personal phones to do this stuff.

They gave me the rattiest old truck when I got the superintendent job, the old Ram Charger, but when they tried to take it away from me, I didn't want to give it up. I liked it. It was big, and it had manual locking hubs so when I did four-wheel drive, I first had to get out and turn the hubs. I got a smaller Cherokee after that and I missed the old Ram Charger.

~~~

When I was there, each ranger was assigned a preserve where they monitored and maintained trails, signs, fences and culverts. Rangers would come to me saying, "We should do this, and we need to get that," and I'd say, "Well, you guys are in charge of these areas. You have more experience and know what should be done." I wanted the rangers to tell me about the problem, but also to outline the solution. Then we could talk about time and materials, and I could authorize whatever was required. They were the ones who had to figure out how to fix stuff, not me. They would look at me like, "Uh, this is different," but they liked it, because they had some power and responsibility. It was fun. I liked working with them and learned a lot. I had fun with the staff.

Thank you, Annette

Some comments on Annette's interview:

I don't know if there are still great horned owls nesting in that eucalyptus tree, but there were during my time as a ranger at FFO. I happened by one day and found a crowd gathered around an adorable fuzzy baby owlet sitting on the ground under that eucalyptus tree. We would normally leave such a bird as the parents might continue to feed it and defend it even on the ground, but this little guy was sitting next to the busiest trail in the whole District, and some visitor would probably have "rescued" it home to their house, where it would have died. We took it to a wildlife rescue center.

Wheel litters are now standard equipment for most park districts. Even with the wheel bearing a lot of the weight, they are the cause of back injuries. I keep thinking that someday soon somebody is going to invent a motorized version with a gyroscope to help keep it upright.

Ranger Frances: Wayz Out

I tried to remember to ask everyone I interviewed about new equipment, or computer technology, or consumer electronics that had changed their working lives at the District. Annette mentions buying film cameras for the field staff, as well as the District's first wheel litter. The first desktop computers also made their appearance at the field offices during her tenure. They multiplied quickly. When I first started as a ranger at the FFO, all the rangers there shared a single desktop computer, and a single email account. The same was true at SFO. I thought it was great. My technophile co-workers would constantly be checking the email--I mean, like every single day! If there was something for me, they would holler as I was trying to make my escape out the office door, "Frances, you've got an email."

~~~

GPS navigation devices in vehicles and cellphones first appeared and then became ubiquitous during my time as a ranger. Their quality may have improved since the time of the following stories, I suppose, and perhaps there are actually fewer lost and misdirected drivers out there than before their advent. Are we simply more willing to forgive and forget about humans giving one another poor and misleading directions than we are machines for doing the same thing?

Journal entry 12/6/2014: On Tuesday last week, I was on foot on the Betsy Crowder Trail when Dispatch called saying there was a tow truck driver at Gate WH05 who needed to get through. I thought there must be some kind of mistake because Gate WH05, near the lower Windy Hill parking lot in Portola Valley, leads into the preserve, onto the Spring Ridge Trail, which is a dirt patrol road. Why would a tow truck driver possibly need access there?

I made my way down to the parking lot where I found the tow truck driver, and a young Hispanic man, who turned out to be the driver of a Kelly Moore paint delivery van. The delivery guy told me that he had been driving up Alpine Road taking a delivery of paint to The Sequoias retirement community, but he had had no actual map and was relying entirely on the directions of his electronic navigator, Siri. He must have somehow missed the right turn to The Sequoias at Portola Road. He said that Siri had then told him to turn right off Alpine Road onto the Spring Ridge Road, which, for the first couple hundred yards, is concurrently the Kabcenell's driveway up to their private inholding within Windy Hill OSP.

"But," I asked, "how did you get through the electronic gate at the bottom of the driveway?" Unfortunately for him, (in the long run) a garbage collection truck just happened to be entering the driveway, and he had snuck in right behind it. He might have been all right had he simply followed the garbage truck up to the house, and, realizing his mistake, turned around. But Siri had it in for him that day, and directed him to turn off the well-maintained gravel driveway and onto the dirt Spring Ridge Trail. Oh dear. This trail does pass directly behind The Sequoias, but, when wet, is one of the slipperiest, slimiest, gooiest roads in the entire District. The paint store van actually made it about halfway to Gate WH05 before becoming stranded. He explained that all four tires were still on the roadway, but he could move neither forward nor back. At this point, he said, he got scared and didn't know what to do. He didn't really know where he was, except somewhere near The Sequoias, but he was in a forest. The tow truck driver, whom he reached by cell phone, wanted him to walk out so they could meet at The Sequoias, but he confessed that he sat in his truck for about half an hour, too scared to leave it.

"Scared of what?" I asked. "I was afraid the mountain lions would get me," he shivered. Yes, I almost burst out laughing, but, of course, I didn't. Poor guy. He eventually met up with the tow truck driver, and they walked back in together. It was actually the tow truck driver who got the delivery van badly stuck in the mud in

his effort to drive it out. They had earlier seen my patrol truck parked near WH05 (where I'd left it while I went on foot patrol) and now, with the paint van decidedly stuck, they agreed to call for my help. It looked hopeless to me, with both left side tires up to their axles in mud, but they initially convinced me to allow the tow truck driver access to attempt extrication. The tow guy said he would have to go get a knobbier-tired tow truck from his shop in Redwood City, but that he would be right back.

So, the paint store guy and I sat in my patrol truck and waited and talked for an hour as it rained and the sun set and it started to get dark. Feeling like a rat, I then rescinded my permission to enter, much to my supervisor's relief. It just didn't seem safe dealing with this problem in the dark, in the rain. Meanwhile, I was amazed to hear that not only had the paint store guy never before driven off of a paved surface, he had never even been outside of an urban landscape. Now I felt bad about my earlier amusement. I ended up giving the young man a ride back to the Kelly Moore paint store, where I got an earful from his boss. Somehow it was all my fault that her only working delivery van was hopelessly stuck in the mud.

Photo by Frances Reneau
Kelly Moore Paint van stuck in mud at Windy Hill

The van was there, stuck in the mud, for almost a month while we waited for the Spring Ridge Trail to dry out. The regional director of Kelly Moore Paint got involved, and thus our legal department, because they wanted their van out right away, and we were denying them access. I agreed that there might have been a small window of opportunity to get it out that afternoon had the tow truck driver arrived with the knobby-tired truck in the first place, but it then poured rain for three days, so the van was even more inaccessible, which they didn't seem to understand.

~~~

Less than a year later, I had occasion to rue the existence of GPS navigational devices yet again. Such devices had certainly been around for several years by the time of these stories, but the problem of misdirected motorists continued. Of course, in both the preceding and the following stories, the drivers themselves can be accorded a good deal of the blame.

Journal entry 7/21/15: Two nights ago at about 2000, I stopped to talk to two boys, ages 16 and 17, whom I'd noticed more than an hour earlier in the same location, hanging out at Gate WH01. They said they were trying to call a tow truck and trying to call their parents, but had no cell phone reception. They had gotten their vehicle stuck on the side of a dirt road. Why had they waited so long, as the daylight hours waned, to deal with their situation? Maybe they thought the problem would just go away, or an easy solution would magically present itself? "Where exactly is your vehicle?" I kept asking. It took some digging to get a clear answer as the boys probably realized that they shouldn't have been driving on this particular road at all. I eventually figured out that their vehicle was on one of the Town of Woodside trails. This trail (road) hits Skyline Boulevard just north of Gate WH01, but mostly traverses private property. The driver, the 16-year-old, a cooperative and polite kid all in all, said that it was his Wayz app that had gotten them into this mess. It had showed this trail starting from the Portola Valley town center, right behind the tennis courts, and leading clear up to Skyline Boulevard. It had looked fun and adventurous. Now, however, they had to face up to the consequences of their impulsive behavior: being stranded without cell phone coverage with their vehicle stuck on the side of a cliff on private property, and being interrogated by a park ranger. They knew they were in trouble, and were sitting around not wanting to face it, and not knowing what else to do.

I have no jurisdiction on private property, so I called San Mateo County Sheriff, as well as Ellison's Towing, and the kids' parents. The on-duty District supervisor, Brad, also showed up. Ellison's wanted to be sure we understood that AAA doesn't cover four-wheeling tows. I got Brad's permission to walk down with the tow truck driver and the boys to look at the stuck vehicle. Meanwhile Brad was working on trying to locate a phone number for the private property owner, Mr. Neelie. By the time we reached the stuck vehicle about a half-mile down, it was almost dark. The tow truck driver looked at this Nissan Xterra teetering on the brink of a steep drop-off from the edge of a narrow dirt road, and said, "No way." Had it been a District truck on our own property, I think we could have easily winched it clear, so I felt sort of sorry for those boys.

The Sheriff's Deputy seemed uninterested in the whole affair although he looked to be enjoying yacking with Brad. He never took any action, never even talked with the boys themselves, even though I told him that the driver kid had only a provisional license, and thus wasn't supposed to be driving his friend around at all. Both kids got released to their folks. I left a message on Neelie's phone machine, but never heard back. Too bad. I am plenty curious about how they ended up getting the car out. It's rather ironic that these kids had made it most of the way up the trail before chickening out and attempting to turn around and go back down, which is when they got stuck. Had they simply continued, they probably would have made it out onto Skyline Boulevard, and no one would have been the wiser. The gate at Skyline Boulevard, at that time was completely unsecured.

Photo used by permission of Mark Casaretto

Mark Casaretto, Open Space Technician, EMO (Equipment Mechanic Operator)

That's me on the dozer down at Loma Prieta Ranch in Sierra Azul. When you got down about halfway, there was a spur road that went off on the right to a flat and a wellhead. It had been due to be developed. We used to hide equipment out there because we figured nobody would see it.

~~~

I grew up right around the corner here in San Carlos. My early experience in the outdoors was with Boy Scouts. Camping was the primary reason I wanted to be in Boy Scouts. I wasn't interested in learning first aid or other stuff; I just wanted to go camping, the weekend camping trips. I had friends that went to Scout summer camp, but I never did. After grade school, I left Scouts, but would go hunting and fishing with my dad. I was in the woods quite a bit as a kid. My two cousins, Frank and Bill—usually referred to by their nicknames Poncho and Tuba-- had a pear orchard in Walnut Grove, and we'd hunt pheasants in the back. Dad had been deer hunting over by Mt. Hamilton, on the other side of Lake Del Valle, since he was a young man back in the 1920's, and that's where he'd take me.

I spent 12 years at parochial school and I can still feel the guilt. After high school, I enrolled in a two-year culinary program at Canada Community College. In my second year I got on as an apprentice at the Burlingame Country Club in Hillsborough. The Swiss chef there knew guys in Switzerland and he got me two different seasonal jobs there. They liked to bring in outside people so they wouldn't have to pay them as much. It's similar to how minorities here are all waiters and housekeepers. In Switzerland, the waiters were all Spaniards and Italians. I didn't make a lot of money, but I got free room and board and I got to be in Switzerland!

In my 20's and early 30's I worked as a chef in the Trattoria Romana restaurant in Palo Alto for about nine years. At that point I decided to look for something with better hours because I had two kids by then, and I thought it would be nice to be home on the weekends and not working holidays and nights in the craziness that is a restaurant. I didn't have any experience in parks, other than visiting them.

So, I looked around at different public agencies. It wasn't easy, as you know, getting hired. People would tell me, "Oh, you're a white, straight male. You might as well forget it." Guys who'd been in the military had a leg up on me. But I thought, "If you don't try, they're not going to come knocking at your door, offering you this job." My wife was supportive, and financially we were okay. She was working mornings at a publisher, and I was working in the afternoons and evenings at the restaurant.

First I got a volunteer job, just to see if I'd like doing parks for a living. I volunteered for a year with the Fish and

Wildlife Service at the Don Edwards Wildlife Refuge down on San Francisco Bay. I'd go a couple times a month on my days off.

Then I applied with California Land Management, which had the contract with Menlo Park for Bayfront Park. I would go there one day a week on my Saturday off and work an eight-hour shift. I had a little Datsun pick-up and I'd drive around, talk to people, and pick up litter. I did more than most people. A lot of guys were just driving around. Once you'd done a couple of laps of the place—it's only about 200 acres—you had to figure out something to do for the rest of your shift. There were no restrooms at that time and not many visitors because it was only partly developed. My wife, Paula, would bring me lunch, and bring the kids.

Then I got on with San Mateo County Parks as a seasonal at Huddart Park, which was 1,000 hours supposedly, but the County bent the rules all over the place. In the summer there were about five seasonals. Early on I was told by a ranger named Leon that when it comes to working in the parks, every day you are either digging a hole or filling one in. That often proved true. The other seasonals would leave and go back to school, but I stayed. They liked me because I gave a good eight hours, and didn't cause any problems, so I got to stay on even beyond my 1,000 hours. They fudged it.

We did the Sheriff's Work Program where they would bring the guys who'd gotten DUIs and had to work off their hours. Most of them were okay. There were a couple of hard cases. I'd say, "We're either going to get through this, or you're going to be here for a long time, pal. If you want to sit on your butt, you can do that down at the jail." Nobody wanted to be there, clearly. It was embarrassing. They weren't all working class guys. Some of them were doctors and dentists. My supervisor wanted to make sure we got our money's worth out of them. We got stuff done that we never would have done otherwise. We had this whole fleet of wheelbarrows, 40 wheelbarrows, and they'd get a ten-wheeler load of bluestone dumped at some trailhead. The work program guys hauled the rock half a mile down that trail and spread it until the pile was done.

~~~

In the meantime, I had applied to the District for the permanent OST position. After I finished the initial interview at Midpen, the interview panel folks were talking amongst themselves, and they said I should fill out a seasonal application. Their seasonal position paid about four bucks an hour more than San Mateo County, so that was a no-brainer. Plus, once I got my foot in the door, who knew what might happen. It could only be good. At that time, Midpen was hiring people, whereas the County didn't know where their next pot of nails was coming from.

So I started work as a seasonal OST sometime in April, either '91 or '92; I can't remember. John Kowaleski was the maintenance supervisor. The permanent OSTs were Michael Jurich, Paul McKowan, Stan Hooper, and maybe Ralph Molica. I was only there about a month as a seasonal before they offered me the permanent job. I was fortunate. There was a woman who had been a seasonal for a couple years already ahead of me, and everyone thought, "Oh, she's going to get it. They want to hire a woman." But she didn't show up for the practical. She had some conflict, and she just didn't come.

That was before they built the new Foothills office and shop. You went in the door of the old office building about where the breezeway is now. There was a hallway, and then you were in the ranger office. It was really cramped with three desks and some wet boxes. There was a big round table where we'd eat our lunch, right there in the ranger office. If you went on farther toward the back, there was the tool room and then it opened up into the vehicle bays. There was an upstairs, too, that used to get really hot.

I remember in the old ranger office they had posters on the wall, and they had this one that showed some partial beers and a pitcher. It was supposed to be an anti-drinking thing. It said, "If you drink a lot of beer, you drink a lot." I was sitting there staring at this poster— this was like my third day — thinking, "What the hell is this about?" and this ranger, Tom Karnofel, came in. I didn't know who he was at this point. He saw me looking at this poster and said, "Oh, don't pay any attention to that. It's just some supervisor horseshit." So, I realized that this was where I wanted to be, and I could see myself doing it until I retired.

I was an OST until '97 or '98 when I became EMO. (Equipment Mechanic Operator) Gus, the only EMO at the time, used to alternate working two weeks at Foothills and two weeks at Skyline. It seemed like every time I worked with him we'd come back to the office and something would be wrong. The first time, he had defaulted on a truck he had bought, and the repo men had come to the office, started up his truck, and driven it away.

The next time he was with me, we got back to the office and the Sheriff and the Highway Patrol were both there to see him. He had stolen Tom Lauston's registration sticker because he was remiss on paying his own registration. He took the license plate off of Tom's car, and took the sticker and put it on his pickup. Well, Tom noticed his license plate was missing and they found it in the dumpster. Gus didn't have enough brains to throw it away somewhere else. Each sticker, of course, has a little number on it that goes with your registration, so it wasn't hard to figure out. That's when they called the cops, and that was the end of him. He was gone, so now they didn't have any EMO. After that, they instituted having two EMOs and Craig Beckman became the EMO up on Skyline.

They hired this other guy, Ryan, who came from Caltrans, as the next Foothills EMO. I don't think he was even there six months. He was always late, and he was always disappearing and sleeping. We'd find him hiding upstairs or over in the Annex. I remember this one time, I had gone out to make sure all the trucks were locked, the ones that wouldn't fit in the bays. I open the door of one of the pickups, thinking I'd just push the lock button down and then close it, and here's this guy asleep on the bench seat. Kind of startled me a little bit, you know. He was let go. He left, and went back to work for Caltrans again!

So they opened up the EMO position again, and that's when I applied. I didn't have all that much tractor experience, but they knew me, and they knew that I was willing to learn, and I wasn't going to be sleeping on the job. It was a pretty low bar that I had to bring myself above given this guy and the previous one. So, I got the Foothills EMO position. I got my commercial driver's license, and went to various trainings. I did that until I retired in 2011.

I remember when Jeff Smith got hired. It was around the time of the Christmas party. I had paid for my seat at the Christmas party, but then I got called to go to court because I was an alternate on a jury for an attempted murder trial. I was driving over to Fremont Older to pick up the tractor, and I had the trailer with me, when the court called and said I had to come in right away. Somebody got dismissed and so..."You're on. We need you here now." But, of course, I couldn't just pull over and leave this giant trailer. I managed to get Craig Beckman to drive down from Skyline and take over what I was doing at Fremont Older. I think Phil Heron drove me back to the office so I could pick up my own truck and drive in to court. By the time I finally got there, they were just getting back from lunch, so it was all okay. Anyway, I couldn't go to the Christmas party, which was that day, so I gave my ticket to Jeff Smith. I remember that. And the defendant went to prison.

Photo used by permission of MROSD
Installing splitrail fence along the Cordilleras Trail at Pulgas Ridge

When I was an OST, we put in that fence at Pulgas. It took us a long, long time. We thought we would never finish. When you went in past the Redwood Center there was that low splitrail fence. We put in all those posts, about 300 posts; it was crazy. Prior to putting up the splitrail fence, we had built the trail. One day when we were working on the trail, I looked up and saw Michael J running and screaming at someone, and I thought, "What's the matter with him?" Then I looked down the length of the newly built trail and saw this woman from the Administrative Office. She was driving her black Mercedes and, instead of being on the pavement, she had two tires on the freshly laid golden fines of the trail. Oh God!

There were various trail-building projects that I worked on with Gene Sheehan, some in Fremont Older, some in Pulgas. By the time we re-did the trails in Fremont Older, I was running the trail machine myself. We built the Prospect Trail, the one that comes up right out of the Prospect parking lot. The Cora Older Trail was there already. They always wanted to put a net over the parking lot to catch the golf balls before they hit the cars. Everybody laughed about it, but I guess it's there now.

~~~

Another big project at Fremont Older was rehabbing Hunter's Point. On the original Hunter's Point Trail, you drove right over the top of the hill, but when you crested the hill, you couldn't see if there was anybody below you. You were just looking out into space. They wanted to make a lookout up there, so I made the road go around the side of the hill, on the left. Now the lookout has a little fence around the top. Then, in the second phase, we ripped up the connection to Rainbow Knoll, which was also really steep. That was a couple years after the Hunter's Point rehab. Now the only way to get out to Rainbow Knoll is off Regnart Road.

I was also in charge of building the Dick Bishop Trail at Pulgas Ridge using the Sweco and the mini-excavator. The Sweco is a little bulldozer. Starting with that trail and a lot of trails after that, they hired that consultant, Tim Best, and he wrote up the plan. You weren't supposed to deviate from the plan. There were a couple places in building that trail where some deviations happened. The plan called for bench cutting some places where I thought, "If you bench cut this, you're going to have to cut all those roots and kill that tree. It's not going to die tomorrow, but it's going to kill it." There were a couple places where I did my own thing and later was able to convince the boss that it was for the best.

We couldn't build like we used to back when we were with Gene Sheehan, where you'd brush out a wide swath and then come in with the trail machine. The dirt was all cast-off. Now they didn't want any of the spoils going over the side. Now instead of doing a half-bench cut, where you'd be half benched into the hill and the other half of the track was fill that you'd compacted so you could drive forward onto it, now you had to move over farther and make a bigger bench cut. You couldn't put the spoils over the side anymore. We had those Canycoms, which were like a toter but bigger, and they dumped. One of those would be coming along behind the excavator. You'd swivel the house around and dump the spoils into the Canycom until it was full, and then those guys would haul it away. It was slow going. That was one of the first trails where we had to do it that way.

~~~

I know the Umunhum Air Base is totally different now. I should go for a ride-along up there. It may have been broken into since, but I was the last person to go down into the bomb shelter. I was up there with Michael J. The normal way in, you went down a staircase and then into a hallway, and it kind of zigzagged underneath. They had a decontamination showerhead thing. Oh yeah, that's gonna save you! I had welded up these big iron plates, and we shoved one of them up against the door, spanning the whole door, and then we crawled in through the manhole on the other end of the bomb shelter, the escape hatch. You climbed down a ladder. From the outside it just looked like a sewer cover. You wouldn't have known what it was unless you'd been told. You went down a pipe with a ladder inside it and came out at the back end of the bomb shelter.

The bomb shelter was good sized, about the size of a Quonset hut buried in the ground. It had a domed roof of corrugated steel. It was in three sections: the first part you came into, through the walk-through door, there was a two-hole outhouse off to the left. The shit? Well, I guess if you survived a nuclear holocaust, the shit is the least of your problems! On the right was a storage room for the food. Then you went a little farther in, and next there was a kitchen. Then it opened up into these two rooms. One was living quarters, and then in the back was the bunkhouse. In the very back was this hole in the ceiling, which was the escape hatch. Not only was there the lid on top, but also this heavy steel door on hinges, like a blast door, that you could only open from the inside.

Once we got this iron thing on the outside of the walk-through door, we had this other similar piece of iron with holes in it that matched the ones on the outside piece. Then we put on nuts and washers and cinched it all down so you couldn't open the door anymore. Then we exited by the escape hatch. Michael J went out first, and then I took a piece of chain and went partway up the ladder and hooked the chain onto the blast door and pulled it up, and that slammed and locked it. Then we locked the chain to a ladder rung. If they'd got behind the metal bars of the door, they might have cut the bolts. It's like anything else: if you've got the equipment, you can bust into anything. I know the bomb shelter was like the Holy Grail to all those guys who were breaking into everything up there. So, that was it. I was the last one in there.

~~~

There were three residences down Barlow Road in Sierra Azul. One was a wood-framed house with various people living in there. One guy was real sketchy, him and his girlfriend. These guys were actually tenants of the District; Brant was his name, I think. There was some question of whether he was poaching deer. His girlfriend was a fairly young woman who didn't have any teeth.

One day we were up on Umunhum Road working on something and Brant knew we were there and he came out to help us. We were cleaning out ditches or something. He brought a shovel and a little hand-truck with a cooler on it. The cooler was full of all his beer for the day.

The Barlow House was made out of cinder blocks with a flat, sloped roof, basically one big room with a '50's era circular fireplace in the middle of the floor. All those houses are gone now. One of those houses was called the Sink House. Those houses were all held together with a wing and a prayer as far as their water systems.

One day they sent Stan and me over to the Barlow House, because they had no water and we had to go figure out why not. The water came from way up the hill somewhere, going up toward the monolith. We found the tank behind the house empty, then we started following the black plastic pipe. We must have followed it for what seemed like miles, but I know it wasn't that far. There was a trail that followed alongside the pipe. We finally found the source, but in the meantime this storm had blown in and it was foggy and raining. If we hadn't known where we were, we'd have been stuck. It was like we were in Iceland. You couldn't see more than 40 feet. The source was just like a wallow where the water collected and then the pipe went in there. You know those nuts that fall off the bay trees that look like green olives? Well, one of those had got sucked into the end of the pipe and had stopped it up like a cork. That was it. That was their water system.

These tenants always seemed like people who wanted to get away from the authorities. There was only one guy I remember who seemed like he was a straight shooter, but he didn't last. His girlfriend didn't like it. It was too remote. I think he was in the Sink House after this Mark guy got booted out. You never knew what these people did for a living.

One time I was up at the double gates with Tom Karnofel. We were painting it MROSD Oxford brown. It was right after they had passed the motorcycle helmet law in California, and this guy, Burkie, came along on his old motorcycle. Karnofel knew him and so they were talking, and then Burkie went on his way, and I said, "Tom, that guy had a pot strapped to his head." "Yeah, he figures that way he won't stick out so much, and won't get stopped." He had taken a cooking pot and a bungee cord and he had it wrapped around his head. Karnofel said that was nothing for up there.

I remember this one time when I was out with Holden. Crazy Jerry had a crude water system up off Umunhum Road. The water came out of the side of the hill right next to the road. It looked like a mineshaft. Holden and I had the Bobcat, and we were scraping up rocks that had fallen, to get them off the road. We went to ask Jerry about his water pipe, because we figured it probably wasn't down too deep, and we didn't want to cut into it. So, we went into Crazy Jerry's place, to see him. I'd never been down in there before. We parked on Umunhum Road and walked in. As we got back in there, there was just more and more junk everywhere, and we were thinking, "Okay, which one of these old trailers is the residence? Somebody's gotta be in here, someplace." We started yelling and out came Jerry and this other guy, Boomhauer, that nobody could ever understand. That was his uncle, I think. They came out and this was about 11 in the morning and they've got these matching bathrobes on, and rubber boots!

They came out of the trailer and we told them what we wanted, and while we were talking, I saw this other guy from one of the other trailers, and he was kind of hiding, and he maybe thought we didn't see him. He was looking at us from around the corner. As we were leaving, I said, "Hey, Holden, did you see that guy looking at us?" And he said, "Yeah, What was his story? What was that all about?" I don't know, but he didn't show himself. He was just checking us out. We found out where the pipe might or might not be, and we went about our business, but they were quite a pair in their rubber boots and matching bathrobes!

~~~

Tom Randall was living at the old air force base up on top of Umunhum for a while with his wife. Originally they weren't in the commander's residence. At the end of the block where the commander's house was, there were all these four-unit apartment buildings, and they lived in one of those apartments.

Maybe they were duplexes. Then Chris Sanger died. He was the caretaker with the phone company up there who lived in the commander's house, and so Tom and his wife moved over there. They lived there for a couple years when Tom was the resident ranger.

There was a lot of nasty stuff up there. I can remember getting sent up there with the deck mower on the tractor to mow the firebreak. We would also do some discing. We only did the disking up there a couple times, and then we figured, "What the heck; let it burn up. Who cares?"

All those apartments still had appliances in them. They'd send you up there, "They need a new stove at So-and-so's residence. Go up to Umunhum and get a stove out of one of the apartments and bring it in." The appliances were disgusting, all full of rat shit. Are you serious? The District couldn't afford a stove or a refrigerator? Get an old refrigerator that hasn't been running for years and you're going to waste all kinds of time fixing it. The fridge would work for two days and then quit. Finally even John Kowaleski had to admit, "You know, this is counterproductive. We can't be doing this."

~~~

This is a story from shortly before I retired. There was this woman who was asleep at the stoplight on Moody Road at Foothill College, in her car with her foot on the brake. At the time I wasn't sure she was asleep; I thought maybe she was having some sort of episode. I was on my way up to Skyline for one of those joint work parties at Monte Bello. I had gotten off the freeway, headed up toward Skyline and there was this car stopped there in the road and everybody was just driving around it. I pulled up past it and saw this woman, probably in her sixties, leaning on the steering wheel. I thought, "There's something wrong here," so I pulled over. I put my flashers on and then tried to get her attention, but...nothing. I called it in on the radio and asked to send fire and paramedics. I couldn't get any reaction out of her, but I could see her breathing, and she didn't look like she was in distress. The motor was running. The doors were all locked. I put some flares down.

Finally, looking way down the road toward El Camino, I could see the red lights coming, and hear the sirens. I'd been banging on this car and yelling. Finally, I took my hand-pack radio and banged it on the windshield really hard, and suddenly she was awake. She wanted to just take off, but I was like, "No, no, no. You can't go anywhere. You've got to stay here. These gentlemen in the fire trucks need to talk to you." I had to jump out of the way so she wouldn't run me over, but she just pulled over to the curb.

The fire department got information from me and it turned out that they had witnessed this before with this same woman. She had told me, when she rolled down the window, "Oh, I'm just exhausted and I fell asleep." One of the firemen said, "Yeah, we were on a call like six weeks ago where she just nodded off in traffic." I went on my way and when I got up to Skyline, they had all heard this incident on the radio. "What's going on down there? Can't just come up and see us?" I only had two more days until I retired at that point.

Of course, I've nodded off myself many times in a chair at meetings. I was known for it. Jim Mort and I were having a little competition there by the end. It's after lunch, and they've got you in the Annex, and it's warm, and they're droning on.

~~~

One time they needed people who knew the Bear Creek Redwoods Preserve to look for this at-risk teenager. It was a girl who was maybe suicidal who had left the house in agitation. How they knew she was there, I'm not sure. Maybe there was a vehicle associated. So they called Michael J and me in on this, and we brought the trailer with the two ATVs.

We parked at the old college buildings where the lake is and met up with the rangers. I think Kerry Carlson was there.

We split up and got our assigned areas and went off searching. I was on an ATV, and I skirted around the edge of the college past that little firehouse building, or maybe it was a garage, straight through to the playing field. There were two big overgrown stone pillars just past that field, toward Highway 17. You went past the stone pillars and then the road curled around to Radio Hill and eventually to a three-way intersection that took you back towards the college.

Anyway, I ran into this girl. She fit the description, but she didn't seem too lost. I was pretty sure it was her, but I thought, "Well, I don't want her to just take off on me." I told her, "We are out here looking for somebody who needs some help. So, what's your name?" She gave me a name where the first name matched that of the missing person, but not the last. I thought, "I bet this is her. She's just trying to bullshit me until I leave." I told her, "Well, we're parked up at the parking lot. If you see anybody, you let us know," and then I drove around the bend and called it in on the radio. The way she was dressed--she had on a T-shirt, shorts, and flip-flops---she wasn't going very far, right? By the time I got somebody on the radio and got back to where she'd been, she'd made it all the way up to the college buildings, where Kerry had found her. She was probably trying to get back to her car and get out of there. She moved pretty fast considering her footwear. It all worked out okay. Participating in searches almost never happened. Crew was always called in last, after the rangers had already gone over the area. I was on other searches in Rancho where the person wasn't in the preserve at all. They'd be out wandering in the neighborhood someplace.

~~~

As far as equipment goes, chainsaws and weedwhips have been around a long time, just not the variety of sizes and weights. Even laser levels have been around a long time, just that they weren't always available to us unless you went out and rented them. Unless you are a big construction company, you're not going to put down the thousands of dollars it takes to get one and then not use it all the time. The power pruner did come into being during my time there. Before that, it was one of those saw-on-a-stick things, with a string that you pulled for the loppers. It would get stuck up there in the tree. The original weedwhips I remember didn't have the bicycle handle grips with the metal blades on them. With those you can cut down small trees. Those came later. The old radios were bricks. We got the old bricks, because the rangers got the better ones, the lighter and smaller ones. We had the bricks until I retired. They just held onto them until they no longer worked anymore.

Photo by Frances Reneau
Michael Jurich and Mark Casaretto working on my truck

One of the things that changed while I was there was that maintenance didn't get the hand-me-down trucks anymore. They would actually budget to buy a truck that was built and designed for maintenance that had side boxes for equipment. The first one that I remember was the Dakota, and it wasn't any more than just a pickup with a lift-up locker in the bed. They bought that about a year before I started, so it was still new.

That was the first dedicated maintenance vehicle that didn't start out as a ranger truck. Even the flatbeds had been ranger trucks and they had just taken the utility boxes off to make them into flatbeds. Then, during my last two years with the District, they started purchasing true service trucks for the EMOs. They were larger than the old ranger trucks, and had a dual rear axle to carry more weight, a crane, oxy/acetylene tanks for cutting, a welder, an air compressor, drawers for storing small hand tools, and jump-starter cables off the front bumper like on a tow truck.

The ranger-on-crew thing was still going on for a couple years when I first started. The rangers would rotate through and they would work with us. They would do whatever we were working on. It helped to keep their skill level up and they got to do something different, too.

As the agency got bigger, there were new people down at the administrative office. I knew their names, and I kind of knew their job titles, but exactly what they did I wasn't 100 percent positive.

The only times when we were ever asked to go work on Skyline was if somebody was hurt and they were shorthanded. Then they would ask if maybe someone could go work up there for a month. I never was able to do that. Then it got to the point where we had hired enough maintenance people where if one person was out, it wasn't a disaster, like the whole crew was cut by 30 percent. But we did work together sometimes. It was more just people reporting to the other office on a temporary deal and swapping with each other. As far as the rangers, you would just meet them at all the meetings and trainings.

~~~

We were doing a controlled burn at some big facility, this place where they made rocket engines down in the South Bay hills. It goes by some kind of acronym. It was out in the boonies for safety, but it wasn't parkland. They had their own fire department because of the nature of what they did there, but it was small. Because it was a training, there were all these other agencies on scene too.

They briefed everybody beforehand. They told you the plan, and you got assigned to different squads. Kerry and I were sent to go with these other two guys from the private fire department of this company. One of them was like a chief. These two felt like the burn plan for this exercise was not burning enough brush. They wanted to see more burn, so they could really get something accomplished, rather than just putting the fire out right away. So, these guys told Kerry and me, "You guys drop a line of fire here," and we were like, "Okay, this is cool." I had the fusee out and we were lighting it all up. Pretty soon, the two firefighters that instructed us to do this had disappeared and now somebody from the legitimate exercise was all over us. "What the hell are you guys doing? Who told you to light this off?" We said, "Well, it was those guys in the white hats over there," and we pointed to where they were driving away. Our fire hadn't gotten big yet, but it wasn't on the plan, you know. So now it was, "You guys go put that out." We got in Kerry's truck and we put it out fairly easily; it wasn't a big deal. That was cool. We got to actually do something. A lot of the time you just stand around and you get to put out one little thing.

Later that same day, in the afternoon when we were supposed to be doing other exercises, all of a sudden there was this big commotion on the radio. "There's been an escape! There's been an escape!" There was fire burning where it wasn't supposed to be burning, and they were calling everybody back to where the problem was. In the meantime, they were trying to evacuate the people who worked at this place, to get them out of there because the fire was burning toward them. Midpen was the only agency that had trucks that could actually get down into where all this brush was burning. The other guys all had these big engines, and unless they were going to do some long hose lay, they couldn't get in there. We were able to get in there and actually put out the escaped fire. Even though our pumpers were small and didn't carry enough water, the trucks were also small and we could drive down there. I guess there had been some kind of fuel leak on one of the pumper units and it had caught fire, and somebody got burned, so they had to stop the whole exercise and actually do a medical. I think they sent us all home after that. Maybe this wasn't the same day.

Used by permission of MROSD
Ranger Craig Beckman, EMO,
Maintenance Supervisor, Area Manager

Continuing on with the fire stories: this was the one and only day I ever really worked on Skyline. They had me bring a tractor up to Russian Ridge. They were doing roadwork down near the bottom of the preserve someplace, on a driveway going to one of the rentals. I pulled into a big flat and offloaded the tractor, and then met up with Craig Beckman and the rest of the crew there. At first I was doing tractor work in this one spot and then Craig had to leave. I think he was going to a ballgame, so he left early. I was going to take over driving the water truck where they were laying down gravel. There were all these private truckers coming in and dumping gravel on this long driveway, and there was a private grader operator. The trucks would dump their gravel, and the grader would spread it, and they would call for another truck, so there was a series of dump trucks lined up in a queue. I was putting down water to keep down the dust and help compact the gravel as this guy was blading it. I can't remember where we got the water from. There must have been a hydrant.

This was the original water tender. It was built on an International body. There was this one valve that, if you couldn't get it open, you couldn't get any water. It was always troublesome. I had gone down to the end of the road and had put down a little water before it got stuck. I turned everything off and I was coming back up the driveway and, all of a sudden, I heard on the radio that there was a fire, and I could see the smoke over the top of the hill. One of the dump truck drivers, sitting there waiting in line, had flicked a cigarette out into the grass. When I got up the road a ways, Steve Reed was there, and I said, "Hop in! Hop in!" We drove to the fire, which was burning down the hill from the road. The grader had come over to see what he could do but he could only get so close.

Steve and I went driving off-road with this water tender trying to catch the fire. We weren't supposed to take it off-road, but it didn't look too bad. He was on the hose. We had a hose hooked up on the back of the water truck and also on the front because it was designed for both roadwork and firefighting. It had a full complement of hoses and nozzles. You could put an inch and a half hose on it and pull it ahead of the truck, walking ahead doing mobile attack. I was driving along and Steve was putting the fire out. We had already called it in and Sango had come up on the radio to help because I was trying to drive, and I had no idea where I was, other than what preserve I was in.

We got it out before the fire department actually showed up. We never put on fire gear. I mean, what were we supposed to do? Let the fire burn clear to La Honda while we're sitting there getting geared up? The funny thing was, the only reason we even had water was because earlier, when I was trying to use it, the damn valve wouldn't open. But I was able to open it then, and so we had an almost full tank of water. Afterwards there was a little bit of teasing about how we didn't follow procedure, not that we got in trouble or anything. How many rangers have pulled out their hose and put something out? They didn't stop to put on all their gear, right? This fire could have been bad. It was late summer when this happened. There was a fire investigator there soon afterward. Hopefully they figured out who flicked the cigarette. If the fire had got past where we could reach it with that water truck, it would have just kept on going. Who knows what it would have destroyed. So, that was my one day of working on Skyline.

~~~

This is a humorous incident. I was still an OST; I'd been there probably a year, and Paul McKowan was still at FFO, so pretty early on. Paul and I had gone to buy some stuff at Orchard Supply Hardware. We were getting out of the truck in the parking lot when we saw this elderly Asian man who was struggling along, taking really small steps. He had this pole like a big staff, and he'd plant it and then shuffle up to it. He looked like he was about to fall over. Jesus Christ, this guy is out here by himself? We helped him inside and got him sitting down, and asked, "Are you here by yourself?" He spoke enough English that we could communicate with him. He said, "I'm all right. My daughter's around somewhere."

We never did see her. He was a little incoherent about where he was and what he was doing there. He said he was supposed to be taking blood pressure medicine, and that he had it with him. We said, "Maybe you should take your medicine.

You'll feel better." We had called for police, thinking that somebody had to deal with this guy. We couldn't just leave him there. By the time the cop showed up, his medicine had kicked in, and now the guy could pretty near sprint up and down the aisle! Paul and I look like a couple of boobs. We were telling this officer, "You should have seen him ten minutes ago."

~~~

When pot-bellied pigs were the big rage, there was this one that used to get away from somebody in the St. Joseph's Avenue neighborhood near Rancho. One time I remember it escaped into the preserve, and it was running around where the old ball field and the tennis courts were, in the brush and trees along the creek. It was a good-sized pig. Tom Karnofel and maybe Phil Herron and I were trying to catch this thing, but it wasn't happening. As soon as you thought you were going to get it, it was gone. It was just running us in circles. We never were able to corral it. Eventually they got ahold of the owner and they were able to coax it over and put a rope on it, and lead it back to their house. It was comical because we thought, "Oh we can take care of this." We looked like the Keystone Cops.

~~~

I once found a desert tortoise that someone had let go in Fremont Older. I was doing roadwork and this seasonal was spotting for me. All of a sudden he stopped me, "You're going to run over something." "What is it?" He looked down and pointed. It wasn't a turtle. There isn't any water anywhere around there. This was on the Coyote Ridge Trail, up on the high spot where it is hot and brushy. This was a desert tortoise that must have escaped from someone's yard. Michael J came up and took it off our hands so we could continue working. He probably took it to some agency to take care of.

~~~

One day we were closing off an illegal bike trail from Soda Springs Road to Alma Bridge Road in the Cathedral Oaks area of Sierra Azul. We had dropped the Sweco off at the top and I was running it down this illegal trail. I would scoop up a bunch of brush and dirt and pile it up in a big berm to try to block the bikers' trail, like a bunch of big tank traps, one after the other. You didn't want to leave too much of an opening, though, because then they would just move the trail over there, around the side. We'd take heavy wire, heavier than baling wire, and take a pile of brush and wire it together, so they couldn't just pull it out, especially when it had dirt piled on it. Even when the chaparral is just growing wild and nobody is disturbing it, there are still spaces where they could get between bushes, and zigzag their way through.

Anyway, one of the OSTs riding the ATV had got onto the wrong trail and realized that he was headed toward Lupine Lodge, the nudist colony, and he needed to turn around. He didn't turn around properly and he tried to muscle through and ended up driving it up on some brush. The machine just kept going and he flipped over. He broke his nose and it flattened a couple tires on the ATV. We had to get the kid out of there and get him first aid. That incident initiated the use of full-face motorcycle helmets. Prior to that, we just had like football helmets.

There was another bike trail off of Priest Rock Road where we did much the same thing, the Moody Trail it was called. They did more work at the top there because they figured, if we made the top more difficult, they were not going to want to do it.

~~~

There was this old guy, Clyde, who lived with his daughter off the end of Mora Road, just outside of Rancho San Antonio, on one of those side streets. Her name was Clydine! He was an old rancher from Montana or Wyoming. He had a Rascal that he used to ride into the preserve. It was like a motorized wheelchair, but more like a little scooter. He would leave their house and drive this thing around the preserve until the battery ran out and then he'd be stuck. His daughter, back at the house, would be wondering where the hell he was, but figured he was in the preserve, so she would call the office and they would send out rangers to look for him.

A couple times I happened to be with John Kowaleski, coming back from some meeting and there was Clyde, almost to the Mora Gate with a dead battery. We'd put the thing in the truck, put him in the truck, and take him home. He was a crusty old guy, but he was friendly. Clydine would be pacing up and down the driveway, waiting. We'd unload the scooter and reassure her that he was okay. She'd scold him and he'd give her some sass back.

One time when he was missing, Kerry and I went looking and we found him down on the Mora-Ravensbury Trail right where it bends around and leaves the grassland. He'd gone off the side with his Rascal. There were no broken bones, but he was a little scraped up, and the Rascal was flipped over. We got him stabilized and called for fire. When the paramedics got on scene, they packed him up, loaded him on the stretcher, and drove him up to the water tank. They took him out in a helicopter. I don't know if he ever was able to come out again or not after that. His daughter would always get so upset with him, "I don't want to just baby him and keep him home, but..." We asked whether she could get him a cell phone, which were around by then, but pretty archaic. "At least with a cell phone he could contact you." I don't know whether she ever pursued that.

~~~

I remember when cell phones first came out and I got one. It was in a box, with this big battery, and an antenna. This was my personal phone. If I had to make a call, like if my car was in the shop and I needed to talk to the repair guy, and I was out somewhere working on a trail, what was I going to do? Wait until the end of the day to call him? Eventually phones got smaller and smaller to the point where they are now. I had one of the early cell phones.

I remember when Steve came in as general manager and there was supposed to be this big push toward technology, to keep everybody informed, so then we had these video conference meetings. They'd have everybody in the Annex, and Steve on this video screen, along with little pictures of all three offices. It was supposed to be a whole staff meeting, but in three locations. It never worked. There was always some glitch, and we'd all be sitting there twiddling our thumbs for half an hour while Michael J tried to get the thing to work properly. It turned into a big waste of time. Man, if this was where we were going, maybe it was time to retire.

~~~

Recently on the news I saw something about the old resort at Twin Creeks. I guess all the dilapidated cottages and community swimming pool are still there. The owner had always been at odds with the District because I guess he had been caught hunting on District land. If you drove farther up the canyon, you came to some other properties where I did some dozer work. The farther you got past the little resort area, the more ramshackle the places got, with falling over buildings. I couldn't believe anybody still lived out there with the broken-down cars and washing machines. What a dump! It was just one after another of these places in there. They were always saying the District should buy it, but I thought, "I don't want to have to clean this up." You'd be there for years. There's gotta to be 1,000 old car batteries alone, and tires, and all the other shit that goes along with places like that. I don't think the District ever bought anything back there, other than what they already had. They did have one property at the end of Twin Creeks, from that old guy who finally died, Fleishman? He had all this weird stuff in his garage, some nasty chemicals. They didn't know what he was doing, maybe trying to turn lead into gold or something.

There was another guy who had a place I went with Michael Newburn before they cleaned it out. You went down Wrights Station Road, off Summit Road and onto Cathermole and then up toward the "Bedsprings" Gate. Not the Signarovich place, where the emus were. There was a two-story garage structure just full of stuff. Why would you haul all that shit all the way out there? There were stacks of doors and windows. My God, this was out in the middle of no-place, and not easy to get to. He had broken-down old trailers. There was no water there. I can't see why they never drilled a well. There were hundreds of gallon wine jugs everywhere, a whole variety, all of them full of water. Wherever you could stick a jug of water, there it was. How long would it have taken to get this stuff up there? It was incredible.

Photo used by permission of Mark Casaretto

This is a picture of the water truck on its side at the top of Montevina Road. The gate is right up here, out of the picture. This happened just outside the gate. I was going in, and I had stopped, opened the gate, and was back in the truck ready to pull forward. Fortunately I had put my seatbelt on. The brakes weren't holding the truck with all this weight in it. It wanted to roll backwards, even though I was on the brakes. That's how I remember it. On these kinds of trucks, they have an emergency brake, but it's not even connected to your brakes. It has a big disc that's around the driveshaft, like a disc brake on a bicycle. It just grabs it. It's not going to stop you, so pulling on that didn't do anything.

I always remembered what Gene Sheehan had told me one time: when you're in a tricky situation, always have a plan in your head for what you're going to do because you're not going to have time to think about it when something does happen. You just have to do it. For whatever reason, I had that formulated in my brain.

The uphill bank there, the cut bank, is fairly steep, so when the truck started to roll back and the brake wouldn't hold, I turned the wheel so the truck went toward the embankment. You can't see it in this picture because I'm past it. The other side was a cliff; I couldn't go that way. I would have put this thing through a neighbor's house, and somebody would have been killed and it wouldn't have stopped there. There was nothing to stop it, just brush. I just cranked the wheels until the back of the truck went up the cut bank, thinking that was going to stop me, and it did, except that it also made the truck roll over. All I remember is that it was real rough and noisy. The next thing I knew, I was on my side. I was able to cut the seatbelt with my knife and climb out through the passenger window. The window was probably down when I was driving. This whole thing took just seconds. When it started to go, it was an, "Oh Shit!" moment. I just turned the wheel and the truck went up the embankment, and "Boom!" it landed where it was.

I cut my head and I had to get some stiches in my arm. I called Michael J on my portable radio and told him what had happened and where I was. Luckily I remembered the name of the road. I knew where I was. I didn't lose consciousness or anything. I told him I was okay, but we had a problem. He came up Bohlman Road through El Sereno with Michael Bankosh and they met me. Michael J stayed up there while I went with Michael Bankosh down to get checked out and stitched up.

That was kind of a fiasco. They took me first to the clinic on Matilda, but the place was a madhouse. Some immigration law was changing and there were all these people there who had to get physicals that same day or something bad was going to happen. So, I was bleeding from the head and they were like, "Oh, we can't take him just now." We ended up at some other place.

One funny thing about this story: I was standing there next to the truck, waiting for those guys to show up, and this woman drove up, and parked her car right there. Obviously this accident had just happened. I was cut up, and kind of dazed and the truck was on its side. She started asking me, "Is it okay if I park here? I want to go hiking."

While this was kind of a scary thing, I realized afterward, "Hey, I could have been killed." Just about a week after this, there was another guy who rolled one of these same trucks not too far away. He got thrown out and it crushed him. He died. It was the same type of rig and everything. I don't know what caused it. It was a construction site.

~~~

The snail's pace was one reason I got out of there. It was like, "What takes so darn long for everything?" I realize that it's a lot more complicated now than it was. Toward the end of my career, it had gotten to the point where you couldn't just go in and build a trail. You had to have a consultant and they had to pass all this stuff. When I first started, if we were going to build a trail, we'd go out, and John Kowaleski would lay it out, and the next day we'd be in there brushing it out. Gene Sheehan would show up with his machine, and away we'd go.

When Stan retired last month, I went to the party. I got there kind of early, and was talking to Grant Kern because he was helping to direct cars at Cindy's house. He said, "Yeah, Stan is retiring at just the right time," and I was thinking, "Wait, you guys said that to me five years ago. " So I guess it's like the old, "Same shit, different day." For me, I was thinking, " Well, the kids are out of college and I have enough years in, and I have other income. This is a good time." Paula had retired about a year before, although she didn't have a lot of years in with the school district as a school librarian. I just figured it was time. I've got plenty of stuff to keep me busy. I'm not lacking in that department. Other people are thinking, "What am I going to do?" I'm just thinking about all the things I can get to now. You never know what the future holds. I was still pretty young, not quite 55. I've known too many people, especially of my parents' generation who worked until they were 65, 70 years old. Now what are they going to do? Their health isn't all that great, and all that fun stuff they were going to do doesn't sound so fun anymore, because it hurts too much. I don't regret it at all. I enjoyed my time there, made a lot of friends, learned a lot of skills, and it was time to move on.

Thank you, Mark

I helped install that endless stretch of splitrail fence at Pulgas Ridge Open Space Preserve as a seasonal OST. I second Mark's comment that it seemed like we would never finish.

Loro Paterson (see interview below) also talks about the training burn at the rocket engine facility, although not in as much detail. She gives the name of the facility as UTC.

Ranger Frances: Firefighter

Marc and Steve's heroics putting out the wildfire in Russian Ridge with the water tender earned them some well-deserved kudos. That story became legend around the Skyline Field Office. I certainly find their actions heroic: jumping into firefighting mode, driving cross-country against policy in the water tender to reach the fire, and realizing that they could stop the fire only if they just plunged in immediately and didn't stop to put on their fire gear. Marc and Steve just happened to be in the right place at the right time. However, I'm not so sure what my own actions would have been under those same circumstances. Good job, guys!

~~~

District rangers were required to participate in the District's fire program. OSTs could choose to participate or not. All fire program field staff attended a one-day, in-house fire training every spring, but seldom got to experience real, live fire. We were lucky to get to go to a prescribed burn or a training with live fire every four or five years, not nearly enough to feel comfortable and confident as firefighters. There just weren't enough live-fire trainings held locally to which to send us all.

Photo used by permission of MROSD
**Stan Hooper and Kristin Perry in
Nomex "monkey suits" in helicopter**

Periodically an effort to amend or augment the existing fire program came up. Certainly with the District trying to reduce its carbon footprint, getting rid of the fleet of Ford F350 pickups lugging around their pumper units and 125 gallons of water all summer would help. One proposal was to have a few true Type 3 fire engines, such as those used by Cal Fire, with rangers specially trained to operate them. The rest of the rangers could then drive small SUVs

I was always fairly dubious about the District's fire program and especially of my own value as a wildland firefighter, but cannot deny that there have been occasions when having that pumper on the back of the truck saved the day, preventing a small fire from becoming a conflagration.

~~~

The District's enabling legislation from the State of California requires that the District maintain a firefighting force. This firefighting capacity may have been included to help sweeten the deal for skeptical rural voters, who at the time of the

District's inception viewed the District as land grabbers, and District visitors as litter- and firebugs. But these rural homeowners, whose million-dollar homes were surrounded by volatile chaparral, loved firefighters. Their starry-eyed view of the District's fire program as a fleet of small fire engines roaming the Santa Cruz Mountains, staffed by crews of trained and competent wildland firefighters, may have tipped the balance in favor of a vote for the District's creation. But now we are stuck with this unwieldy fire program.

Many healthy, strong, fit, young rangers love the fire program. The special clothing, the truck bed-mounted pumper units, the associated equipment and tools, and the specialized fire training, all add interest and excitement to the ranger job. I may even have felt this way myself at one time, but as I neared the end of my career, I realized that 58-year-olds do not belong on the fire line. Just look at Cal Fire, the primary agency fighting wildfires in California. Do you see anybody who looks to be over the age of 40 digging line or humping hose? Not likely. The 40-somethings have all promoted up and out of the frontlines, or moved on to other professions. Firefighting is a young person's job, and by the summer of 2017, I realized, "I'm too old for this."

My realization that I had become a liability, not an asset on the fireline was brought home to me while taking part in suppressing two small wildfires in the preserves that summer. While overtly doing my bit fighting the fires, I felt lucky to have avoided exacerbating my old back injury or passing out with heat illness. I knew I was in over my head, and made every effort to preserve my wellbeing, as opposed to directing that effort toward putting out the flames. Not the focus you'd expect from the person responsible for saving your house or land.

Journal entry: I have been meaning to get down this entry about the little fire last week, on 7/22/17. It was Saturday, right about 1430, because we had all just logged on for the late shift.

Alex was strolling back across the office from the base station radio when Marianne, who had also just logged on at her 10-10 (employee residence) at the INE ranch, suddenly came back up on the radio anxiously calling, "Power lines down on Highway 35, right at my driveway." Alex and I barely had time to agree that he would go fill when she was back on the radio, "We've got fire on both sides of the highway!" I remember saying, "Shit," as I headed for my truck. Code 3 down there, lights and siren, with Alex right behind me.

I found two patrol trucks just pulling in ahead of me, north of the fire—Andrew and Kyle, I think—and presumed they would be dealing with southbound highway traffic, so preceded through the gauntlet of flames. I must have driven right over the power lines; I didn't even notice them. Didn't even think to look. Stupid. Just south of the flames, I saw Marianne beside her truck struggling into a road safety vest and hauling out her stop sign for dealing with northbound cars. I quickly decided to head for the chestnut orchard over on the west side of Skyline Boulevard, to stop visitors on the Chestnut Trail from continuing north on foot directly into the path of the flames. I slowed down, rolled down my window, and yelled out my plan to Marianne. "Go! Go!" she yelled back.

Being first on scene, she had faced quite the dilemma. "Do I stop traffic? Do I change into fire gear? Do I start fighting fire? Do I race back down to my house and rescue my dogs?" The opening minutes of any incident are always hectic and confusing, but she who is first on scene is, by default, the IC (incident commander) until a higher-ranked person arrives and takes over. So, for the time being, Marianne was in charge. When she came up on the radio with these questions, Supervisor Brad did a good job of assisting from afar. "Get the traffic stopped; others are coming who can fight fire."

Up at the chestnut orchard, I first drove on up to the nearby District rental house on the hilltop, just to make sure no one was home. I didn't, however, think to check on whether the leaseholder, Hans, happened to be out working in his chestnut orchard. As I was changing into fire gear, and then struggling to get my pumper started (all the while imagining the fire burning up the other side of the hill, and seeing a wall of flames cresting over it in my mind's eye) Hans drove up out of the orchard. He must truly have wondered about my competence as a ranger as I had clearly failed to thoroughly check the premises for people, and now seemed incapable of operating my own pumper unit. It turned out the bypass valve was slightly cracked open, keeping the pump from priming.

My role for the next three hours was to stand in the chestnut orchard turning around the almost non-existent stream of visitors. The fire never got anywhere close. I couldn't even see it from where I was, and I felt useless, a complete fifth wheel. On the other hand, I didn't envy those rangers—Andrew, Chris, Kyle, Alex, and Kristin—who helped Cal Fire put wet stuff on red stuff. I was miserable, and on the verge of heat exhaustion just standing around in my thick Nomex fire gear in the hot afternoon sun. I was incapable of any actual physical exertion in that heat. I chalked up my poor heat tolerance to increasing age, and felt even worse..

Two airplanes were there dropping fire retardant and/or water from overhead within ten minutes of my arrival, and the first Cal Fire engines were on scene not long after that. Poor Kyle had left the windows of his truck wide open and his truck got hit hard by a retardant drop. All pink, inside and out. It took him hours and hours the next day to clean it. Eventually a hand crew arrived and dug a line around the burn, including the almost vertical road embankment. Plenty of excitement for a mere .75 acre burn.

Journal entry 9/12/17: Ours was just one of many small lightning-caused fires around the San Francisco Peninsula yesterday. A bizarre lightning storm had arisen suddenly in the *afternoon. I headed up to Borel Hill in Russian Ridge, per Brendan's orders, to look for smokes (fires in the distance) and could see dozens of wonderfully dramatic lightning strikes all around, but no smokes. Then headed north to where Andrew had found a fire in the upper part of La Honda Creek Preserve, off of Allen Road. A small fire, and almost out by the time I got there, suited up, and walked in. It was also completely dark, so I was able to feel at least a little useful by providing headlamp batteries from the supply in my truck to some Kings Mountain Fire guys. I helped them finish digging the scratch line around the perimeter of the black, following along behind Brendan. Judging by the line of bobbing headlamps ahead of me, there looked to be some ten guys whacking down ferns and chopping out roots, leaving little for us at the end of the line to do. Fine with me.*

I had only been back to work for three days following sick leave for yet another remission of my old back injury, and I was in no hurry to return to the couch with the ice and ibuprofen. Fortunately, it was dark under the trees and easy to go through the motions without anyone noticing that I wasn't putting in a lot of effort. I was working hard to be hardly working. I was nervous about hurting myself, but too embarrassed about being exposed as a worthless old lady to ask to be excused. I felt guilty and silly pretending to work, but too proud to do otherwise. An uncomfortable set of feelings for me.

Andrew and I volunteered to spend the night out there babysitting this one big tree that was still on fire. It was spouting sparks like a volcano, but was so tall that Cal Fire couldn't hit it with their hoses. They wanted to cut it down, but had only an insufficiently experienced sawyer on scene. Our job was simply to keep an eye on it and make sure the sparks didn't start another fire. It was a long, sleepless night for both of us, even though we took turns watching. It was clear, starry, and beautiful, if not especially warm. In the wee hours, a half-full moon came up, turning the grassland silver, and the forest black. When I volunteered to take this watch, I had already secretly decided to retire at the end of the year, and I really wanted this all-nighter experience. I would never again have another opportunity to do anything of the kind. Maybe, too, I was assuaging some of my guilt from my earlier pseudo-effort at digging line.

Kristin and Kyle relieved us at about 0445 this morning. They logged on at 0400, but took 45 minutes to get out to us. We showed them their task in the dark. I then had the half-hour drive back to SFO, and the 45-minute drive home, where I arrived at 0600, and tried to get to sleep. Finally gave up, bathed, dressed, made another box lunch and headed back up the hill for another late shift. Brendan did grant a two-hour reprieve, letting Andrew and me start at 1500 instead of 1300. Not looking forward to dragging through the next five hours. Hope nothing happens.

Photo used by permission of MROSD

Cindy Roessler, Biologist

I was a biologist with the Midpeninsula Regional Open Space District. I had various titles - resource management specialist, senior resource management specialist – and worked in various departments, but I was the primary biologist for the whole agency. For decisions about how to take care of the natural resources, I would be the lead person. When I started there, about 15 years ago, in 2003, I was the only biologist on staff.

Jodi Isaacs was the first biologist, or resource specialist, at Midpen. She was there for about five years, and I actually knew her professionally during that time, as I was working for the nearby Santa Clara Valley Water District. We would see each other at professional meetings. She had a strong background in wildlife and did a great job setting up the District wildlife protocols, such as the wildlife incident reports, feral pig control, and mountain lion sighting response protocols. I'm primarily a botanist, so it was so nice to get into the District job and have these strong wildlife protocols all set up.

I think my first boss was John Escobar. Right away I was in the field working with Stan Hooper and Michael Bankosh, the maintenance supervisors. In a lot of ways I felt like they were my bosses. They would ask me for advice, and for help in setting priorities. After Escobar, my supervisor was John Maciel, and then Sango. Originally I was in the Operations Department, and then, in my last four years, the District finally created a Natural Resources Department. Kirk had worked in the Planning Department as a biologist in the design of projects, so we were coordinating, but working in different departments. Eventually, when the Resource Management Department was created, Kirk became its manager, and therefore my boss.

~~~

My parents were both university professors in the sciences, but also both first generation off the farm, and that certainly influenced me. I loved gardening and plants, and my dad always had a garden. Every summer we'd pack all seven kids in the station wagon and drive from Florida to Minnesota, where we'd spend two months with my grandparents on their farm. We ran around everywhere, and helped my grandpa out in the fields. It was a midwestern farm with corn, wheat, cattle, pigs, chickens, and cats and dogs. I spent a lot of time outside there, but not in wild areas. We didn't do much camping. I'd never been to the Grand Canyon until I moved out to California and I stopped there on the drive out. I think the sciences, and gardening, and the farm were my early influences.

~~~

Most people have an innate pull toward nature, although others seem to have an aversion, which I don't understand. For many the out-of-doors is a true passion. Some of it is early exposure, but it is also part of our human roots. It's sad that some people don't have it.

I once had a volunteer helping me collect wildflower seeds. We didn't do this often because it is pretty difficult. You see the wildflowers when they're blooming and they're beautiful, but by the time you're collecting the seeds, the plant is all dried, shriveled, and brown. This woman was training as a nurse, and her community college program required her to volunteer a certain number of hours. She was trying to get in her hours at the last minute, and this was the only volunteer project that still had openings, so she joined us. She'd spent very little time outdoors, had never before done seed collection. She was just there to get in her hours, but she was good at it, and was so excited about doing it, that she wanted to bring her dad out that weekend. It was amazing for me to give her this experience and see how fulfilling it was for her. It must have changed her life, that one day, that one afternoon that she just happened to walk into.

~~~

A few months after graduating from college, I got a job with a Florida county government agency in coastal zone management protecting the beaches and waterways. I worked a lot on the beaches on the Gulf Coast of Florida. I found that I liked working for government. It was more meaningful and it was a longer-term investment. I worked there for five years, and then moved to California.

For years the only work I could find in California was in consulting, which was interesting and where I learned a lot about writing environment impact reports and the California Environmental Quality Act (CEQA). We worked all over the state. One of my employers was contracted with the U.S. Army and we were doing evaluations at the Mountain Warfare Training Center, near Sonora Pass. It was kind of cool getting zipped off to places like that. But a downside to doing consulting work was that you got deeply involved in a project for a few months to maybe a year, and you did the environmental review and you made recommendations, and then you were gone. You never knew whether they followed through or not. Working for government, you're there for a long time, and that land that you're taking care of is there forever. That type of investment was better aligned with my vision.

Next I got the job with the Santa Clara Valley Water District whose primary mission is flood control. After I'd been there awhile, I worked as a project manager on a big creek maintenance project that ended up taking about four years. It involved all the creeks in the Santa Clara Valley, hundreds of miles of creek. I worked as a biologist doing ecological reviews and environmental design, which involved taking damaged areas and returning them to more natural conditions. For example, Coyote Creek. They were doing a flood control project on the lower end, so they'd bought up farmland and bayland and designed a flood control project.

They didn't just go and ream out the center of the creek and line it with concrete, which was the old design. By that point we were working with a new design where, when the floodwaters came down the Coyote Creek and the water got to a certain height, it would pop out into what they called an overflow channel. The big farm fields were re-contoured to have this large, earthen, secondary channel. The floodwaters would go into that channel and soak into the ground until the water levels went back down again, and then the water returned to the creek. It basically was like a second creek. My job was to plant riparian forests around these flood control channels, which was fun and exciting. These were huge multi-million dollar projects, funded by the Army Corps of Engineers, and I would hire contractors to do the installation, maintenance, and monitoring, and to write reports to the permitting agencies.

We even had a bird-banding program at one of these sites, to learn how the birds were using the new plants. We had planted a 20-acre riparian forest. We worked with the Coyote Creek Riparian Station, a volunteer group out of San Jose State University, which is now the San Francisco Bay Bird Observatory. They put up mist nets to capture the birds, which had to be checked every 15 minutes. You didn't want the birds in there struggling for long. It was a way of seeing what kinds of birds were there. You carefully pulled the birds out of the nets, which tended to ball up around them. You noted the species, and the breeding status, and then weighed and banded the birds, or recorded the information if they already had a band. They did that year-round for ten years. We were able to see how the birds changed as the riparian forest grew.

Our conclusions were that, when you first planted an ecological restoration site, the first three years you would find birds that liked grassland, even though you may have planted trees. It was still like grassland to the birds. Between three and five years, things changed; you got a different mix and variety of birds. You started to have a forest-like ecology, even though you didn't have giant trees yet, and you started to get the forest birds. We planted a lot of willows and cottonwoods, with oak trees around the upper edges. When we got a yellow-billed cuckoo in the re-vegetation site, I knew it was working. In the more bayland areas we planted salt marsh vegetation. When we bought that property, it was farmland, fruit orchards, cornfields, or wheat, or something similar. My favorite part of that job was re-creating these more natural areas. It was cool working with the bird biologists, learning about the birds, and making presentations at conferences. And then that project was finished.

I then got assigned as manager of this creek maintenance project, which was not such an exciting thing to do. Some of our creeks were just inverted concrete channels, but some were a little more natural. With the older, concrete designs you had to keep dredging out the sediment, so the challenge was how to do that in the most environmentally friendly way. My job became to do an environmental impact report and get ten different regulatory permits. It took about five years to do that. They had given that job initially to a different biologist, and she wasn't getting anywhere. They reassigned her and asked me to do it.

They sent me through project management training. The Water District is a big engineering firm; it's 90 percent engineers. Once a week for a year I'd be at a training with all these engineers learning project management skills. They brought in various experts, like for the budgeting part. It was a good experience that I used all the time moving forward in my career. On the one hand, creek maintenance wasn't my favorite thing to do, but I realized that in this major metropolitan area, these flood control systems had to be maintained. The older ones weren't going to be redesigned any time soon, and for the newer ones, the maintenance could be done in a more environmentally protective way. I was supposed to get this environmental review done and get some changes made. It was a lot of data management. I was the manager of a team of engineers, which was the inverse of the norm for that agency. Usually the biologists work for the engineers.

It ended up being pretty exciting, and I had almost finished, when I ran into Jodi Isaacs, my Midpen predecessor. The Water District EIR had been finished and certified. We had gone through all the public hearings, had resolved all the controversies, had all the major permits, and at that point I was looking around for what the Water District would have me do next. I didn't want to go back to my regular job as an environmental scientist, where I would just be working on these dinky things. There were no big restoration projects coming up, no big, new, exciting project waiting for me. The managers were happy I'd gotten this big project done, but they didn't say, "You did such a great job, now what do you want to do next?" It was just, "You got that done. Now go back to your old job." I felt like what I had just done was amazing, and now I had all these skills that I wanted to use.

Then I ran into Jodi Isaacs at a meeting, and she said, "Well, actually, I'm leaving the Open Space District." You can guess what I was thinking right away: I want your job. But I didn't want to be rude and just say that to her. We talked for a while and then she said, "You know, you should apply for my job." She was leaving because she and her husband decided that they didn't want to stay in the San Francisco Bay Area. They moved to San Luis Obispo and Jodi now works for State Parks. She was at the District for five years, and I followed her for 15. Of course now there are many more biologists, including various specialists, and the program has grown a lot. But that's how I ended up working for the Open Space District. I ran into Jodi right at a time when I was ready to try something different. I applied for the job, and they hired me.

~~~

I remember Matt Freeman was on my interview panel and one of his questions was, "How would you define 'biological diversity?'" and I said, "Texture." I remember looking around the panel and seeing that two people had blank looks on their faces, but Matt's eyes had just lit up and he smiled and I could see that he knew exactly what I meant. Then we discussed it in more detail, but he knew what I was talking about. There is this fine texture in the natural world, this incredible detail of everything all woven in together. I remember that bit of the interview.

When I first started working out of the AO, back when we were still leasing out the east end of the building to some other business, I had a cubicle way on the southwest corner, just outside of Sango's and Gordon's offices. Bunny Congdon, the accountant, sat right across from me. When you're new, you put in late nights, and Bunny often seemed to be also working late nights, and we'd start talking about raising our kids, and stuff like that. At some point in there I was also breaking up with my boyfriend, and Bunny was so calming and helpful.

That was a neat spot. When I was applying for the job, I had asked Jodi, "When I need to figure out how things work at the District, who should I go to?" She said, "If you need help, just ask Gordon Baille. Gordon knows everything." Later I told him this story, and it's so true. He knows how to handle things. Not only does he know how to get things done, he also has a calming way of getting people to work together.

Bunny and Pat were in District housing when Pat got hired by the Open Space Authority and left the District. They got kicked out of their District housing and it was a mess. They were in the Saratoga Gap house, off Charcoal Road, which is gone now. They couldn't find a place to live because the economy was in the dot-com boom, but the General Manager was after them to move out. They finally found a house off Skyline Boulevard, the house at the INE Ranch, back when it was still privately owned. They lived there for a long time and were very happy. When the District bought INE, Mike Williams knew that Pat and Bunny had lived there, and invited Pat to come walk the property with Mike and me. Did you ever see that little bench beside the pond? It's kind of gotten covered up by coyote bush, but Pat built it, and he carved their two initials into it, inside a heart, and then he carved the back to match the mountain silhouette. Pretty cool.

Photo used by permission of Patrick Congdon
Patrick and Bunny Congdon at a fun committee barbeque

Jodi had set up every Thursday as a crew resource management day, when she would be out with either the Skyline crew or the Foothills crew. I just continued that schedule. Every Thursday I'd be out with one crew or the other. At first I was working on a lot of the legacy projects that Jodi had started, like the eucalyptus and acacia removal at Pulgas Ridge, and the French broom removal at Saratoga Gap. Those were always fun days because I got to be out with the crew all day.

I remember the first day that I did this up at Pulgas Ridge. This was when Michael Newburn was still area superintendent. Those guys worked so hard! We were cutting acacia and I was swamping (pulling away the cut vegetation behind the saw operator) for Michael Bankosh and Holden. They were working so fast. I didn't have on a long-sleeved shirt and there was poison oak on the branches, and I guess I was just kind of new at this part of the job. At one point Newburn came out and said, "You know, there's poison oak in here?" He got a coverall for me, but I still got a real bad case of poison oak. I was so exhausted by the end of that day, I was thinking, "I don't know if I can keep up with these guys," so I actually started working out to get in better shape. Well, years later Michael Bankosh told me that Newburn had come into his office the morning of that Pulgas Ridge project and said, "So, today is our first resource management day with the new resource person. I want you guys to work as fast as you can. I don't want you to stop. I want you to show her how hard you can work." I did learn to wear long-sleeved shirts on RM days.

I started by continuing with the RM projects the crew had been doing, and then figured out new ones. It gave me a chance to work with the crew supervisors on setting priorities. For the first few months they took the lead, but that gave me the chance to get out into the preserves and see what was out there—where there were invasive plants and erosion issues. Eventually I could start saying, "You know, there are more efficient ways to do this."

I brought in this guy, Ken Moore, who was treating French broom seedlings with propane torching. He did a great hands-on training for field staff. There was always that sort of controversy about French broom. The seeds can last 50 or more years, so why are we bothering to do this? Won't we just be doing this forever? I would respond that after three to five years there will be fewer seedlings, and it will take you a fraction of the time to go through an infested area. You might not even need to come back every year. "Let's look at some more efficient ways of treating the seedlings, once you get the big broom trees out." The crew loved having somebody like that come in. The field staff didn't like to be lectured at; they wanted to know how to do it, and see how to do it. Ken Moore had been doing invasive plant control in state parks for decades, mostly with volunteers or on his own. He was this wiry guy who really knew what he was talking about, and he was their type of people. So, I learned that that was important when working with crew, to get the right sort of trainer. It was about equipment, too. "Oh, we get to buy some new equipment!" I remember that some of the crew were wearing safety glasses on the day of the training, and Ken had asked me about them. They were these nicely contoured safety glasses, so afterward I sent him a thank you card, and a pair of those safety glasses, too. He never forgot that.

~~~

I think another early project was the Christmas tree farm restoration at Skyline Ridge. When the District bought the Skyline Ridge property, which was one of our early purchases, it had the Christmas tree farm on it. It was planted in the 1960's, and was one of the first commercial cut-your-own Christmas tree operations. That property may have been planted in hay or wheat before that. When Midpen bought the property in the '70s, they saw that there was erosion from parts of the tree farm causing sedimentation in Horseshoe Lake. The arms of the lake and the creeks were filling with sediment, and the trail around the lake kept getting buried. One condition of the purchase was that the tree farm tenants could continue to operate it, but that some parts would be pulled out of production to deal with the sedimentation. When the Christmas tree farmers had planted the first few Christmas tree fields, they had made the rows go up and down the slope. Then, to control the weeds between the rows of trees, they would disc up the soil every year. Every winter each of these disc-lines became a deep rut that washed soil down into the lake. At some point the tree farmers changed to contour planting the rows of trees, so it was only the older, original, up-and-down tree fields that were supposed to go out of production. That had been the agreement since the '70s, but nobody had ever gotten around to implementing it, so I took it on.

We split the tree farm into four sections, and we cleared the trees from the first section with a bulldozer. One of the EMOs took the bulldozer to the bottom of the tree field and then just slowly drove it up the hill, knocking all the trees over with the blade, and pushing them up to the top. The trees were shallowly rooted. As they pushed the trees along, the branches and the trunks combed and re-contoured the land. It had been row-furrow, row-furrow, row-furrow. The crew didn't have to do that much grading afterwards. They had thought they would have to bulldoze it a lot, but just pushing the trees up that way got rid of a lot of the ruts.

Our initial design was very low investment. We didn't have a lot of money, so we planted acorns, and watered them with buckets for the first summer. We put in a lot of erosion control fabric, especially around the drainages, and we seeded the area with native grasses. It did fairly well. In the last few weeks before I retired, I toured one of the sites that I had worked on. I found one of the original trees and got my picture with it towering over me. We didn't put in an irrigation system. We did only minor weeding. The design was to plant in what we called balloons. Instead of doing the entire two acres with acorns, because we couldn't find that many acorns and we didn't have that much labor, we planted ten acorns in a group, a balloon, all close together. Then we left a gap and then planted another balloon. That gave the oaks a chance to start their own little mini-forests, which modified the environment immediately around them. The next year we went back and planted more little balloons. We did that for about three years, and then we let it go.

Photo used by permission of Cindy Roessler
Cindy under oak grown from acorn

Some years the acorns did better than others, depending on the rainfall. Planting oaks with acorns using volunteers is really cheap. You can do it year after year, and if one year out of five is a good one, and the rest are low yield, you can still get a forest planted. Instead of planting the area with saplings in 15-gallon pots and installing an irrigation system, which is costly both to install and to maintain, why not just do it more gradually? We'll own that land forever. There's no reason to make this huge investment. When you think about it, you're planting a forest that's going to last for hundreds of years. So what if it takes you five years to get it planted? That was my original design. Planting oaks from acorns is the way to go. If you plant them from containers, they often don't do very well. If you plant one oak tree from an acorn, and next to it, you plant another as a sapling from a 15-gallon pot, in five years they'll be the same size. The acorn starts slower and may not germinate, but you're going to get a healthier tree.

Photo used by permission of MROSD
Stan with Lisa Bankosh at Skyline Tree Farm

When I hired Lisa Bankosh, I handed the tree farm over to her. She thought it was important to get a greater mix of plants in there, a greater understory. By that time we had more funding, so she started using more nursery plants. The next phase of the project, which she did, she also put in more wildflower seed mix. It turned out well, and it was gorgeous in its first year when the wildflowers bloomed, but they eventually washed out. Wildflowers need fire, or some other type of disturbance, to keep them blooming year after year, and we don't have that disturbance, but the native grasses grew well there. Lisa also used maintenance contractors to water.

Ironically, ten years after this process of slowly re-vegetating the tree farm, the problem with the root phytophthora came up. These are root diseases that were being spread through the native plant nurseries. We found out that the sections of Skyline Ridge tree farm where we had the greater diversity, where we had used the nursery plants, were the parts contaminated with this root disease. Some of those nursery plants were now dying.

The first Midpen property identified as contaminated with root phytophthora was not actually the tree farm, but just across Skyline Boulevard, along Skid Road in Monte Bello. A consultant working on sudden oak death found it. Being an observant person, he noticed something unusual along Skid Road, and he started testing the soil underneath the valley oaks. We asked him to do some spot testing within the Christmas tree farm, and that's when we discovered the soil phytophthora there. We had thought that the plants were dying from the drought. We'd been going through a five-year drought during the planting of those later phases. We'd been thinking that we'd just have to go back and re-plant. But now? One of the last things I did before I left the District was to hire a phytophthora expert who would test all of our re-vegetation sites to see which ones were contaminated, and then help us develop a plan to respond. It was just ironic to me that the cheap, simple design that we started with was the one that was more successful in the long run.

Soil phytophthoras don't spread very fast, so the oaks-from-acorns sections might be safe from infection. Both soil phytophthora and the sudden oak death (SOD) phythophthora are in the same genus of plant diseases. Most phytophthoras, like the one that caused the potato famine in Ireland, cause root diseases. The SOD phytophthora is unusual. By the way, I just learned at the California Native Plant Society conference where SOD is from originally. They have now determined that the SOD phytothphora is native to Vietnam.

~~~

Sudden oak death was another one of my early projects. SOD is still killing millions of oaks in California. It was first seen here in like, '97 or '98. People noticed a lot of oaks dying but didn't know what was happening to them. They finally figured out that it was this pathogen. Early on Jodi had started the testing for it on District land. By the time I got there, the public and the Board of Directors were really worried about it. They wanted the problem fixed, and it was my job to find the solution and fix it. We had many public meetings about it. There was no solution, no cure, but that wasn't good enough for our Board. They wanted something done. It took me about six months and the help of two temporary interns to research what was known about SOD. We did a lot of testing and mapping of the preserves, and we made vegetation maps of the susceptible oaks and projections about where SOD might spread.

I thought we needed something even more comprehensive, and so we put together a 10-year work plan. Over the course of 10 years we figured out how SOD was being transmitted in tan oaks, and studied whether there were any resistant tan oaks. We tested some possible preventative measures like removing bay trees which act as carriers of the disease, and we funded further research. I read lots of SOD literature and talked to SOD researchers, and went to technical meetings, because I wasn't an expert on this type of organism. We needed to figure out how our agency could fit into this larger picture with other agencies. Then I went to the Board with a proposal to be worked on over the next 10 years. I asked them for about $400,000 of funding. In those days, that was a lot of money to recommend for a resource management project, but it was spread over 10 years, and they approved it.

I started going to the annual SOD conferences, sponsored by the National Forest Service. At my first conference, I asked the organizers, "Hey, can I organize a pullout meeting over lunch with all the other park districts here so we can figure out who's doing what?" They said, "You and the National Park Service are the only park districts here, the only ones involved." I asked, "What about state parks? Don't they have SOD?" "Oh yeah, It's really bad at China Camp, but they're not here. They're not funding it, researching it, or responding to it." Researchers would occasionally go to a state park and ask to do a study, but in the early years, nobody was doing much about it.

Since then, more local parks have gotten involved, but I remember running into a former Midpen manager at a meeting after he moved over to work for East Bay Regional Parks. He told me, "I heard what you are doing on sudden oak death. It's a complete waste of time and money." I said, "You know, the oak trees are important to the ecology." He responded, "You can't do anything about it." I disagreed, "Okay, you have your opinion, but someday you're going get this in East Bay Parks, and you will have to deal with it." He was like, "Nah, we'll never have it. We're too dry." Five years later they had SOD and they were funding research and calling me for advice. Unfortunately, it had spread. It was a problem without a solution, and people just wanted a solution.

The bins with the disinfectant we made for field staff to clean their boots and truck tires are a good example of how much we didn't know, and how things changed over time with more information. We didn't know how SOD was spreading. A researcher did a study in Big Basin State Park where they took swabs off the boots of hikers exiting the trails. Back in the lab, they grew the SOD pathogen from these swabs, so the question was how much people were responsible for tracking the spores around. We were also wondering how much the spread was due to wood collection and logging. You'll remember that we were very restrictive about moving firewood for a while. But, over the years, we learned that most SOD pathogen movement was by wind, which we cannot control. So, we gradually became less careful, less restrictive, about how equipment could move, or about visitors cleaning their boots. We realized that cleaning off boots wasn't going to make a big difference in preventing the spread of SOD.

We had installed boot cleaning brushes and bike tire cleaning brushes at many trailheads, and they were very popular, and I don't think they were a waste of money because of all the weed seeds they stopped. We definitely carry weed seeds around on our boots and equipment. Any effort to brush off a piece of equipment or clean the mud off our boots is going to result in fewer weed seeds getting spread around, and not just in our preserves, but also elsewhere, like up to Yosemite. We are now learning that the soil phytophthoras probably get spread mostly by dirt. So, I'm careful. Yesterday, before we went hiking, I looked to make sure my boots were clean. Especially if I'm going somewhere like Southern California, and I know I'm going to go hiking, I will scrub my boots down and spray them with alcohol. I make sure I don't move dirt around. So, even though boots and bike tires turned out not to be the main vectors for SOD, cleaning boots and bike tires is a good practice for all these other pathogens and weed seeds.

Sometimes when I reflect on how effective I was in my career, I think, "How many times did I say to field staff, 'You're not only cleaning your boots for SOD, but for weeds seeds too' and 'It's really important to clean the disking equipment when you go from Monte Bello to Los Trancos, because we've gotten the yellow star thistle out of Los Trancos, but not yet out of Monte Bello.'" How many times did I say that? But I still run into people who never got the message. Is that because I didn't tell them? The communication has to be constant and repetitive, and it can never stop. I've learned not to get too upset when somebody says that they didn't know. I've learned not to say, "But I've already told you that how many times?" I have to tell myself, "No, Cindy. This is the business. You have to communicate all the time. Stay calm and keep on repeating."

I now own two boot dryers. You know how nice it is to put your feet into clean, dry boots every day? I think the public will never get to the same point that I am with boot cleaning, but, with enough repetition, there will be some reduction in the dirty boots. You have to also just realize that, as human beings, we move around, and we move stuff around, and this is going to create problems. We just have to respond as best we can. You can't get like, "We have to be perfect, and if we can't be perfect then we give up." You can't do that. You have to just keep looking for the best solutions you can find as you go along. I'm still trying to do that. Humans want stuff to be perfect, and we want to find ways to reduce the amount of work. So, if you can't make it easy to be perfect, people just give up. I'm not willing to give up on the whole world. I also know that I can't make it perfect.

~~~

Another project I worked on was mountain lions. After Jodi left the position, there was about a six-month gap before I got there. Stan Hooper filled in during that interim. My first two days at work, he was out in the field, but I was sitting at what was still his desk, seeing his stuff, reading his notes. Then one day I remember I was standing in the hallway talking to Gordon when he looked over my shoulder and said, "Oh, there's Stan." I turned around and Stan said something, and...you know he has that deep voice? I went, "Wow! I get to work with this guy?" Then we spent about two weeks every day out in the field together.

I remember one day we were driving out of El Sereno, and he asked, "What would you do if, right now, over the District radio, somebody said there had been a mountain lion attack?" I didn't know, so he filled me in on Jodi's mountain lion and wildlife response protocols. Over the years, after various incidents, we refined it, but it is still a great document. It seemed like I spent a lot of time learning about mountain lions, and talking to people about them. We were taking reports of mountain lion sightings, and I learned how to interview people to get the best information. I wanted to know what they had seen, and I wanted to know about the animal's behavior. I could then judge how reliable the report was, and what type of response was called for. There was also an element of education with the person on the phone. You had to be delicate about it because everybody wanted to believe they had seen a mountain lion, and often they hadn't. Often it was a bobcat, a house cat, a dog, or a coyote. You couldn't tell for sure because you weren't there, but the rangers would go and check the locations of the sightings later, looking for tracks and scrapes. It was an interesting combination of wildlife biology, public safety, and psychology. Sometimes the witness would send you a picture, which clearly showed a bobcat. They so wanted to have this fantastic experience of seeing a mountain lion. How could I tell them, "No, that was a bobcat?" I found that an interesting challenge, and sometimes I turned out to be wrong.

There were a few months when we were getting a lot of mountain lion sightings near Rancho San Antonio, but they were all vague. One lady claimed to have seen a mountain lion with kittens, and I was quite skeptical, but I took her information and was very polite with her. Then we got a second, very reliable reported sighting from almost exactly the same location. I went back through the records (because we were keeping records) and we could see a pattern to these sightings which showed that there was a female mountain lion with kittens in that Los Altos Hills neighborhood, and the adjacent parts of Rancho. It was a problem, a public safety issue.

Newburn and I decided that we should have a community meeting. About 50 people showed up, which seemed pretty good. I had been thinking, "Everybody's going to be so scared, and this will be so controversial," but everybody was interested. They wanted to know more about mountain lions, and how to keep themselves safe. They didn't want to kill them. It was neat to be able to share these safety tips with people and have them be invested in their local wildlife and open space.

For many years I was able to say, "There has never been a mountain lion attack on a human in a District preserve. The last attack in Santa Clara County was at the turn of the last century," and then we had the attack on the little boy in Picchetti, and I wasn't able to say that any more. However, the wildlife response protocol worked in that instance. I was out of town, down here in San Luis Obispo when that attack happened. Actually I was on my way back to the Bay Area when the phone calls started coming in. I was driving north on Highway 101 and I was like, "Hold on. I'm pulling off the highway." My heart was racing and I couldn't believe that this was really happening. I think it was Ranger Jeff Smith who called me. I asked him, "Did you do this? Have you done that?" The protocols worked beautifully. They'd gotten the preserve closed, and had gotten everyone out of there. They'd called Fish and Game. The District media people were lined up. So, I wasn't there, but Clayton and the rangers were all trained and were doing everything that needed to be done, like clockwork.

I learned later that there had been earlier sightings of this mountain lion behaving aggressively in Picchetti on that same trail, but because the sightings were by people heading down the Zinfandel Trail toward Stevens Creek County Park, the people had told only the County park rangers, and those rangers had never informed the District. If they had, we would have done something. I would have put signs up on that trail. If there had been repeated sightings, we would have closed the trail or even the preserve, which could have prevented that attack. So, in a way, the protocol worked, but the communication hadn't spread far enough. After the attack I talked to Jeff and others, and they said they had told the Santa Clara County rangers that they should let us know about unusual mountain lion sightings. It was terrible, of course, that this child got attacked. Fortunately he recovered quickly. We don't know more than that because the family wanted to keep it private. It certainly raised people's awareness.

~~~

When I had been with the District for five years, I got the opportunity to move into employee housing at the Big Dipper Ranch in Russian Ridge. There were a lot of mountain lions on the Big Dipper and I started putting up wildlife cameras and noticing scat and scrape marks. (The District had two wildlife cameras, but they were big, clunky and slow. We used them for a while until I started purchasing my own.) I put a camera at what I called Cedar Junction, since there were two big incense cedars planted there. This was the intersection of the Old Page Mill logging road and an old farm road. The amount of mountain lion activity on that camera was amazing! We went through all the photos for one summer and could see that there had been seven different lions through there. There was definitely a male, and a female with two cubs, and a female with three. Because of their size, and the timing of their appearance, and little nicks in their ears, we could tell that they were all different animals. The road was a corridor for mountain lion movement along Peters Creek and probably formed the edge of several different territories. Creeks and ravines and canyons will often be edges, and I think that was what we saw happening there. By starting to use more sophisticated wildlife cameras, and working with Ken Hickman on them, and just looking at these photos, I learned a lot.

Moving out to the Big Dipper Ranch, living there, wandering around on my own through the woods and down the creeks, putting up and monitoring the cameras, and just spending so much time out there, I learned a lot more about wildlife. Living at the ranch was an adventure. For nine of my 10 years there, I lived by myself, and spent my three-day weekends out there alone. But I'd have parties, and invite people over and take people hiking. Ken and I did a lot of wildlife camera trapping there, so I was sharing the ranch too, and writing about it in my blog, sharing it in that way. Writing the blog was all on my own time, as was the hiking around, so that was 24/7. There was the maintenance of the fuel breaks, and the road, and the cattle infrastructure, and the fences, but it was an adventure, and a really good time in my life. When I moved up there, my son had just graduated from high school and was headed to college. I was ready to do something different. For many years it was a 24/7 adventure.

Photo used by permission of MROSD
Cindy leading a hiking group, maybe at Big Dipper

At some point it did get to be too much for me. It wasn't what I was doing on the Dipper Ranch, so much as it was the rest of my job. I was hiring more people and turning into more of a supervisor. The nature of the business, the nature of the District, and my own responsibilities were all changing and piling up. So, did I stop the adventure part of being at the Dipper Ranch, walking out on the trails, running the wildlife cameras and sharing the photos in the blog? Should I stop doing all that so I'd have more time to work on budgets, planning documents, Board reports, and phone calls? I couldn't stop doing those things. That was my job. That's what my manager wanted me to do. That was the track of my career. I was supervising more people, and hiring more consultants. The District was growing and my workload was building up. Buying more land meant more time doing vision planning. But I didn't want to give up on the adventures. My job did actually get to me after a while. That's when I started to think about retiring. I think I had a different experience of the 24/7 than the resident rangers did.

I liked being out on the property and sharing it, but with the water system constantly breaking down, and having to do the fuel break maintenance, it was also getting physically difficult. It was too steep to use wheeled equipment to mow; I had to use a brush cutter. It would take me weeks and weeks, or rather weekends and weekends, which I called "weed-ends." There is one hill above the driveway gate, which I recognized had more native grasses than the rest of the property, so summer evenings I would go up there and pull yellow star thistle. I adopted those 30 acres. I hand-pulled all the yellow star thistle off of it. You develop this relationship with the plants and you see so much when you are weeding. You start to notice the badger digs, bees, ant tracks, and owl pellets. Right as we were coming out of the drought, there was this magical, natural combination of suppression of the annual European grasses by drought, the perfect timing of the cattle grazing, and my own weed work all combining to bring out the most fabulous bloom of wildflowers on that hillside. I would go up there around sunset, because it was cooler, and it was beautiful to watch the dusk settle over Mindego Hill, and spend a peaceful two hours up there pulling weeds and watching nature. It was a reward for my efforts. But it took eight years to get that reward. No easy solutions.

Photo used by permission of Cindy Roessler
Lupines on hill above Cindy's driveway

A lot of resource management in parks is invasive plant management. This beautiful land has suffered human impacts for a long time: logging, mining, cattle grazing, and water diversion. And we've brought in weeds. An invasive plant, in the context of the District, is a plant that is not native to this region, spreads on its own, takes over large areas, and hurts native plants and animals. It takes away resources from this intricate interrelationship of the native plants and animals. It's not just any non-native plant that we would call an invasive plant. We defined it as meeting all these criteria. It had to be adversely affecting the mission of these lands. French broom, yellow star thistle, purple star thistle, eucalyptus, stinkwort, and many others are disturbing natural functions. We spend a lot of time and money trying to control them. Instead of having a field of annual European grasses and yellow star thistle, you could have deep-rooted native perennial grasses that do a better job of erosion control, and native wildflowers that support native pollinators. Square inch to square inch, you'd have different species present instead of a wide-spread monoculture of invasives.

It's a big job. There are a lot of invasive plants in the San Francisco Peninsula, and you can't take on all of them at once. A lot of my job was about picking priorities, figuring out where we could be most effective, operate most efficiently, and follow up, because none of these things would be taken care of in one visit. It takes three, to five, to eight–plus years, depending on the weed. We used a mix of field staff, contractors, and volunteers to do the work, depending on various factors. We had this invasive plant, goat grass, in Los Trancos, but a much smaller population, mostly along the edge of about one mile of trail. Goat grass is hard to recognize until, all of a sudden, it goes to seed, at which point you've got 10 days to get it out. In Los Trancos, we could pull it by hand.

We started by using field staff, but then we realized that the window of time when the goat grass set seed in early summer was also exactly when the summer camps started calling, asking for projects for their kids to do to help out in the parks. Kids could spot the goat grass. It's easy to pull, and they didn't have to wander far off the trail. They'd pull the plants and get a big bucketful, and feel satisfied that they had done something. Can you read about that in an RM textbook anywhere? That line of goat grass slowly went away. That's an example of how to crack these complex problems. It helps to know your field site, and your local community, not just the books and the experts' advice. And there always has to be a backup.

You won't be successful at everything. We wanted to use prescribed burns at Russian Ridge to control the Harding grass. We had learned a lot up there, using prescribed burns, and were making progress. I have before and after photos where we had been burning at Russian Ridge for about four years, showing all the native wildflowers, lupines and poppies and owl's clover, in what had been solid invasive Harding grass. Then we got stopped from burning. This member of the public felt like he had expertise in grassland management. He thought we should hire him to do it, and should listen to him. He had some good ideas, but he didn't like us burning up there and he threatened to sue us if we kept doing it.

We used prescribed burns, herbicides, and mechanical means like mowing and hand pulling on invasive plants. My emphasis, once I got there, was not to go after everything, but to be selective. Where might we be effective with the means we had? Where did we know we could follow up? We shouldn't take on a new project site unless we were sure that we could be out there for the next several years. I started getting strict with the crew about that, so we added a few projects but not others.

There is legitimate concern about using herbicides, which have some bad consequences, like the effects of DDT, so you have to be careful, and you need good training. The public in particular is concerned about herbicides, because this is their land, and they don't always have good information about what the District is doing. All they know is that sometimes they see somebody out there with a backpack sprayer.

Eventually we needed to do this Integrated Pest Management (IPM) program and Environmental Impact Report (EIR). Doing these would set up a more formal program. Integrated Pest Management is about evaluating what the pest is, whether it's invasive weeds, stinging insects, or rodents getting into buildings. What's your pest and what are your options for dealing with it? How can you treat it as safely as possible both for people and for the environment? It doesn't always mean using pesticides or herbicides; it doesn't always mean mowing. You have to look at each situation: can we do this safely and can we keep up with this, or will it be a waste of effort?

First I looked at all the existing data, the records of what we had worked on, like maps of invasive species. But it wasn't comprehensive enough. Then I questioned the field staff, asking mostly about invasive plants, but also about other pests. A true IPM program looks at all pests. We definitely had ant problems and rodent problems in the buildings. These were sometimes native animals, but they were still pests. Some District employees were using pesticides, and we needed to evaluate that versus other options. So, we added rodents and stinging insects to the IPM-EIR. Then too, when we "brush cut" roads and trails, whether cutting invasives or natives, it was still vegetation management, and that still fit within the definition of a pest, so trail brushing got included in the IPM program. We didn't add fire, because we knew that it was too controversial. We wanted to make sure we didn't completely lose our invasive plant program in the controversy about fire.

The data gathering when preparing for the IPM-EIR was similar to the creek management project I had worked on at the Santa Clara Water District: a lot of data gathering and discussion of the District's mission. There was a new understanding of what our options were. It wasn't just about how we had dealt with this pest in the past. Should we be using rodenticides in buildings? What if that building was out in the middle of a preserve and that rodenticide was getting out into the bodies of native predators? How might we avoid this? Was it how we were using the product? Could we be using a different product or a different method? There was a lot of analysis, and it took five years. I had to get consensus from the field staff, the managers, and from different public interest groups. We had a whole series of public hearings. We then hired a consultant to write the IPM-EIR, and the Board adopted it.

Midpen had done a lot of previous EIRs, for different activities. Every time the District bought a property, we had to do an environmental review. When we bought Mt. Umunhum from the federal government in the 1970's, we didn't do an environmental review, because back then they weren't required. But our neighbor, Loren McQueen sued us. He claimed that an action by a government agency that will eventually have an environmental impact had to have an environmental review. Purchasing this piece of property was the first step toward doing something with it. Umunhum used to have a military base on it. There was a lot of bad stuff up there, asbestos, lead, you name it. You're going to change it and you could contaminate that land. Anything could happen. You've got to do an environmental review. It went to court. It was a classic CEQA (California Environmental Quality Act) court case that I studied as a consultant when I first came to California. Since that court case, long before I even had an inkling that I would one day work for Midpen, every government agency that purchases land has to do an environmental review, not always an EIR. The banks now require environmental reviews, because they're not going to give you a loan on a property if there's a problem, right? So, yes, Midpen had done a lot of environmental reviews, but never an EIR on our invasive plant control program.

We were using herbicides based on the directions on the labels. We were careful to use them as directed, to follow standard practices and safety standards. There are provisions under CEQA, that if you follow other regulations, you don't have to do a separate review. There is a gray area surrounding when following pesticide label directions is enough, and when are your actions are bigger than that and you have to do a review. Because we were putting together this comprehensive, District-wide, many-years program, we decided to just go straight to doing an EIR.

Integrated pest management is actually a science, originally developed for agriculture. Farmers used to always spray their fields on certain dates, because that's what the manufacturer's label told them to do. It used a lot more chemicals and it wasn't always effective. This science started to develop out of UC Berkeley that said that we should only be using these chemicals when we needed them. First you needed to make sure the pest was actually present. Although developed for agriculture, it has been recently applied to invasive plant control in wildlands.

I think we finally finished up the EIR about three years ago, and then we hired Coty. He had a background in IPM, so he's now the manager of that program. It requires a lot more reporting than we used to do, and that is somewhat aggravating. We have to record how much herbicide we use, on which plants, over how many acres, on what date. We were doing that before, but now we are doing it all electronically, because you want be able to look at the big picture, to see all the projects. You want to be able to figure out if, say, using Milestone herbicide on yellow star thistle at Long Ridge is working after three years. How does using the Milestone compare to a similar area where you are mowing the yellow star thistle to control it? And if there is a difference, what is it due to? It is a much more scientific approach. To achieve this, you spend a lot more time record keeping. In theory, this makes your job safer and more effective. For field staff, however, it is aggravating to spend so much time recording and evaluating information. With time, I think we will realize increased effectiveness.

~~~

The deer surveys were discontinued last year, and, like the boot and equipment cleaning, I feel like I've been repeating this explanation of why for about 1,000 years. I have to keep telling myself to calm down, because, even though there are rangers who still don't understand it, their ignorance is not their fault. It's a communication failure. Okay, so: Deer surveys were started by Jodi. She tried to mimic the California Fish and Game's statewide deer survey program. They don't do comprehensive surveys, but they do have some places that they try to track every year. She followed their methods as far as time of year, and what you do. I had the same questions when I arrived here. How helpful is this? Where does this data go? How can you compare from season to season? I spent a lot of time talking to Stan and Loro about it. From those and other conversations I heard that rangers and volunteers all enjoyed the actual surveys; the rangers got fun people to chat with, and the volunteers got a unique opportunity to be out in the preserves after dark. I have to tell you: it was all about the experience.

I once did a deer survey with Loro in Russian Ridge, and I learned so much from her that night. She knew that preserve like the back of her hand, and she knew animals. At one point I spotted a deer and said, "Look, a doe on the top of that hill," and I started to mark it down. Loro said, "Wait. Did you see what she just did?" I said, "Uh, she turned her head and looked behind her." Loro said, "That means there's more deer coming behind her." Sure enough, within a few seconds three more deer came over the ridgeline. The whole evening was like that. Here I was the biologist learning stuff from Loro, who is, of course, a deer hunter, but she knew about other animals, too. She said, "Usually there's an owl in this tree," and sure enough, there was a great horned owl in the tree. I personally enjoyed being out there, and learned a lot.

So, we decided to keep the program going. Statistically, scientifically, we weren't covering enough area to get meaningful results on the deer population, even though we were being as consistent as we could be. If you did what we were doing for 50 years, you might have some statistically significant data. Or if something dramatic had happened, like some sort of disease outbreak, it would have shown up right away. Our method would have caught something like the blue tongue disease outbreaks that were happening in Northern California, which were first noticed by hunters.

Every year we looked at the data and we compared the number of deer seen per hour in each preserve, and the total number for all the preserves, to see if there were any big jumps. We'd make a graph of the data and send it off to the California Department of Fish and Game, which became the Department of Fish and Wildlife. They always told us that they found our surveys interesting and liked seeing them. We would send the graphs to the area superintendents, and ask them to share them with the field staff. People would ask me about them and I would pull them out and show them what we had. We talked about whether we could actually use this information for anything, and we talked about the experience.

I turned deer surveys over to Clayton, who handled a lot of the wildlife stuff, but I told him that it was more about the experience, and he agreed. He too liked being out in the preserves after dark. He liked working with the rangers, and doing deer surveys. Probably as the agency has grown and gotten real wildlife biologists on staff, they've been looking at all the work they have to do, including a lot of endangered species protection, and have decided that this was an activity that they weren't going to spend their time on. They looked at it purely from a wildlife perspective. I'm a little sad about it because I know how much fun the deer surveys were for a lot of volunteers and rangers.

Photo by Frances Reneau
Me holding red-bellied newt in Stevens Canyon

Discovering the rare population of the red-bellied newts was something I had no idea would happen in my career. If you want to read about it, you can go to the Dipper Ranch blog. There's a whole series called The Mystery of the Red-bellied Newt. One of our trail patrol volunteers, Chuck, reported seeing what he thought was red-bellied newt in Monte Bello near Stevens Creek. I had not only never heard of them before, but when I researched them, I found that their range was only in Northern California. The closest spot to here was in Sonoma, 80 miles away on the other side of the Golden Gate. Originally Chuck didn't send pictures. He eventually saw another one and carried it out. Chuck was a marathon runner, who'd regularly cross five preserves and 20 miles in two hours, but he was also very observant. So, when he saw this second red-belly, he put it in his pocket and he ran out and found the crew, who were working on a tree down across Page Mill Road. He waved it in their faces, and they took pictures of it.

I walked into the office on Monday and saw the pictures rolling on my computer screen and I shouted, "That's a red-bellied newt!" In the background of the pictures was the wall of the main office, which meant that the newt was actually in the office. I bust into the Monday morning crew meeting and demanded, "Who took the pictures of the red-belly?" It went from there. We were able to confirm that the newts were there, and that they were a breeding population. We got the Museum of Vertebrate Zoology at University of California Berkeley salamander experts involved. They did some genetic studies, hoping to figure out where the newts were from, but couldn't. The genetics were too much alike, which is very unusual for salamanders.

When they are ready to breed, salamanders go back to the same location in the same creek where they were born. We had had genetic studies done on giant salamanders in the preserves and found that, from one creek to the next, the genetics would be distinctive. The populations get so isolated that every animal in that population is similar. They took samples of the red-bellies from Stevens Creek, and compared them to red-bellies in their collection at the Vertebrate Museum. They hoped to see some patterns, so they could say, "Oh, these red-bellies match those from this population near Humboldt, and were probably introduced from there," which was the most likely scenario, even though it's hard to introduce salamanders. The introduced populations just don't survive; they try to crawl back up to Humboldt to breed and get run over or something, poor confused newts. But the Stevens Creek population's genetics were almost identical to all the other red-bellied newts in their collections. Extremely unusual.

What this tells us is that red-bellied newts have evolved as a species more recently, and at some point when San

Francisco Bay wasn't there, the population was more continuous. This might be a remnant population, or it might be introduced. We don't know. In doing this research, I learned about this Stanford professor, who originally had discovered the red-bellied newts in the '60's in Northern California. He had done experiments with their breeding and movement patterns in Sonoma, but then had committed suicide. He may be the key to this whole mystery. On the one hand, it's kind of annoying because I want to know: were they introduced, or did we find an isolated, previously unknown population? On the other hand, it's kind of cool that it's still a mystery. We will know one day. These genetics analysis tools we have now are still new. Sometime in the next 10 years, somebody will do another analysis, with more powerful tools and they'll be able to tease this out.

I'm a botanist, but I landed at the District and this zoological mystery was handed to me. I spent a lot of time, including my own time, reading papers from the Stanford Professor, Dr. Twitty, and I called up his graduate students, trying to figure it out. Pretty cool that I got to do that. You and I talked earlier about people having an innate connection to nature? That's just one small, but fascinating detail. This type of story is repeated throughout all of the preserves, both known and unknown stories.

~~~

MROSD is 64,000 acres of land with the Pacific Ocean on one side and San Francisco Bay on the other, and these major cities squeezed in between. There are so many people and so much development, and then there's this greenbelt with so much wildlife. All this ecology is going on, almost as if the human beings weren't here at all. That to me shows the health and the uniqueness of the District lands. It's this bit of nature that's churning along, to a large degree on its own. We're influencing it, but most of the time, the wildlife doesn't care. Nature can continue flowing along here, and people can come and experience it. Not only is it beautiful to look at, but also it's fulfilling to see wildflowers and understand their relationship with fire, and to see signs of Native Americans, and see pollinators interacting with plants, and over-wintering birds, and predators. You can see so much complicated life. That's what attracted me to working in this field. It was an honor to be part of protecting and restoring these lands. Working in Open Space was so special, and I feel fortunate to have been a part of it. I don't say "lucky," because I worked hard to get there, but I feel like my life was enriched by this job. I got to be part of preserving these lands. Sometimes I'd look out my window at the Dipper Ranch and I'd think, "I can see millions and millions of trees from here and underneath all those trees there are more plants, and mountain lions and bobcats, and birds and salamanders."

Agencies change, times change, and we change. I wanted to do a good job setting up the IPM program, to hire and train good staff, and make sure the budgets were dependable, do 10-year budgets on some special projects, and communicate well with the community. All of that was important to me, but I didn't want to only do that. There was a point when I just said, "I want to spend more time outside." Now I can pass my job on to these three other people!

Thank you, Cindy

Some comments on Cindy's interview:

Cindy says she was the first biologist at the District, but she may not have been aware of Alice Cummings' work, which had Alice wearing many different hats. Alice used her biological training to write acquisition reports, use and management reports, and grant proposals.

I, too, worked on the acacia removal at Pulgas Ridge as a seasonal OST, years before I became a ranger. Mark Casaretto and I spent a couple weeks up there doing nothing but feeding the trunks and limbs of cut acacia into the chipper. I cursed the person who thought planting acacia was a good idea. The big flat in the middle of Pulgas Ridge was once a tuberculosis hospital, landscaped with all sorts of exotic plants. Now it is an enormous dog off leash area. The exotics keep rearing their ugly heads and we keep beating them back. The dogs and their owners love it.

The Christmas tree farm is an interesting example of the District's willingness, even in its "purist" early years, to compromise its mission in order to close the deal. A Christmas tree farm is not a natural forest. It is a monoculture of Douglas-firs, devoid of understory. Even a "green" tree farm like Skyline Ridge (which uses no herbicides) has none of the "texture" Cindy talked about. It is a dubious sort of agriculture. Space, soil, and water are being sacrificed to make a commodity that, in about a month's time, will be added to the compost pile. Preserving the Skyline tree farm was political expediency.

I love the bit of succinct Cindy-wisdom about perfectionism. I have passed on to many others given its relevance to other aspects of life. It certainly hit home with me. As soon as she said it, I knew it was true, oh so true, of me. With Cindy's admonition in mind, I now try to acknowledge both that the results of my endeavors will likely be inferior to my expectations, and that it is worth carrying on, nevertheless. Enjoy the process because the result will never be good enough.

Many of the open space preserves contain houses that came with the purchase of the property. Many get torn down. The nicer ones are rented out to the general public at full market rate. Some are rented out to District employees at full market rate, and others are rented out to employees at half market rate. The half-market-rate houses usually go to rangers who get to pay half market rate in exchange for being "on" 24-7. They are the first rangers to get called out for an incident in the middle of the night or on their days off. These half-market-rate "resident ranger residences" are scattered around the District, usually not more than one per preserve. Some half-market rate houses also go to OSTs, who also sometimes get called out in the middle of the night and on their days off. Cindy was the only non-ranger, non-OST half-market-rate rental I know of. I'm not sure how often she got called in afterhours, but I know she got called in for wildlife issues on her days off.

All rural homeowners in California are advised to keep the weeds mowed back at least 100' away from their houses. For those renting District houses, this is part of the lease agreement. In recent years, both the price of housing in the Bay Area and the competition for District housing have skyrocketed.

I asked Cindy about the cessation of the deer surveys because as a ranger I had come to doubt whether this smidgeon of data we were collecting could possibly be useful. I was right: it wasn't. Cindy couldn't believe that I had never been given any feedback about the ongoing deer surveys, since she dutifully collected and reported this information to the area superintendents every year. Information frequently failed to trickle down to field staff. Mostly I was dismayed to learn that for years, we rangers continued to collect this data, but the program existed only to keep us happy and busy.

Ranger Frances:
Mountain Lion Attacks

I enjoyed hearing Cindy's story of the Picchetti mountain lion attack, and comparing it with my own, as well as hearing her views on dealing with lions in District preserves in general. Rangers field a lot of public reports of mountain lion sightings, and my experience jives with what she had to say. Maintaining a living space for large predators in the Santa Cruz Mountains is a balancing act. Modern technology such as motion-trip cameras and lion collars that ping to satellites have helped wildlife biologists learn more about mountain lion numbers, mountain lion behavior, and the lion carrying capacity of the land. I hope the increased knowledge and understanding gained from these high-tech devices may lead to increased safety for both species. It is sad to me, however, that the "king of beasts" now has to live with a big collar lodged around its neck. This symbol of wilderness can't escape from Big Brother.

Photo by Frances Reneau
Mountain lion print in Russian Ridge

Mountain lion attacks are such rare, dramatic and news-worthy events that I feel I should include them here, even though both of the following attacks, one on a deer and the other on a child, were down in my old stomping grounds working out of the Foothills Field Office. I moved up to the Skyline Field Office in 2013. In general, the preserves in the Foothills get many more mountain lion sightings and encounters than those up on Skyline. The obvious explanation is that there are many more visitors and residents down there to see and encounter lions, and there is greater encroachment of residential development into lion habitat. There are more early morning and late afternoon hikers, bikers and joggers out on the trails during the week getting in an hour of exercise before or after work, during exactly those hours when crepuscular mountain lions are most likely to be active. There may even be more food for mountain lions down in the "urban interface," since lions preferentially feed on deer, and deer love the landscaped yards of Los Gatos, Los Altos Hills, Woodside, and Portola Valley. As I often say, "If you have deer eating your roses, you have mountain lions eating your deer."

Up on Skyline, what we have instead are reports from our grazing program tenants of mountain lions killing their cows. We have filled the grasslands, where once elk, deer, and pronghorn antelope grazed, with domesticated European ungulates, but are then shocked and frustrated when our large native predators happily eat our meat. We displaced theirs, after all. The California Department of Fish and Wildlife will readily issue a depredation permit to hunt down and kill any mountain lion thought to have killed a domestic animal. This is standard practice throughout the West. District preserves, however, are intended as wildlife habitat, including habitat for large predators. So far, the District has resisted allowing the slaughter of cow-eating lions on District grazing-lease lands, much to these ranchers' disgust. Instead, if it can be certified that the cow, calf, sheep, goat, or llama was truly killed by a lion, and didn't die of some other cause, the District will compensate the rancher for the market value of the dead livestock. A District representative or a Fish and Wildlife warden has to certify that it was indeed a lion kill. If the animal is already starting to decay by the time it is found, the cause of death can be hard to determine, and there can be some argument over whether that carcass can be counted as a kill. I think an occasional animal lost to predation is the cost of doing business, and should be passed along to the consumers of "environmentally grown" beef, not taken from the coffers of the taxpayers.

Mountain lion attacks on people are extremely rare, but attacks on deer are daily, even hourly, occurrences. There are an estimated 5,000 lions in California, and each of them needs to kill at least one deer a week, more if they are feeding kittens. That's a lot of deer. If we humans are scared of mountain lions, imagine how the deer must feel. They live under constant threat from those long teeth and sharp claws, those huge night-vision eyes and big, sensitive ears. Deer are a mountain lion meal ticket and always have been. Like other species of deer and antelope, newborn fawns have evolved to run within an hour of being born, and a mature deer can outrun a lion if given enough head start. But the lion is stealthy and a better sprinter. All this drama of stalking and chasing, hunting and killing is going on out there all the time, under our very noses; we just don't see it. Even rangers, wardens, and wildlife biologists rarely if ever witness the bloody business of a large predator capturing and killing its prey. Wildlife photographers spend years of their lives trying to film such events. And then some innocent, oblivious visitor to Rancho San Antonio Open Space Preserve just stumbles onto the scene, and, being a modern American, has his phone open and at the ready to record the whole thing.

Journal entry 1/11/15: Big excitement today at Rancho. Right about noon, I was sitting on my butt in the Skyline Office working on a supplemental incident report, when Mountain View Dispatch came up on the radio, "Any unit near Rancho San Antonio? Visitor reporting a mountain lion attacking and killing a deer on the Wildcat Loop Trail." What? I had just been doing my little "Not me, not me!" dance in my head supposing this would be just another Rancho parking lot dispute. Not fair; I would like to go to this one. Anyway, Tracy headed out to meet with the RP (reporting party), who had photos confirming the incident, and Supervisor Chris started getting trails closed, and getting the higher-ups notified—CA F&G, Cindy and Clayton, and SO (Sheriff's Office.) Once the Sheriff was there, they walked in to the spot. I would love to have gotten in on that. FFO rangers were busy the rest of the day closing and guarding trails and putting up Mountain Lion Encounter signs. This happened at noon, on a beautiful, clear day, on the main trail, absolutely crammed with visitors, whom the mountain lion reportedly ignored.

Journal entry 1/12/15: The mountain lion vs. deer attack at Rancho yesterday has gone viral on YouTube today. Lloyd found it for me (and others) at the Skyline Office. It sounds like there were three people who witnessed at least part of the kill, and at least one had a decent video camera with a zoom—either that or the guy was friggin' close! When the video starts, the lion already has hold of the muzzle of a 4-point buck, and they are wrestling, the lion trying to hang on and the buck trying to break free. Poor thing. I'm sure he couldn't breathe and was suffocating to death in terror and pain. The buck is on his feet for most of what I watched, trying to skewer the lion with an antler, but the lion is crouched incredibly low, almost sprawled on the ground. Eventually, the buck drops over dead, or exhausted, and the lion goes for its throat. Only at this point does the lion look up at the camera. You see the eye shine in the video. If I were the photographer, I'd be thinking,

"Oh shit." I had a hard time watching, to my own surprise. It was so ghastly to imagine the terror and agony of that buck.

This same lion, or its brethren, have been in residence at Rancho ever since, going on two years now. The District labeled this lion-vs.-deer event an "encounter," meaning that the lion's behavior was not considered entirely kosher. Kosher kitties, per District standards, are expected to flee the minute a human appears, which in this case would have meant abandoning its freshly snagged buck. Following this very public deer kill, the early shift at Rancho moved to 6:00 am, back an hour from the standard 7:00 am start. These early shift rangers' task has been primarily to prevent illegal, pre-dawn visitors from entering the preserve and potentially exposing themselves to an unfortunate meeting with our resident lion. (District preserves are open to visitors from "dawn" to a half-hour after sunset.) This lion continues to leave spoor, and bloody deer parts and startled, excited visitors in his wake. He has found himself a territory and doesn't seem to be in a hurry to leave. He seems comfortable living on the fringes of human society, but just how comfortable should our visitors be, knowing not just that this lion might be in the neighborhood, but that it most likely is? Does the fact that he hasn't attacked or harassed a human in these two years mean that he is "safe" to be around? Like land managers of other parks where other even larger and more dangerous predators roam, such a grizzly bears, the District is challenged to keep visitors safe from a predator that is so inured to their presence. Visitors who behave stupidly, and approach this dangerous animal too closely, may soon learn a deadly lesson. We'd like to prevent that, for all our sakes, human and lion alike.

~~~

Attacks on humans are rare, but not unheard of. Since 1986 there have been 14 attacks in California, three of them fatal. Until 9/7/14, I could say that there had never been a mountain lion attack on a human in the District, and I had always assumed that there never would be. If lions were so prone to attacking humans, why hadn't they eaten *me* a long time ago? They've certainly had plenty of opportunity. I saunter around the mountains all the time, as do tens of thousands of others. This attack, therefore, was a real shock to my complacency, and a real political dilemma for the District, pitting public safety against wildlife protection. Public safety has to prevail, of course. We can't have rogue lions attacking and killing small children, but in the courtroom of District policy, at least for now, wildlife still has standing. We still seem committed to maintaining a legal space for dangerous, "man-eating" predators. We've remained committed even after a lion nearly killed an innocent child in one of our preserves.

Journal entry 9/7/2014: Picchetti Ranch OSP, the equestrian entrance below the winery. I'm here standing guard beside the taped-closed entrance. I can't believe it, but I guess we have had an actual mountain lion attack on a six-year-old child here, out on the Zinfandel Trail a couple of hours ago. It seems to be substantiated. The kid is reported to be okay, but was sent to the hospital. It sounds like it was not that far from the winery, between the Orchard Loop Trail junction and the Zinfandel Creek Bridge. The sheriff is out there now searching for evidence, as well as for the lion itself, and has reportedly found some tracks. Fish and Wildlife is already here, now waiting for a trapper with his dogs. I imagine we won't be released until the cat is dead.

New ranger Kristin reminded me that she took a report of an aggressive lion stalking people at Picchetti a few weeks ago. I was incredulous at first. I just couldn't believe a lion would attack in broad daylight, at midday. I'm wondering about extenuating circumstances like the kid holding food, or wandering alone. How about the lion? Is it sick? One good aspect of killing it would be the information from the necropsy. I'm heartsick about this. Why did this have to happen? It just stokes all the paranoia. Kerry just pulled past to go guard PI02. He says there have been two attacks on Zinfandel in the past month. Maybe he is thinking about the aggressive encounter that Kristin is remembering. Maybe this cat is a bad apple.

(Now four hours later, about 1800) A boring last four hours, other than curiosity about what's going on over at IC. Various rangers have passed me and chatted, so I have a little more information about what's going on. Jeff just passed on his way back to FFO to write the report. He was second on scene, right after Anthony, and got to see the victim and talk to the family. He reports that the lion jumped on the kid from above, and the kid has puncture wounds to the back of his head and neck. There was a second child right next to the victim, and the family was about 50' back. The two fathers ran to the rescue and the lion took off, jumping off the side of the trail. Amazing but true. That child would have been killed if the family hadn't scared the lion off. What a nightmare!

Every Fish and Game warden in the Bay Area must have driven past me here, and two different "hounds men," although one has returned back down the hill, maybe headed over to Fremont Older. Kristin just now took a report of a mountain lion sighting on the Tony Look Trail at 1600, so that might be the same animal. Marianne came by and dropped off an Area Closed sign. I think we are closing both Picchetti and Fremont Older. Aren't there also Mountain Lion Attack signs we are supposed to put up at this point?

I stopped a boy riding his bike alone up Monte Bello Road here. He said he was 11, but he looked about 7. He said his family let him ride the road alone regularly. I said it was not safe tonight and made him wait with me and call his father to come pick him up. I had to tell the dad the whole story, of course.

Brief interaction with X27 (Mike Perez). Sounds like just killing one lion won't be enough. They will have to kill every lion in the area. I hope not.

Further information eventually trickled down. The boy was one of a party of four adults and five children, two families, who had walked out to the nearby pond from the lawn and picnic tables at Picchetti Winery, and were on their way back. Suddenly the lion jumped out of nowhere, viciously attacked, and tried to kill their son. The parents responded instinctively to rescue the boy, and saved his life. The lion was chased off. The child suffered no permanent physical injury. The lion was eventually "dispatched." After three days of effort, during which the surrounding preserves remained closed, Fish and Wildlife hunted for and finally trapped and killed the lion close to the site of the attack. Forensic evidence verified that this was the lion responsible, so that ended the lion hunt. It was a healthy, young, male lion, thin, but not starving, not rabid or otherwise diseased.

Why that lion chose to attack that child where and when he did, against all odds, remains a mystery. Young lions, having left their mothers, have to find and claim a home territory. They don't share, especially not with other males. Their territories do not overlap. These young animals are stressed and hungry, being unable to find any land not already claimed by another lion, or by humans. Could this lion have learned from his mother to regard humans as prey? Or maybe, being hungry, this cat threw his natural caution of humans to the wind and followed his instinct to chase, kill, and eat small running mammals? It was unusual, out of the ordinary behavior. If all our local lions behaved like this, we would have many more attacks and, in short order, no more live lions.

Certainly the child who suffered the attack and his friends and family who witnessed it, will bear the scars, physical and emotional, for the rest of their lives. I can only believe that such a terrifying experience must have severely shaken those peoples' enjoyment of any future excursions into natural areas. If I myself had been the victim or, perhaps even worse, my own child, I can easily imagine instantly and permanently losing all trust in wild nature. My illusion of invulnerability, that bubble of self-confidence built up over a lifetime of outdoor living, might well pop in that instant. What happened to that child's psyche? How did his family move on and deal with this awful experience? Were they, from that day forward, forever fearful of forests, mountains, ponds and meadows? Did they ever again leave the familiar safety of the pavement?

Photo used by permission of MROSD

Stan Hooper, Maintenance Supervisor

My love of the Santa Cruz Mountains began in the 1960's with family visits to relatives in Brookdale, a place of redwoods, bikers and hippies near Boulder Creek. It was an hour's drive and worlds away from my suburban home in Santa Clara. I always looked forward to going, even if it meant getting carsick in our Rambler station wagon, the one with the back seat that faced backwards. There were also family camping trips to Big Basin where I explored the redwoods with my older brothers. When I was ten, I started tagging along with my brothers bicycle camping. We would strap our sleeping bags to the handlebars, shoulder our backpacks, and pedal off in the predawn darkness up Highway 9 into the mountains looking for adventure. This was before Highway 9 became a major commuter route. We made overnight trips to Henry Cowell, Big Basin and Castle Rock State Parks all without parents. Bicycle camping cost 25 cents per person per night. I remember my friend Thad carrying a cast iron frying pan and a coconut, which dislodged from his pack and rolled back down Highway 9. I scooped it up as it rolled past me.

Bicycling was great, but as I approached age 15½ I longed for a motorcycle. My parents weren't the type to spoil me and they usually made me earn what I wanted, so I was surprised when my father told me to go get the classifieds to look for a used motorcycle, which he would buy for me. The first motorcycle we looked at was a red Yamaha 175 Enduro. I loved it and he bought it for $300. A week later he died unexpectedly of a heart attack. Stunned by this loss, I rode my motorcycle every chance I got day and night exploring the Santa Cruz Mountains and mourning my father. I've always felt he knew.

At my high school many kids believed that "a clan of albinos" lived in the upper reaches of Stevens Canyon and they were afraid to go there. I intended to find out if it was true. One afternoon my buddy Bill and I went exploring a roadcut high up on the south-facing slope of Stevens Canyon, deep in "albino country." Eventually we parked the motorcycle and hiked. Up ahead we could hear a repetitive metallic sound. "Albinos!" we imagined. Creeping closer, we realized we were hearing a branch scraping against the corrugated metal roof of a shed. I decided the albino myth was just that. That land is now part of Monte Bello Open Space Preserve.

Bill and I used to explore the Voss property bordering Rancho San Antonio when we had double-period lunch breaks. We motored up the steep fire roads riding double on my Yamaha, me standing over the gas tank and Bill perched on the rear rack, hanging on like a rodeo cowboy. We always wanted to go a little farther but our watches told us to hurry back to class, smelling of two-stroke exhaust. I wonder if kids do stuff like that anymore.

My mother was active with the Santa Clara Valley Historical Society so we had many books about Santa Clara Valley history. I also spent time reading about Valley history when she would take me with her to Historical Society meetings. I read about Mountain Charlie and his encounter with a grizzly bear in 1851, and the early loggers of the redwoods, but that was about all. The Santa Cruz Mountains had less written about them and therefore were more mysterious.

The Santa Cruz Mountains are not large geographically, but they are diverse, very rugged, and heavily vegetated. This meant I could hike a short distance from a town or road and feel very remote. I might hike a ridgeline but know nothing about the mid-slope or creek below me because of the rough terrain. So the Santa Cruz Mountains have been changed very little compared to the Santa Clara Valley over the last two centuries. These mountains can provide a lifetime and more of wonder and exploration.

There are many sources of wonder in these mountains, like some of the tallest trees on earth, elusive mountain lions, fantastic, otherworldly fungi, and views from ridgetops peaking out of a sea of fog. But what I loved best were the tafoni sandstone formations; we just called them rocks. These rock formations were prizes to be found and climbed. We would sometimes climb exposed faces without ropes to heights I wouldn't think of now! Some evenings we'd sit on a comfortable rocky vantage point in the still forest, look down on the valley lights and listen to the distant rumble of the city. We felt safe there from wild creatures, real and imagined.

Castle Rock State Park is known for its rocks, but there are lesser-known rocks to be found. They often have shallow caves with sandy floors. To teenagers like us, caves were fantastic places where Indians had lived, bandits hid and bears slept. Remote caves made us wonder when the last humans had visited and who they were. I always looked for that prized grizzly bear tooth hidden long ago by an Indian boy. Caves were places to camp where candlelight transported us to another time. Or they were simply places to get out of the rain. I scoured topo maps looking for rocks, and would then enlist friends to join me on off-trail hiking adventures to find them, just relying on my sense of direction. When we found a new rock, we would give it a name of our own—TJ Rock, Frankenrock, etc. We weren't always successful, but we always had an adventure.

On one night visit to TJ rock (which now is skirted by the Achistaca Trail) with Thad (TJ) and Bill, I chose to stay overnight. I told them, "You go on home without me." They didn't believe me at first, but eventually they left. Other than a great horned owl calling, it was a peaceful night. I was up at first light and hiked down to Stevens Canyon Road, where I hitchhiked and then caught buses home. I called to Bill to let him know I was home; he wasn't even awake yet!

A high school aptitude test suggested careers as a motorcycle mechanic or a park ranger. I loved working on my motorcycle and on cars. After my father died, I had learned to repair appliances and do home maintenance, so being a mechanic made sense. I also loved being in nature, learning about it and protecting it, so being a ranger made sense too. Being on the maintenance staff at Midpen allowed me to do all of this in one job.

My senior year in high school I was in a program called CEBAS (Community Experiential Based Alternative School), which incorporated elements of Outward Bound. It included two trips, one to the Sierra and one to the Santa Cruz Mountains. We backpacked from Big Basin to Sanborn County Park in the rain. I was introduced to non-native invasive plant management when we spent a day pulling French broom in the rain along China Grade Road. I didn't know it at the time, but it was the beginning of a long relationship I would have with French broom.

Another part of the CEBAS curriculum was a career exploration project. I shadowed the Castle Rock ranger, Larry Thomas, for two weeks. One project he had me work on was painting the metal railing at the Castle Rock Falls observation deck. Years earlier I had scratched STAN HOOPER into the green paint beside dozens of other names. As we stood together on the deck, just feet away from my name, he demonstrated the use of the wire brush. I figured he had to know, but he never said anything. I learned about karma on the project, as well as about rangering.

In the late 1970's I was only vaguely aware of the fledgling Open Space District. My friends and I would park on Skyline Boulevard a couple mile north of Highway 9, cross the road to the west, hike cross-country up through the forest and out onto the ridgetop grasslands with amazing ocean views. We saw old ranch equipment contouring cow trails and spring-fed repurposed bathtubs full of water, which suggested recent grazing, but we saw no cattle. On one visit we heard a truck coming up the dirt road so we hid in the brush and peeked out as a white pickup with an agency logo on the door and a red light on the roof rattled by. It was a ranger and we were in a park! That was my first experience with the Midpeninsula Regional Open Space District in what would become Long Ridge Open Space Preserve.

After high school I enrolled in the Industrial Arts Program at Chico State University. I soon discovered Sinkyone Wilderness State Park on Northern California's Lost Coast. I was camping there that November, in 1986, when I heard they needed a volunteer campground host to staff the visitor center the following January, so I signed up. I got to work alongside staff and see firsthand what it took to run a park. For the next five years for my winter break from Chico State, I worked as campground host at Sinkyone. It was this experience that convinced me to work in parks, rather than teaching Industrial

Arts. This led me to Midpen where I experienced the Santa Cruz Mountains in an entirely new way, as a land manager. I would make a career of caring for the lands I had trespassed on as a teenager. Since my retirement from the District, in coming full circle, I have been re-hired as the January camp host at Sinkyone.

~~~

The bicycle trips of my youth in the late '70's were really fun despite the skinny tires that shook our bones when we'd end up on dirt roads and trails. If only there were better bikes! Then in 1984 my buddy John Butera bought a Univega mountain bike and I bought a Mongoose mountain bike from Stan's bike shop in Cupertino. We had a new way to explore the Santa Cruz Mountains! We rode our bikes everywhere and rarely saw another mountain biker. Our cycling kit consisted of Levi's 501 bluejeans, white crew neck T-shirts, lightweight hiking boots, small fanny packs, and no helmets. Life was good!

When mountain biking gained popularity in the '90's and I was hired at Midpen, the "trail wars" were already in full swing between hikers, equestrians, and mountain bikers. Mountain biking had started on Mt. Tam, just across the Golden Gate. I saw the controversy from three sides being a nature-loving hiker, a mountain biker, and a land manager. The shenanigans of a few in the mountain bike community turned me off to the sport. They were riding closed trails, acting aggressively toward other users, damaging trails, building illegal trails and vandalizing park infrastructure. At Midpen we were able to resolve most of the issues and learn to share the trails. Happily I have rediscovered my love of mountain biking; there is nothing like riding the trails I helped to build such as Crossover, Blue Blossom, Virginia Mill, Methuselah, Giant Salamander, Mt Umunhum, and Ancient Oaks.

~~~

In my early twenties, well before the Internet, I wrote a letter to the District asking about career opportunities. They wrote back saying something like, "Thanks for your interest, and these are things we look for in a candidate." It would be fun to have that letter now, to see who wrote it and what they said. They told me when to apply for seasonal, which I did. I drove down from Chico for the interview, which was at the Old Mill administrative office. David Topley and Carleen did the interview. I was offered the seasonal position, and they let me start work after my semester ended. I started June 1, 1990. After my first season at the District, I went back to Chico. Two openings came up for OST, which went to Paul McKown and Brian Malone. Brian was a seasonal on Skyline; Paul had worked at Loch Lomond, for the City of Santa Cruz. I graduated from Chico and came back again to work as a seasonal, and when another permanent opening came up, I got that job. Brian eventually became Land and Facilities Manager and then an Assistant General Manager and Paul went on to become the Volunteer Program Manager. We called ourselves the Class of 1990.

My first season I was on mini-crew. There used to be crew, and mini-crew. Mini-crew did the recurring maintenance, and crew did the capital improvements. Ironically, that is exactly how the crew will be structured again, starting July 1, 2018. When Don comes to Skyline, he's going to be the supervisor of the special projects crew, and the remaining crew will do the recurring stuff. John Kowaleski was the crew supervisor doing capital improvements with Warren and Renita and Travis, and I was on mini-crew with Michael Jurich. My second seasonal season, I was on the capital improvement crew. I remember that John Kowaleski, as crew supervisor, worked in the field every day, which supervisors can't do anymore. Once in a great while he would say, "I gotta go to a meeting; you guys go work on this today."

Photo used by permission of MROSD
John Kowaleski, Mainenance Supervisor
I never heard that John had been a ranger,
but that is a badge on his shirt.

That second season, I often worked with Gene Sheehan, the District's hired trail consultant and trail builder. He built many of the District's most popular trails, the earliest trails. Gene was ornery and wise and you had to earn his respect. He was a highway engineer from Canada and he built trails the same way: a maximum ten percent steady grade, just busting through anything that was in the way. Then he would put in these little water bars, inside ditches and tiny culverts, which took a ton of maintenance. The art of trail construction has evolved a lot since then, no discredit to him. Everybody built them like that back then. The whole thing of rolling dips, outsloping, and climbing turns all came later. In the early '90's we built the Coyote Trail that goes behind the Foothills Field Office, and the Farm Bypass Trail that goes behind Deer Hollow Farm. We built the redwood bridge that connects the paved road to the Coyote and Farm Bypass Trails. There was no connection there previously, just solid poison oak. We built the Seven Springs Loop Trail at Fremont Older, and the Zinfandel Trail at Picchetti. The Zinfandel was a nightmare; I'm not proud of that trail. You know, it went through that crumbly shale, and kept falling off the hillside. When we acquired the Vidovich property, we re-routed the Chamise Trail, grading and re-routing the old road, and we did some work on the single-track part. It used to be a rollercoaster right up the ridgeline. We build trails all in-house now. Ken, Holden, Eric, Grant, Warren, Brendan and the rest of crew do a fantastic job.

~~~

In the last couple months before I retired, I taught the resource management unit of the new ranger-training manual to some of the new rangers. We went in the conference room, and I got out all the materials, the IPM-EIR-FGM (Integrated Pest Management Environmental Impact Report and Field Guidance Manual) binder and the Sensitive Species binder, the Pest Control Recommendations, the Work Plan and various other documents and maps, and I started describing my experience with resource management at the District. I was glad to be doing it because I had a lot of experience, not only with weed work, but with the politics of weed work. I was going to be taking this knowledge with me, and at least I got to tell these new rangers, so they would have some idea of where we had come from and where we were.

The ranger job is now mostly law enforcement. The people that are attracted to the job are going to change over time, but historically, rangers with an interest in RM (resource management) could pursue it, and those without didn't have to. There were some rangers who were pretty motivated. Cindy once tried to require that all rangers would do a small amount of weed work each week, pulling star thistle at Los Trancos. I thought there would be a revolt. And there was a revolt.

Under CEQA (California Environmental Quality Act), which was a landmark regulation about 50 years ago, government agencies have to have EIRs (Environmental Impact Reports) on all their practices with impacts on the land, and we never had one for our staff to do weed work. We just went about our happy way doing good, conscientious work, until along came one of our District gadflies, a thorn in our side. This man was critical of our RM methods, especially our prescribed burns. He did some research and said, "Where's your EIR to support these burns?" We said, "Well, Cal Fire does the burns and their EIR is this old, historic one, and we just tag on to that." He felt like that didn't fly and management agreed, so we stopped burning. Right around that same time, we hired a new general manager and he was opposed to how we used herbicide, which shut down a lot of our weed work as well. We decided to do an EIR, and the District never does anything half-ass. Driven by Cindy and consultants, we produced a comprehensive EIR that was so good that other agencies are now copying it. Cindy brought copies to every convention and conference and put them on the table, and said, "Take one."

Our IPM-EIR is a two-part document. It's the EIR, and then it is also a guidance manual for field procedures. It defines what a pest is--a plant, an animal, a pathogen; it's really broad. It talks about thresholds, and impacts on the ecosystem. When is the impact tolerable and when does it cross the threshold of when you have to take action? What choices of action do you have? What action is the most effective and has the least impact? This is how we will manage yellow jackets, rodents in buildings (snap traps only), and yellow star thistle, etc. It gets down to how to spray and which chemicals, if any, to use under which circumstances.

~~~

Years ago I noticed that there were acres of this unusual grass out in Long Ridge, barbed goat grass. It looked pretty nasty. The subject came up at a training at the Department of Agriculture, and the commissioner asked me, "Did you say that you have barbed goat grass in one of your preserves? You've got to get rid of it." It wasn't a formal directive by the commissioner, but more of a personal one saying, "I want you to get rid of that barbed goat grass." I knew it was a bad, noxious weed, but what made it worse than the other invasive, non-native grasses was its economic impact on the cattle industry. Physically, it is a nasty plant that does bad things to the insides of cattle, and probably anything else that eats it, but nobody studies other animals, like deer, because there is no money involved.

So I set out to learn how to manage it, and started observing it. It's a hard one. You can look for it one day, and not see it, like if you go out there May 1st, and look. Where is that goat grass? Next thing you know, it's completely mature and gone to seed by May 10th. That raises one of my big frustrations: if it had been my job to manage that goat grass, I could have done it, but it was only one tiny part of my job. I couldn't focus on it. I did do some strategically timed mowing with the seasonals, but I never had the crew spray it, because there were already acres of it, and I didn't have the desire or the capacity to use that much herbicide. We did a lot of mowing, which was ineffective because we didn't follow up properly, going back to the same spot, at the right time, year after year. We had other priorities.

Then, when they hired Coty as the IPM coordinator, he identified the goat grass as very high priority. He said, "Stan, thanks for what you've done, but I'm going to take it from here." He did have me coordinate with Rangers Marianne and Kristin for the observation, because rangers patrol there regularly and could easily look for it in passing. They did a great job. Coty got contractors all lined up and got them out mowing and spraying and hand pulling, and the volunteers, too. I wish him luck. I was thinking just the other day, "Oh, it's May 17th. They should have treated the goat grass by now."

~~~

The District never formally did weed work in the early days, other than some rangers like Kerry Carlson, who used to pull thistle here and there, before thistle was everywhere. I was at FFO from '90 to '96 and I can't think of anything we did that was weed related. Then, when I went to Skyline, I worked for Patrick Congdon, who was the maintenance supervisor. You know, Pat was interested in everything, and one of the things he wanted to do was to get the French broom out of the meadow at Highway 9 at Highway 35, on the northeast corner. It was solid broom there, seven feet tall, in what's now that grassy meadow. He had the crew up there weedwrenching, and then he had the Morgan Center, the autistic adults, come and hand pull. We pile-burned, too. Ken Moore, the pioneering weed worker from Santa Cruz County, was an early visionary in weed work. He came and gave the crew a training on the propane torching of broom seedlings. That was about '96 when we started managing the broom at Saratoga Gap. Then we started working on broom at other locations, within our capacity to keep up with all of our other responsibilities.

Along the way, the District's Board of Directors changed and we got Deane Little and Ken Nitz and they were both highly weed-focused. In 2004 the Board created the Maintenance and Resource Management Supervisor position to oversee the weed program and that's when I was promoted from lead OST to supervisor. Michael Bankosh got the same position at FFO. I was excited and ready to rid the preserves of invasive weeds.

Weed work became more important at the District. We were doing joint RM days, where the crews from both offices would get together and do these big projects on acacia or English ivy or French broom. We got to work together, to see each other; that was one of the big reasons for it—team building. We were doing these projects every couple of months, alternating between Foothills and Skyline. It was a challenge to come up with a useful project for whatever season it was, so we asked, "Instead of doing a project every month, can we do a certain number of hours every year?" They said okay. I think the number was 2,700 hours. We then had more flexibility about when we did the work. There was a lot of enthusiasm, interest, and pressure to do weed work. Ken Nitz or Deane Little would call me up, "I was hiking at Windy Hill today and saw a lot of purple star thistle. When are you going to get on it?" And I'd be like, "Yes, Sir! We will," and we would. That was just the climate back then. We did a lot of good work, and had more and more sites that needed up-keep. That's when we started using herbicide. It was unregulated, you might say, in that there was no EIR, or Pest Control Recommendations.

We didn't have guidelines except for those that Craig Beckman had put together when he was maintenance supervisor. I had the good fortune to work with Craig for 21 years. Our work relationship changed as we held various positions. I was a lead OST and a supervisor; Craig was an equipment operator, supervisor and area manager, but he was always the same great co-worker. He had the rare combination of intellect, wisdom, and interpersonal skills to rise to the top of any profession. Stories of Craig's selfless heroics and contributions could fill volumes. We were lucky to have him and I am a better person for having worked with him.

Aside from the Beckman guidelines, all I had to go on was the product labels, the advice of other land managers at multi-agency conferences, and the training I had received earning my Qualified Applicator Certificate. Different field staff had different ideas about how to use herbicides. Some avoided it altogether. Others were mounting boom sprayers on the back of the spray truck saying, "Hey, no more brushing! No more mowing! Just spray it!" To me, that seemed excessive and inappropriate, but I just had my opinion, not any authority to say no. So I welcomed the EIR and Pest Control Recommendations. Eventually the

District's Resource Management Department came to be on the cutting edge of scientific knowledge about glyphosate, even funding new research. This was before the controversial finding that glyphosate is a "probable" carcinogen.

Over time, Deane Little, and Ken Nitz, and Operations Manager John Maciel left, but no one ever announced that the program had changed. In the meantime, we bought more land. We bought Driscoll, Mills Creek, Big Dipper and all the Sierra Azul properties. We added a lot of property, but, "Oh, by the way, you still have to brush all the existing trails and roads." We also had more houses, with more water systems to take care of, as well as more meetings and trainings, and so the slice of the pie for weed work kept getting thinner and thinner. It was frustrating for me, but I agreed that, if you're going to make me choose between brushing the trails and getting rid of the French broom in Saratoga Gap, I gotta go with brushing the trails. I just can't justify not doing that. If I have to choose between having safe drinking water at one of the residences, or doing yellow star thistle in Los Trancos, I'm going to work on the water system. So, little by little, we just did less and less, to the point where I got discouraged. I kept tracking our RM hours, but eventually I thought, "If no one cares, then why should I?"

During this time, the economy also did its dotcom boom and then the bust, and then the real estate boom and then the bust. Morale of the crew went up and down with that. We always needed more people, but there was a hiring freeze. Then the new general manager came on and, through Sango, issued a directive: Stop all spraying. I responded, "Wait a minute. You can't. If you do that, we'll lose 15 years of work. We'd be throwing it all down the drain because the plants are going to go to seed, and the clock is going to start all over again. Are you really saying to do that?" Sango said, "I'm being told to tell you, 'Yes, do that.'" I kept trying to find an angle where we could spray under certain conditions until I pushed Sango too far and he lowered the boom on me. I don't fault him at all. Sango was great and I appreciate his mentoring over the years.

Then Cindy stepped in, with her smarts and her creativity and cut a deal with management. She came to Michael Bankosh and me and asked, "If you could choose ten sites, where you would still get to use herbicide, what sites would they be?" So, out of 300 sites, I chose ten that I just didn't want to give up. Saratoga Gap was one of them, and the acacia at Mills Creek was one. I can't remember them all now. So we operated under those rules that Cindy got management to accept for several years, while they worked on the EIR. The EIR now allows us to use not only Roundup, but also five different herbicides. I'm kind of amazed. The crew only uses Roundup, but contractors use the others.

At about that time Ellen Gartside was hired as Volunteer Program Lead, a new position, and she and her volunteers picked up much of the workload and took on new sites and projects.

There is how I feel philosophically about herbicides, about their impact on the land, and about the corporations that make them, and then there are my feelings as a supervisor doing weed work. I'd rather not use herbicides at all, but if we're going to use them, then we need to be very good at it. I've been advocating for ten years to have a dedicated resource management crew. Weed work isn't for everyone. It's hard to make someone do weed work well if they don't want to. Yes, you can tell someone, "If you don't do this today, you'll be disciplined," but that's not how the District is. So, of the crew, the seasonals were always willing to do anything, so they did a lot of it. But that meant you first had to train them and then their season would end, and they were gone. Then you had new seasonals to train the next year. Of the regular crew, I had just a couple who had the motivation, the knowledge, the mindset, and the physical ability to do the work, and it wasn't enough. We were just limping along.

To be good at herbicide application, you have to spend time with it, and with the equipment. You have to be able to go back and review the work you did at set periods of time after you sprayed, not just a year later. You have to go back a week later, and two weeks later, three weeks later, and closely observe how it's affecting the plants, both the target plants and the non-target plants, if any. Did you miss 20 percent of the plants? Were you careless about being thorough? Then you could adjust your mix and adjust your application technique. It's an art, and crew just didn't have the time to do all that. If you missed half the plants, or 20 percent, and you got back a week later, you could get those you'd missed, but if you came back a year later, they would all have gone to seed, and you had just wasted your time. A specially trained and motivated crew skilled in weed work could accomplish a lot.

When the District wrote Measure AA, we did these visioning workshops with the public. We asked, "What Midpen work do you value the most?" It depended on how you asked the question, but the bottom line was that the public didn't value weed work. The pubic wanted trails. They wanted bathrooms. They wanted to get the closed preserves opened. They wanted parking lots, nature centers, and more land protected. But weed work was way at the bottom. I don't know if we could have educated the public a little bit, and maybe they would have answered differently, but clearly not everyone cares. They don't have the knowledge. Just look around Boulder Creek; there's English ivy carpeting redwood forests everywhere. If you take out the ivy, the native seeds are still there and it's cool to see what comes back. But people don't know what they are missing, and so our directive from Measure AA did not include weed work. I saw the writing on the wall of the District priorities.

A lot of the vision planning started internally. Through the whole process at these Operations Department retreats— when we were still Ops, before the split—we would ask about non-native plant work, and management would always answer, "Don't worry. That will be taken care of." What played out was that the Board approved a big contract for weed work, so the real answer was: it's going to be contracted out. I also once heard a manager say, "The resource management will be there for future District employees to work on." I understand setting priorities and making choices, but I don't think it had to be an either/or choice. Every day you wait, it costs more to get rid of these weeds, and you lose more and more of the native ecosystem. I disagreed with the decision but I couldn't change it.

Supervising the herbicide program meant a whole lot of time spent on training and record keeping, and low productivity. And yet, herbicide is an extremely effective tool, and I feel we applied it carefully and with minimal impact both to the land and to the people who applied it. Just out of curiosity, I once calculated how much glyphosate we used annually. If you looked at it on a per acre basis, it was a ridiculously small amount, like half an ounce per acre. Of course, it's not used that way. It's used at infested sites, with the majority of the land not touched at all. But even those infested sites were incredibly tiny amounts compared to agricultural uses, or what homeowners apply on their own yards. Eventually management asked for these numbers and I had them.

I did see some effects that surprised me at Los Trancos at the "elbow tree," a giant canyon oak, when (under the direction of a plant pathologist) we cut out the bay trees to protect those heritage oaks from sudden oak death (SOD.) Bay trees are the Typhoid Marys of SOD, serving as hosts, and helping to spread the pathogen. We treated the bay tree stumps with glyphosate and we saw a nearby bay tree die also. That told us that the roots were connected, and we had caused non-target tree death. It wasn't killing the oaks, just the other connected bay trees. You weigh your opinions about herbicide versus how much you value healthy native ecosystems. If you think it's important to have a native ecosystem, then you can rationalize using herbicide because it's one of the best tools.

There is a strange partnership between tree-hugging, environmentalist land managers and corporations like Dow Chemical and Monsanto. I learned this early on by attending all those California Invasive Plant Council Symposiums, and the Annual Oaks Symposium, and the Central Coast Weed Symposium, and various continuing education workshops, where I went to get my units to keep my Qualified Applicator Certificate current. The plant lovers see the English ivy or yellow star thistle pushing out the native plants and they think, "Oh, I want to get rid of that stuff. How can I do it?" and the chemical companies say, "Well, we've got just the thing." No mention of non-chemical IPM methods. I actually quit going to Target Industries in San Jose, which is where we used to buy our Roundup. They hosted these weed workshops for continuing education units. They had a classroom with a projector and a screen. You sat there with other land managers, like other park workers, and city park turf people and arborists and such. I was put off because I felt like I was sitting in an herbicide commercial. You do a course evaluation at the end, and I told them just that. I said this isn't teaching us best management practices; this is selling us herbicide. What a surprise.

~~~

Over the course of my career, the District became increasingly bureaucratic, which factored into to my retirement. I felt like the frog in the pot on the stove. After we got the EIR approved, I worked on a lot of the procedural aspects of pest management, and every single one of them was just depressing. It was like, "Okay, this is the criteria ranking form for prioritizing weed work, and this is the committee that will approve it, and this is the procedure for starting a new weed project, and this is the procedure for tracking the work you did." It wasn't just the RM program, but also trail brushing and trail construction.

Management wanted to know how much we spent per preserve, and to us that was an irrelevant number, because each preserve is completely unique. I guess the Board wanted to know this for when they buy land. To me, this was where knowledge and experience came into play and not just a reliance on numbers. You spend all your time tracking your time. It was my job to keep track, and they were paying me to do it, so I kept doing it, but it was slowly killing me. Previously, I got to make the decisions about new projects but all of that was being taken away from me and going downtown for review, approval, engineering, permits, etc. I enjoyed the challenge of involvement and control in a lot of different programs, and the rewarding feeling of achievement that came with it. Little by little, I became a bureaucrat. I was filling in spreadsheets and sitting in endless meetings. I had lost touch with why I worked for Open Space.

~~~

One of the things that upset me was seeing the District buy a property, build a trail, and then name the trail after the owners that had sold them the property. That struck me as wrong! There was an existing history of naming trails after native plants and animals. Then it just dawned me: why not Native Americans? They were the original landowners. They were on this land for 12,000 or more years and the whites for just a few hundred. I happened to be researching this just as we started building this new trail paralleling Skyline Boulevard north from Saratoga Gap. This area was once territory of the Achistaca tribe. I vetted the name with Randall Milliken, a UC Davis archeologist. He said, "It's not inaccurate, but the pronunciation is a copy, of a copy, of an unwritten word." He offered some other spellings but they were getting farther and farther from Achistaca. I chose Achistaca for the trail name because it was the easiest one to say, and spell. I know the name drives the dispatchers crazy, but it's no harder than Yosemite or

Zayante. We have a lot of Native Amerian names in our culture today.

At my retirement party, Brian kind of credited me with the names Oljon and Charquin but I believe that Charquin was from Mark Hylkema and Oljon was someone else, maybe Mark or Matt Baldzikowski. Even the Ipiwa Trail wasn't my suggestion, but Greg Smutnak's. He was intrigued by this concept of Native American names. I think he asked me where Achistaca came from and I got out the book, "The Gathering of Voices," and we went to the glossary of Ohlone words in the back. Brian Malone was in the process of re-naming the Ridge Trail segments in Skyline Ridge. Previously there had been various trails through Skyline Ridge Preserve, all of them called the Ridge Trail. There is that rattlesnake sign on one trail segment, which always frustrated me because there were no more rattlesnakes there than on any other exposed southwest facing trail, and the sign scares people needlessly. Brian was looking for names for these trail segments and Greg said, "Oh, here's 'rattlesnake.'" I thought that was kind of cool, so, that's where Ipiwa came from. It did feel good to bring some of those Native American words back to the landscape. Even if we're saying them totally wrong, those words are still being spoken, and it keeps them from disappearing altogether.

Europeans stole the landscape the Native Americans created. It was such good grazing land because of Native American management practices. They too favored meadows, because of the grass and flower seeds the meadows produced, which were possibly even a bigger part of their diet than acorns, and meadows made good deer habitat. Then the Mexicans and Europeans came along and said, "Look at all this great grazing land!" They benefitted from the Native Americans' practices, but nobody cared enough at the time to ask them how they did it. But when the whites started building flammable wooden houses, they got pissed when the Native Americans continued to burn the land and burning meadows was outlawed. "A Gathering of Voices" documents how Indians went to jail in Santa Cruz for doing their traditional burning, because they might burn down a white man's house. Two centuries later we find out that the Indians knew what they were doing by strategically setting fires to prevent catastrophic wildfires.

~~~

Remember what I said about the strange partnership between the land managers and the herbicide companies? It's the same thing with the cattle ranchers. I grew up hearing the Sierra Club's dogma: the cattle have no business in the sub-alpine High Sierra. I've hiked my whole life in places that have been impacted by cattle, not just the Sierra. The springs, lakes, and creeks were just muddy messes, and there were flies and shit, and trampled bare dirt instead of grass. At an early age I thought, "I don't want to be a part of this. I'm going to stop eating beef," and there were other good reasons to stop eating beef.

Just like with trail building, a paradigm shift occurred and some of the land managers were saying, "You know, cattle could be good for the land, if done right." I thought, "Well, my mind is open to this. There were elk and pronghorns here, and before those, mammoths," but I couldn't forget about all the degraded land I'd hiked on. It's hard to get on board with that being a good thing. The first District "holistic" or "resource management" grazing training we had was led by that couple from Hearst Castle, Orrin and Cindy Sage. I liked them, and they made a good case. They were aware of the environmental impacts of cattle, and they were articulate about the good the cattle could do for the land. They shared a vision of resource grazing that I was open to trying. Fast forward to when we started putting cattle on the properties: something got lost in the translation. We weren't doing what Orrin Sage taught us. We first threw the cattle onto the property and then built the fences around the sensitive areas, instead of the other way around. What started out as timed grazing, in which cattle were only to be on the land for a few months each year, became year-round grazing in some locations.

It was politically driven. The Board learned that if we wanted to expand the District's boundaries to the coast, we had to show the "coastsiders" that we had cattle grazing. Our GM also wanted to show that recreation and cattle could co-exist, because they arguably did so in the East Bay. For me, the reality of our grazing program was nothing like it was advertised, and that was disappointing. I had some say as the resource supervisor; I could point things out. The problem was, I couldn't get out in the field. I was always in the office doing admin. I wasn't aware of what was happening on the very lands I was supposed to be managing. My memory of the Coastal Annexation is that the coastal people wanted to maintain their way of life, and part of that was grazing. They were saying, " You will just lock away more property from grazing." So management said, "Okay, then we'll graze our properties," because they really wanted to go to the coast. The District's political objectives were met; time will tell about the resource objectives.

The row crop agriculture that the District is now supporting, the pumpkin patches and Brussels sprouts fields south of Half Moon Bay, are part of the mission creep that I see in there with the cattle grazing. We're buying the land and then allowing the agriculture to continue under a conservation easement. It's a win-win thing, but definitely mission creep for the District, so we added a second mission statement for the Coastside. Two mission statements for one agency! I don't think that was the vision of the District founders. The District that I went to work for was protecting lands that were near and dear to my heart, like Devil's Canyon. There are really good people working really hard on this project so I feel bad criticizing it.

~~~

As far as technology goes, everything has improved. Cordless tools, specialized trucks, lift gates and hoists now do the heavy lifting. Getting the enclosed cabs on the tractors made a huge difference for crew. When operating the earlier boom flail in the poison oak with the old red Hesston tractor, you'd put on your coveralls and button them up all the way, and wrap a scarf around your neck, and put on a dust mask, goggles, hardhat, and gloves. The dust and the cut material would just settle on you until you and the tractor were all the same color of brown. The enclosed cab with the air conditioning and the AM/FM radio and the joystick controls is so much more efficient and comfortable for the operator. There are two such tractors now, one at each office.

Another big change was getting the mini-excavators for building trails. We used to have Gene on his trail machine, which was the 36"-wide track with the excavator bucket on the front that was controlled by individual levers, a row of six different levers that Gene would manipulate with great dexterity. There was also volunteer Bo Gimbel, who used his little orange Kabota tractor to build trail. When the District bought its own Caterpillar mini-excavators, that was a game changer. Not only was it a more efficient machine, but it was our crew operating it, instead of a consultant. The Achistaca Trail was the first trail that the crew built in-house using the mini-excavator and also the Sweco four-foot bulldozer. That doesn't get used much these days. Given a choice, crew would rather just use the mini-excavator. If you need to dig a trench or auger a hole, use the mini-excavator. It has saved untold numbers of back injuries.

Remember those gasoline augers? Operating those was like a cowboy riding a mechanical bull. "Are you a man, or are you a mouse? Get on that machine!" It was so stupid; it was like this competition to see who could hang on the longest. Two people running at full throttle and just hanging on until the bit hit a root and stopped abruptly pitching the operators. There were so many injuries from those things. We got rid of the bad two-man augers and got newer ones with smaller bores, which were safer. Every tool we bought was an improvement over the old. Like we used to use the Pionjar, the gasoline powered jackhammer. It weighed about 60 pounds, and burned a rich mixture of gasoline and two-stroke oil, twice as concentrated as chainsaw mix. It spewed fumes and dripped oil out the exhaust. I injured my back using it on the Resolution Trail in Corte Madera. Gene would get to a point where his trail machine couldn't break the rock, and he'd yell, "Stan, go get that Pionjar." I'd hammer away until I'd broken up enough rock and he'd be on his way. Then we got the MB60, which was a slight improvement. It was a two-stroke rock hammer but it was a little bit lighter and you had a little better control. I don't think the crew gets either of those tools out anymore, because there is a rock hammer attachment for the mini-excavator. Why beat yourself up?

Photo used by permission of MROSD
OST operating a backpack sprayer

The skid sprayer for the herbicide was a huge improvement. We used to only have the backpack sprayers. Using the backpacks was a mess: either the hose would leak, or you would bend over to go under a fence, or under a tree limb, and the lid would leak, or the nozzle would come apart, all of which was inefficient. Then we got the skid sprayer, where the whole unit is on skids and slides into the back of a flatbed truck. Now when you're out spraying, you just have the wand in your hand, with a long, lightweight tube that goes back to the truck. The tubing is on a motorized reel that has a remote control so you can feed it out or roll it back in.

The radio system got a lot better, thanks to David Topley. When I first started, Midpen was on the Santa Clara County Parks frequency. Maintenance was on the same frequency as patrol, so when maintenance staff had to go on the radio, not only were all the rangers hearing us, but all of Santa Clara County Parks was too. It just made maintenance not want to use the radio at all, so it was a big deal when the District went to using Mountain View Dispatch and we got our own exclusive frequency. That might have been about 1996. At least it was just us. Finally maintenance got their own frequencies with the upgrade to the new digital system. The hand-held radios got smaller; when I started they were big, heavy bricks, but they eventually shrunk to the size of a consumer walkie talkie. Then cell phones came along. Skyline has such spotty cell service that the Skyline crew still uses the radio for maintenance traffic, but Foothills crew rarely does, because they do most of their communicating with cell phones.

~~~

There were so many factors regarding the timing of my retirement. You know, I could retire and get my pension any time after age 50. If you had asked me when I was 47, I'd have told you that I was going to retire at 50. Actually, it was the whole Measure AA thing that made me think, "I can't leave yet, not right now." I wanted to see how it played out. And then we won the election, and I thought, "Well, I can't leave now." And the next thing I knew, I was 55 and everything kind of lined up to where, "Okay. Now's the time." My job was stressful for me, but not all the time. I was co-supervising 12 regular employees, plus six seasonals, and knowing all the regulations and the policies and the laws, and doing the work plan and knowing that the crew was out there every day doing dangerous work. There is so much supervisors are supposed to know, and I couldn't know it all.

April 3, 2017, I retired after 27 years with the District. When I think of what 27 years represent, I think of this old-growth redwood tree on the banks of Slate Creek below School Road in Long Ridge. I first noticed it around 1990, so tall and straight, a fine specimen. It looks much the same today, maybe a bit larger in diameter. Twenty-seven years is just a brief period in the life of a 1,000-year-old tree, but for a person it is the span of a career and a third of a lifetime. I've changed a lot more than that tree in those years, and that's not a bad thing.

I've rambled on and filled all my space without getting to the incidents and accidents, wildlife and marijuana grows. I'm proud of what I accomplished at the District. My co-workers were the best, a dedicated and talented group. Something about this place, these lands, attracts exceptional people. Even if it did become a big bureaucracy, it was a damn good one.

Thank you, Stan

Some comments on Stan's interview:

Compare Cindy's and Stan's narratives about the IPM-EIR. Both complain about being dragged out of the field to sit in an office, compile statistics, and analyze the data required for the

IPM-EIR program, but both express the hope that this program will eventually rescue the District from the deluge of weeds.

I helped build the Zinfandel Trail as a seasonal and agree with Stan that the crumbly shale made for a terrible trail bed. Retaining walls above and below the trail were added piecemeal over the next decade in an effort to keep the trail from sliding off the steep hillside. The Zinfandel Trail is one of few trails in the District closed to horses, for fear that it can't withstand their weight.

I'm so glad that Stan brought up the Native Americans and their stewardship of the land. I've often thought how amazing it would have been to have seen California in the 1600's, before the first Spanish cow stepped off the boat. The pristine wetlands surrounding San Francisco Bay, the virgin Santa Clara Valley just a sea of native grass, wildflowers, and vernal pools, and the untouched Santa Cruz Mountains full of elk, beavers, and grizzlies and covered by a forest of enormous redwood trees and ancient oaks. It must have been a sight to see. But, of course, it wasn't pristine, untouched, or virgin. The Native Americans had been here for 12,000 years, chopping tules, burning chaparral, slaughtering deer, and exploiting the resources to the best of their ability. Land management by native peoples was limited by their near total lack of plants and animals suitable for domestication.

Ranger Frances: The Sacred Cow

Stan and my views of the District's cattle grazing program seemed well aligned, which was certainly not the case with all of my co-workers. Field staff who had grown up with strong ranching and farming backgrounds could see nothing wrong with having cows grazing on District lands, and I heard so many District visitors remark on the "lovely pastoral scenery" when looking across a cow pasture, that I was forced to learn to bite down strongly on my tongue before replying. To these visitors and field staff, grazing of Open Space lands posed no contradiction of values or ideology, and a hillside covered with cows looked like a perfectly normal country scene, so what was my problem?

Photo by Emma Shelton
Lando Cowzillion, my favorite cow

It's no secret that I hate cows. This became more of an issue for me when I switched from the Foothills Field Office to the Skyline Field Office in 2013 and started patrolling preserves in the Coastal Protection Area, all of which are grazed.   The animals themselves are not to blame, but the District's grazing program, of which they are part and parcel, is anathema to my own vision of Open Space.   Our preserves are supposed to be refuges for native organisms.   Our mission is supposed to be about protecting and restoring the natural environment.   The human use of this land is not supposed to go beyond low-impact recreation.   Not all land on Earth has to be logged, mined, and grazed to serve humans.   Some lands are supposed to be protected. This land. My land. Everyone knows how I feel about cows on my Open Space, and I receive a fair bit of teasing about my outspoken opinion that cattle grazing does not belong here. My husband even gave me a plastic cow figurine for my birthday last year.

I fully acknowledge that my objection to the cows is deeply ideological. I don't like the corruption of my wilderness vision with the inclusion of agriculture. Including cows (and Christmas tree farms, and vineyards, and pumpkin patches) under the umbrella of District protection feels like a compromise of our original mission.   In a tacit acknowledgment of this ideological dichotomy, there is even a separate mission statement for the Coastal Protection Area. The Coastal Mission Statement tells me that part of the District's job is to "encourage viable agricultural use" and to "preserve rural character." The Goals of the Grazing Policy tell me that we are helping to sustain the local agricultural economy and preserving and fostering appreciation for the region's agricultural heritage.   I found myself patrolling the public cow pastures, much to my disgust.

In order to appease the San Mateo County Farm Bureau and their constituents, the conservative rural voters, and win their votes to expand the District boundaries to the coast in 2004, the District agreed to do an about-face on the cattle question. To simultaneously appease the tree-hugging, native-creature-favoring urban voters, grazing was re-positioned as a tool of resource management. Rather than their former role as evil European exotics outcompeting and displacing native elk and antelope, and denuding and damaging the land, the cows became perfectly acceptable substitutes for our displaced native undulates, performing the same chore of vegetation management for biodiversity and fire protection. These arguments do little to assuage critics like me. I want the elk and antelope.

How ironic, to my mind, that the District evinces concern about world crises like global warming, (they have invested in a fleet of electric vehicles at the AO, for example) while subsidizing the production of red meat, one of mankind's least sustainable foods. I had a hard time swallowing all this, especially when out on patrol and dealing with the cows. Here are just a few excerpts:

Journal entry 11/28/13: Yesterday went with Ranger John back to Tunitas Creek OSP and he showed me around the cattle pasture part of the property. What we found upset me more than any pot grow site: cow pasture enlargement via bulldozer. The neighbor had scraped several acres of steep hillside, right up to, and maybe crossing over, the preserve boundary. There were additional smaller scraped areas within the preserve, as well as areas where it looked like the dozer had tried to just scrape out individual coyote bushes. I was horrified, and became even more upset when I later talked to the maintenance supervisors back at the office. They told me that the grazers have permission to scrape "brush" back to "historic limits." I appreciate meadows as much as the next guy, but we are talking about cow pastures of nonnative European grasses and weeds.

Journal entry 2/12/14: Resource specialist Cindy had sent Ranger Elisa an email asking that rangers go look for a possible cow carcass in the Big Dipper property. The camera at "Cypress Corner" had captured photos of a mountain lion and of panicked cows. It was fun. Elisa and I found lion scat full of black hair, but no lion tracks and no carcass. It's beautiful wild country that should be open to the public. Since I was last here, cattle have been re-introduced to the property and some parts of the road were complete mires of cow crap and thick mud. Elisa seemed to be even more upset about it than I was. "Why," she asked, "are they putting cows out here when there is nothing for them to eat? They are just tearing up the place." I, of course, agree.

Journal entry 6/10/15: I've been sequestered with the computer attempting to include the pictures in my report on the cows in the creek in La Honda OSP. The question arose in filling out the electronic incident report form as to whether there was, in fact, a violation involved. It's not illegal grazing because the cows are there by lease agreement. Might this then be a "permit violation?" Is a lease a kind of permit? And how about the pruning of bushes along the creek, clearly done to allow the cows easier access to the shade and water? Surely that's not okay, not permitted by the lease agreement? I'm sure the pruning is the work of Silvario, the ranch hand, who probably is doing it of his own volition, his primarily concern being with the cows' welfare, not with the creek's. It's clear that the cows are going around the fence where it ends a quarter mile away up the hill, but there is quite the cow trail coming in off the road where the gate seems periodically to be left open. Hmmm...

Photo by Frances Reneau
Harrington Creek, La Honda OSP, showing cattle damage

Journal entry 2/29/16: Knuedler Pond, Russian Ridge. Poor little pond down here is surrounded by "cow cups," like sun cups in old snow, but they are made of dried mud. Like sun cups, mud cups are hard to walk on. Fortunately, I suppose, I have big feet, so my boot can more easily straddle the foot-deep chasm of a cow track, balanced on the narrow arête of dried mud between pits. The entire perimeter of the pond is thus covered. Pisses me off. Driving down here, the roadway itself is similarly wrecked. The three pasture gates I now have to go through to get here also spoil my illusion of being in an actual preserve. We've installed a new sign up by the new corrals, (which hog one of the nice, flat meadows on Mindego Ridge) explaining to visitors that cattle grazing is entirely beneficial to the land, that the cows eat all those evil invasive weeds but promote native wildflowers. The District's commitment to "promoting cultural heritage" (i.e. ranching) is listed last. Why? Maybe I am not alone.

I was bemoaning the cow situation to a friend, Edith Collin, at the swimming pool and she promptly invited me out for coffee to further discuss my feelings. She was a good listener, and knew something about the issue, as she is active with POST, the Peninsula Open Space Trust, a private, non-profit organization which has been phenomenally successful at saving land. POST has been most recently focused on the coastal properties between Half Moon Bay and Santa Cruz, which were threatened by development into condos, beach houses and luxury hotels. In fact, the very lands whose management philosophy so upsets me were acquired with POST's help, so she knew all about it. Later that day I wrote the following journal entry:

Journal entry 12/23/13: Edith was sympathetic to my cry for wilderness, but pointed out that it is hopeless. The "historic" precedent, the Farm Bureau, the "working lands" inclusion in the vision plan, the lack of any other entity willing to take on management of the coastal ranches POST is saving, all doom my point of view to that of a lone fanatic. (How about a nice agricultural land trust, rather than an open space district assuming this task?) She helped me realize that even a compromise position with the "working lands" folks, like more restrictions and oversight of the cows and cowboys, wouldn't resolve my ideological issue.

I would love to see the District reintroduce herds of elk and antelope. Our native ungulates could perform the same task of grass removal for fire and weed suppression as the cows, with no need for gates and fences and water troughs, and complex lease agreements with cattle companies. But it's not going to happen. The agriculturalists have won, for now. I guess I would just like the District to come out and publicly acknowledge that our present situation actually is a politically expedient compromise. Having two, separate mission statements comes close to an admission, but the coastal version is hidden away on a back page of the web site, not front and center. Yes, the preserves are supposed to be about providing and improving habitat for native species, but subsidized cattle grazing (and Christmas trees and Brussels sprouts) has to be included in order to make it happen. This is about politics, not resource management. Of course, as a political entity, the District does have to put an entirely positive spin on this reality.

If there is anything that ameliorates my frustration and hurt feelings, my sense of betrayal and isolation, it is the one and only fact about the grazing program with which I can completely agree: cows beat condos. The land is still there, thanks to land managers more adept at compromise than I, and the land is still relatively undeveloped, just some barbed wire fences, gates, and corrals. Major development has been averted and, somewhere down the line, the land will still be there. Times change and the day will come when political support for the use of public lands for cattle grazing will evaporate. The enlightened citizenry of the Peninsula will acknowledge that beef production is not a sustainable and wise use of resources, and then we will finally kick out the cows.

Photo used by permission of MROSD
Kerry talking to visitors

Kerry Carlson, Ranger

My first memory of the District is from when my family would drive up to Jimmy Rapley's house for Thanksgiving in the '70's. Jimmy was my great uncle. There were these new brown gates we'd pass driving up there, like at Monte Bello. My dad was like, "That's that darn park district. They're buying up everything, the Midpeninsula Regional Park District." That was the original name.

~~~

When I got out of high school, I didn't know what to do. I graduated from Bellarmine High, so everybody else was going to Santa Clara University and to UCLA, and my parents asked, "Where do you want to go to school?" I was like, "Uh, West Valley College. I'm kind of interested in this park management program." There were four kids from Bellarmine that went to

216

junior colleges, and I was one of them. I got into the park management program, which was run by Tom Smith, "Smitty." I was really into it. At that point, I think my parents were just happy that I was doing anything productive, not just smoking dope. "Maybe he'll do something with his life after all."

Somebody at West Valley told me that there were four seasonal park ranger openings at Stevens Creek County Park, and I thought, "I don't know if I want to do that. That's a lot of law enforcement," so, at first I didn't apply. Then one of the four original hires quit or didn't show up, so I had a second chance. I thought I better try it, and I got the seasonal job. I already had my PC832. It was through that job that I came in contact with Midpen when I started meeting the Midpen rangers. In those days Stevens Creek County Park was crazy, a total biker park. I did more law enforcement in my four seasonal years there than I did in my whole career at the District, honestly. Every day I was writing cites, dealing with fights, going into stuff with the sheriff. It was a crazy time. Pat Congdon, who was a District ranger then, would fill with us, so I got to know him. I got to know Dave Camp, and Joan Ferguson, and Lisa Varney. I thought, "Wow, look at these people. They've got utility boxes and scanners in their trucks." They seemed super professional, a step above County Parks, like they were on the cutting edge.

I got my two-year degree in park management from West Valley College, and then I actually did a provisional job for Santa Clara County Parks because one of their rangers got hurt. It was 30 hours a week, and I liked it. The County then offered me a full-time job, but I had also applied at Midpen. I remember that when I applied, only three out of 300 of us got interviews. That's how competitive it was; you just didn't get a job at Midpen. I interviewed but then I didn't hear from them.

At the same time, I had been hired as a habitat aide for the Department of Fish and Game at Grizzly Island, which also was my internship for Chico State. I was double dipping. Two others got hired at Midpen, and then, finally, when it seemed like I wasn't going to make it, they gave me a job. Jim Bolen said, "Kerry, it wasn't that we didn't want to offer you the job. It was that you were on your internship and we wanted you to finish your four-year degree, so we picked you last."

I lived out on Grizzly Island during the internship, which was fun. The houses were in a square, 12 miles out into the marsh. I got to band ducks, set up duck traps, and run equipment. I worked the check stations, checking in hunters, checking their hunting licenses, and checking their birds. We had to learn all the kinds of ducks, so I was really good at identifying waterfowl. I knew some heavy equipment operation just from growing up on the ranch, and my grandparents' orchard, so I had some experience when I got to Grizzly Island. Not a lot, but enough that they let me run things. It was pretty loose, totally the opposite of Midpen. It was a State Game Refuge, about a quarter of which was open for hunting, while three quarters was a wildlife refuge. It was open for hunting on Wednesdays, Saturdays, and Sundays, and the birds had totally learned the schedule. When it was Wednesday, they all flew over to the closed areas, then, come Thursday, they'd all fly back into the hunting areas. They had the calendar all figured out.

The game wardens were having trouble getting citations to stick because they needed to get the closed areas signed better, so they gave us these Closed Area signs and told us to go put them up. It was easy digging postholes because it was a marsh and we planted a whole bunch of signs. About a week later, we were driving along and..."Hey! What's going on?" The hunters had pulled the signs out. I just couldn't believe that they would do that, especially that many signs that quickly. I got out and looked at this pulled-out sign and I noticed that there were elk tracks all around it. Later I watched as this big, old bull elk rubbed his antlers on a sign and he hooked it and up out of the ground it came. So that's who was vandalizing the signs: the Tule elk. I told the wardens, "Hey, those signs need to be the same width as the post. They can't stick out like a T."

There was elk hunting, but you could only shoot one, and there was a drawing for the permit. Nowadays, I think, you can shoot like three or four. I've never hunted elk. I never had that big a desire. The local elk are Tule elk, not like the Rocky Mountain elk, which are in Arizona, Wyoming, and Montana.

The manager of the refuge was a smart guy, but he had never gone to college, which was a problem whenever there was some task he wanted me to do. He'd be like, "Hey college boy, looking for your textbooks?" I'd been there for about a week, when the shop got broken into and all these tools got stolen. The manager was like, "I need this door welded closed, but the equipment operators are too busy." I was like, "I can weld." "You can weld?" "Yeah, I can weld." He was skeptical of this college boy, but he had me weld closed one of the doors. He came by later and was like, "Huh, that looks pretty good. The rest of the week you're going to be welding." I didn't want to spend all week welding, but by the end of the week he was like, "You should come by my house for some steaks and beer." He told me, "I admit I was a little hard on you because most college boys are worthless, but I didn't know you had skills." After that it was all good.

I kind of wanted to stay there at Grizzly Island. I was working there when Midpen called offering me the job. I told the refuge, "I'm not going to Midpen. I really like it here." But the boss was like, "If you don't go, I'm putting you in the truck and driving you down there myself. Don't be stupid. Take the job." So I did.

~~~

I remember my first week at Midpen, I thought they were messing with me, because someone would say, "Who's going to go Yazoo? Somebody needs to go Yazoo the meadow" or, "You guys go over there and take the Punjar." I thought, "Okay, this is some kind of snipe hunt. They're making these terms up. There's no Yazoo, no Punjar." It's like how we refer to all the properties by the former owners' names, which aren't on the map and mean nothing to a new person. "Go check the Cho property," which now we call the PG&E loop at Rancho.

Photo used by permission of MROSD
Gene Sheehan operating his trail machine

I got put on patrol, working out of Rancho, but I was only there for a couple days, when I was asked, "Do you get poison oak? No? Okay, you're going onto crew." They were building the Seven Springs Trail—just the northern half at that point—at Fremont Older, where there was tons of poison oak and everybody was out on workman's comp with poison oak, so I got bumped onto the trail crew. That's when I met Gene Sheehan and we became lifelong friends. I think I stayed as "ranger on crew" for quite a while. The south side of the Seven Springs Trail got built years later. The Seven Springs Trail used to just stop at

Ranch Road, and then you'd have to go back up Ranch Road, which was undesirable because it was so steep.

~~~

David Topley was trying to impress me this one time saying, "We've got this consultant who'll be working with us on this water line. He's the best equipment operator you're ever going to find, and it's a privilege just to meet him." This sounded just great, so I came by the Rancho office. I went in and around the corner and it was Luigi, Lou Bourdi's son. He was like, "Hey, Kerry. What's going on?" "Hey Lou. Good to see you." Poor David just looked dumbfounded. Luigi told him, "Yeah, we went on the Rubicon together. We've been jeeping together and his family has known mine for the last 100 years." It was fun to have that old time connection.

~~~

Shortly after I started working for the District, I was on patrol at the Monte Bello south gate, at the top of Monte Bello Road, where I found a van parked looking pretty suspicious. I thought something was going on and I better investigate. There was this middle-aged woman with two 18-year-old guys and she was having a grand time. She had a bed made up inside the van and was giving them alcohol. The guys were under 21, so there was a Furnishing Alcohol to a Minor violation and two Minor in Possession violations. I called in the stop and Michael Newburn came up from Stevens Creek County Park to fill for me. He was still working for Santa Clara County then. I wrote her for Furnishing Alcohol and them for Alcohol under 21, thinking, "I am ruining a good time for this woman.

Later I got called in and talked to. This was before the union, before there were formal discipline procedures. It wasn't worthy of discipline. They said, "The south gate is not on District property, so you did law enforcement off District land." "Okay, but it is a District pipe gate, and their vehicle was partially blocking the gate, so it seemed like it was related to District business." That was weird to me. At county parks I would have gotten a pat on the back.

Then, after some other incidents, they called me in again. They drew this graph on the white board, like a number line, with a zero and numbers up to ten. They were like, "You know, Kerry, most of our rangers seem to fit in here somewhere. Some are fours; some are fives; some are sixes or sevens. We don't know what it is with you, but for whatever reason, you are always at 9.9. You are always just inside the line, in the gray area." I was like, "Well, it sounds like I'm inside the limits." After that, I just wanted to stay on crew.

~~~

I worked on building the Peters Creek Trail at Long Ridge, and the Whittemore Gulch and Soda Gulch Trails at Purisima. By then, I was living in Half Moon Bay. Brooke and I lived on Purisima Creek Road. While I was working on the Purisima trails, I'd have to leave Half Moon Bay and drive to the Rancho office and load up chain saws and stuff and then drive back to Purisima, by which time half the day would be gone. We'd work on the trail for a while, but have to leave early because we had to drive back to Rancho. I kept telling David Topley, the crew supervisor, "This is stupid. You could let me leave my house and drive up Purisima Creek Road to meet Gene and I'd be working hours before the rest of the crew even got there." Eventually they said that was okay and I got to report right to the job site.

~~~

Newburn got hired in '86. We'd had had a grand time together working as seasonals for Santa Clara County. We knew what each of us was going to do before we did it. It was like we'd been together for 20 years. We were great at what we did and played off each other. He was going to Cal Poly in San Luis Obispo, but he didn't finish. He took a job working for the San Luis Obispo County Department of Corrections at the jail. He said, "It's a full-time job. I can't pass it up." He was there a week or two and was telling me about beating up prisoners. It sounded terrible. About three weeks into it, he realized that it sucked and he didn't want to work in a jail. I said, "Well, you know, there's a seasonal ranger aide job just opened up here that needs good maintenance skills." Michael had good carpentry skills, and I put in a good word for him, and Michael got the job.

~~~

Ranger aides mostly worked with the maintenance staff, like OSTs. This was before there was a real OST program. Martin was the first ranger aide I can remember. He couldn't drive. We'd always tell him, "No, you're not driving." This one time we were headed into upper Wildcat Canyon where we were putting in those bridges, in 1986. It was a real mess because the culverts had washed out. Those bridges are still there. Anyway, we were driving in to upper Wildcat, where it's super narrow, bringing in concrete and lumber, and he went off the road. "That's it, Martin! You're not driving anymore!" But somehow, months later we were going through the Holmes property into El Sereno, up the easement to the District gate. The old maintenance truck, a Dodge one-ton with a utility body, had a manual transmission, and we had sacks of concrete, and the pipe gate itself, plus all the equipment loaded in the bed. Martin started driving up the hill and around this switchback and he killed the engine. We asked ourselves, "How did we let him drive again?" He got the truck started back up, but he dumped the clutch. The pipe gate, the cement mixer, the cement sacks, everything slid off onto the ground. We were so pissed. "Okay, Martin, that's it. No more driving." This gal, Mari, who was a ranger aide, really lit into him, "God damn it, Martin! You can't drive worth shit!" I should have seen right then that horse trainer gals were dangerous. This was before I met Brooke.

Photo by Frances Reneau
Memorial to Jimmy Rapley
See my comments at the end of Kerry's interview
for more about this picture

There were a few prime instances where being a Rapley came into play. Jimmy Rapley was my grandmother's brother, my great uncle. He was born just before the San Francisco Earthquake in 1906, so he was a young man in the 1920's during Prohibition. He was a wild man and had great stories. One of his best stories was about drinking. This was from before Skyline Boulevard was built, maybe in the 1920's when there was just a graveled road along Skyline Ridge. He and his buddies went down to the Pioneer Inn in Woodside and they all got liquored up. Then they were going back up to the ranch, but they were hammered. Jimmy said, "Well, tonight we aren't stopping for any gates." So, from the Pioneer Inn all the way back to Rapley Ranch Road, they just rammed all the gates. They rammed like eight gates, but when they got up to the Rapley Ranch gate, they stopped and opened it. Down at the ranch everybody passed out. The next morning, all these ranchers came pounding on Jimmy's door yelling, "God damn it, Jimmy Rapley, come on out of there!

We know what you did." and he was like, "What do you mean?" "Come on. We know it was you. You rammed every gate but your own." He laughed that if he'd been smarter, and had rammed nine gates, instead of eight, he wouldn't have had to fix any. He spent the day hung over, building gates.

Another good Rapley story is from when I worked on Skyline, which was like '88, '89, and '90. I went on a hike on Hamm's Gulch, or maybe it was Razorback Ridge Trail in Windy Hill. It comes out onto Alpine Road right by this house. This lady came out and I greeted her, "Hi. How are you doing?" Just then this guy went driving by in a Land Cruiser with the top down, an older-looking guy, like 70. I asked her, "Who's that?" and she said, "That's Jack So-and-so." With that, she launched in, "I'm the town historian for Portola Valley and that's the whole problem with you Midpen people. You know nothing about the local history, or the long-time residents. You have no relationship to this area, no attachment, and no roots. You just come in and buy land." I was thinking, "I'm just going to let her ramble on." She was getting real wound up, but when she finally stopped for a breath, I said, "You're making me feel pretty bad. It has been a while since I've been up to see old Uncle Jimmy. He tells me a lot about the history up here, but I haven't seen him in a month or two. I better go see Jimmy Rapley." Her mouth was hanging open by then, "You're a Rapley?" I told her that my family got here in the 1860's, which just punched the air out of her. It was hilarious. Some of us here at Midpen do have some roots in the area.

~~~

This next is a good karma story that I've shared with other rangers. This was a long time ago, when I was still at Rancho. I was up at the Mora water tank and it was raining. I was sitting in my truck thinking, "What am I going to do? This is boring and there's nothing to do. Well, I guess I'll take a bent shovel and go hike the Mora-Ravensbury Trail and check the drainages. Then I'll feel like I've been more productive." Halfway down the Mora-Ravensbury Trail, here came this guy up the trail with a big German Shepherd. I thought, "Who'd have believed this would pay off? Right?" The dog was leashed and well behaved so I stopped him and just gave him the whole talk about the Dog in a Prohibited Area violation. He said he was really sorry and that, in fact, he knew the rules because he lived in the neighborhood. He said he was taking a shortcut home because of the rain, hoping that he wouldn't run into a ranger. He just wanted to get home and get dry. His information came back to the address he gave, and he seemed legitimate, so he just got a written warning.

Years and years later, we had this nasty mountain bike case that went to jury trial, the Toonie case. Anthony and I were on patrol together when we ran into these two obnoxious mountain bikers at the Monte Bello south gate. One of them had a boom box in his backpack and it was blaring, and they were both wearing full downhill helmets. I just knew this was going to go bad. They were being total A-holes to us. We warned them about the 15-mile-per-hour speed limit and then called Ranger Warren to let him know that they were entering Monte Bello, and he might want to set up for radar on the Canyon Trail.

Warren got into position. I guess he was already in Monte Bello with a radar. How rare was that? He radared them at 25 mph, but they just blew past him, so he called Anthony and me on the radio, saying they'd gotten past. We jammed to the end of Stevens Canyon. I was driving while Anthony was checking the radar with the tuning fork. We wanted to get these guys for something. We hoped to radar them coming down the trail if we could get there in time. The radar thing was a little iffy because we were still coming to a stop when Anthony radared them at 28 mph, but they were just going to blow by us. The first guy had gotten past, but then I threw the truck door open (policy-wise I'm not sure where I'm at with that) but I threw it open and the door hit the second guy's bike. I was yelling, "Park Ranger! Stop! Stop! Stop!" I grabbed the guy, and he started screaming that his arm was dislocated and that I was hurting him, but we got him stopped. We had lost the first guy, but we were trying to keep this one.

Anthony was Big Anthony back then, before he lost all the weight. He was bigger and looked much more intimidating. The guy just stood there for a while, but then he said, "Fuck you," and he rammed us with his bike. Anthony grabbed the handlebars and shoved the bike back so the suspect and the bike went flying backward. With that, the guy whipped off his helmet and pulled it back to hit us with it. I pulled out my pepper spray and started yelling, "I'm going to spray you! I'm going to spray you!" I should have just sprayed him. It would have been totally legitimate, but we were always so scared of getting in trouble. Maybe I was already seeing another IA (Internal Affairs) investigation. Luckily he didn't want to be sprayed, so he complied and put his arm down. We got his ID and the sheriff came, and we were going to get him arrested, but ended up just citing him out for the PC 148, Delaying and Obstructing a Peace Officer. I think later we tried to add Assault on a Peace Officer because he'd hit us with the bike, but the DA dropped that. And we got him for the speed violation.

Months later we got a call from the DA who said he had our guy, Toonie, and the guy just wouldn't let it go. He wanted a jury trial. They tried to plea bargain it down, but in the end we went to trial, because this guy was a jerk. We got assigned this assistant DA, who had only been there for three months. I forget what the legal term she called it was, but it meant that I was going to help her prosecute the case. I was supposed to be a co-something; I can't remember. I would be sitting next to her, feeding her notes.

The defendant's attorney started out by saying that he was going to prove that the rangers used excessive force on his client. Anthony and I were kind of freaked out. It was bullshit, but it was still scary. There was nobody else from the District there. We were just two rangers, and this could get the District in trouble. The attorney was bringing up all this use of force stuff, but the judge was just referring to the Penal Code, which says that officers are allowed to use reasonable force. I was thinking, "Oh my God. If this attorney had looked at our policy manual, this case would be over." District policy actually says that rangers have to leave suspects an avenue of escape, which is so ridiculously stupid. The judge was this older guy and he was like, "Nope, they can use reasonable force as peace officers. Overruled." We seemed to have him on our side. Every time the attorney would bring up some new thing, the judge would say, "Overruled."

The assistant DA and Anthony and I all went to lunch together and then Anthony testified and Warren, but mainly they had me up there on the stand. For an incident that took like 30 seconds, it felt like three hours up there with the attorney cross-examining me. One sort of funny point was when he asked me, "You say the defendant held up his helmet. How long would you say he did that for?" I said, "Eight seconds." So the attorney walked over to the display table, grabbed Toonie's helmet and held it up over me and slowly counted to eight. I looked stupid, because anybody could tell that it hadn't been any eight seconds. Fortunately I was quick on my feet and said, "Thank you, Honorable So-and-so for the demonstration because that refreshed my memory. With your help, I can now say that it was two seconds." The jury started laughing. Whew! Survived that one.

Then Toonie got up and said that his bike shoes were slick and that he had just slid in the gravel and run into us. He said that's what really happened. The judge then asked, "Are those Specialized 541's? I'm a bit of a mountain biker myself." Who'd have thought the judge could identify bike shoes from across the room? The jury went into deliberation and, in passing them in the hallway, I heard one of them say, "I hike at Rancho all the time and I don't know about the bikes," so that was encouraging. The jury returned after 45 minutes, and the assistant DA said that was good, based on her three months of experience. They found him guilty, and the judge sentenced him to ten days in jail and 1,000 hours of community service. Toonie and his attorney were disappointed. The assistant DA thanked me. She had a win under her belt now. She said, "I wish I could always use park rangers instead of police officers. Number one: people believe park rangers and they don't always believe police officers anymore. Number two: You guys are much more articulate on the stand."

Then the judge called me to approach the bench, and I was wondering what I had done wrong. He asked, "Do I look vaguely familiar to you?" I said, "I've been looking at you this whole time, and I feel like somewhere we might have met." He said, "Oh, we did. Do you remember a rainy day and you were out in your raingear and you came across a guy with a big German Shepherd? That was me. You treated me so fairly and so professionally that when the defendant was saying you did all those things, I knew it was all bullshit."

I tell new rangers that story. Treat everybody respectfully and professionally because someday it will come back to you. It's just karma. You never know who you are talking to. Fifteen or 20 years later there in the courtroom, the judge had remembered everything. Afterward we got to meet with the jury foreman and two or three jury members. They said they noticed some discrepancies between me, Anthony and Warren, but it was clear that we all were telling the truth, and we just remembered it slightly differently. "We had no problem with the guilty verdict."

A year later I ran into the defendant at St. Joseph's Hill. He recognized me and asked if I remembered him. He said, "It wasn't so bad. I did my 1,000 hours at a bike park helping out."

~~~

This was one of the funniest complaint letters that I ever got. It had snowed at the top of Black Mountain, and I had decided to go on foot patrol on the Black Mountain Trail to get some exercise. Tom Lauston dropped me off in the snow at the top so I could walk down with my bent shovel. I ran into this woman on her horse and with this little off-leash dog. I was talking to her, trying to deal with her. I didn't want to write her a ticket, but there was no way not to. The woman was so obnoxious, and the dog was so out of control. The lady was going crazy and I was having a difficult time citing her. She got so mad that when she went to sign the citation, she punched the pen clear through the paper, so I had to write it all over again. Her letter here explains what occurred. Annette got this letter:

Dear Supervising Ranger Annette Coleman,

On February 26, Ranger K. Carlson stopped me, my horse, and my dog on the Black Mountain Trail. He said, "You just passed three signs that say No Dogs. I'll be writing you a citation. What's your name?" I said, "Wait a minute. I didn't pass any No Dogs signs. I just want to go up and see the snow." I told him my name but I said, "So, now you're telling me I passed three signs and am lying about it? I'm not giving you any more information. I'll just leave." "Well, It's up to you. If you don't give me this information, then you're guilty of obstructing a patrolman. I'll have a sheriff waiting for you at the base of the mountain."

This REALLY made me mad. He was completely unreasonable. I do not deserve to be treated like a criminal. It was quickly unraveling into a power issue with K. Carlson. "What if I don't sign or pay for the ticket?" "You must comply or else a warrant will be issued for your arrest. You won't be able to renew your driver's license or your car registration. You'll end up in jail. Be prepared to forfeit any estate or property you might own." So, I signed the ticket, but I scrawled all over it. I was as mad as I have ever been. I have zero respect for this officer's ethics or professionalism. I do not like being threatened and bullied into compliance. "That's a misdemeanor, ma'am. I'm going to have to re-write this. If you knew Hidden Villa like you say, you would know that they also have a No Dogs policy." More erroneous information!

Backed into a corner, I signed the ticket. He then blocked the trail and told me that I couldn't go up to see the snow. I rode off in a rage back to the two signs I had passed. Sure enough, I was right! I rode back and I got him and showed him the two signs at the turns I had made, but there was no reasoning with him. He pointed to a third sign and said, "See. This sign says No Dogs." "But it's for a Hikers Only trail and I'm on horseback. I am NOT ON THAT TRAIL." I returned to Hidden Villa and put my dog in the car. Then I got on my second horse and rode back up and took pictures. I'm not only contesting this ticket, I'm lodging every possible complaint against Ranger Carlson's ludicrous, bullying accusations.

Ranger Carlson said Hidden Villa has a No Dogs policy. Wrong. Hidden Villa allows dogs. I've boarded my horse there for 3.5 years. I've volunteered with the farm manager, and we are always accompanied by his dogs, Banjo, Pearl and Bette. Fridays I volunteer with the livestock manager and her dogs, Ginger and Bert. If the nearest area to Black Mountain, Hidden Villa, allows dogs with some restrictions, why would dog owners assume the Black Mountain Trail does not?

I was cited without warning, quoted policies I have never seen enforced, threatened with seizure and arrest, and accused of lying, all based on signs and policies that don't exist. If this is Midpen policy, it leaves a lot to be desired.

I was humiliated, verbally backed into a corner, threatened, stripped of my personhood and dignity, made to acquiesce to the power of a law-enforcement agent, who seems to take this all as a personal victory. I think his style is harassing and abusive.
Thank you for listening,
Lorrie S. and her dog, Pickles

There's a picture of the dog, Pickles and a hand-drawn map, on which you can see that she's on the Black Mountain Trail. This is the reply from Annette:

Dear Ms. S.,
I'm writing this in response to your letter dated March 4th. Thank you for the detailed map and photographs. I spoke with Ranger Carlson and his supervisor regarding your complaints and concerns. Ranger Carlson expressed surprise that you had written because he remembered your last words had been an apology for your behavior and your saying that he had been very fair with you.
Ranger Carlson is very familiar with Midpeninsula Regional Open Space District ordinances and policies. He is known for his calm and informative manner in contact situations. The sign you rode past in photo #4 indicates that dogs are prohibited on the Black Mountain Trail of Rancho San Antonio Open Space Preserve. Additionally, nowhere in District preserves are dogs allowed to run off leash. Ranger Carlson told me that you did not have a leash for your dog. Ranger Carlson checked with the Hidden Villa staff to verify the dog regulations. Dogs must be leashed in the farm area and dogs are not permitted on the trails. I've enclosed the Hidden Villa brochure, which describes all their regulations. I hope I have answered all of your concerns. I encourage you to take care of the citation you received in order to avoid further inconvenience.
Annette Coleman

~~~

Did it get up to Skyline about my Ms. Lemmon incident? Everybody knows this story but Frances. You know, I have more IAs than probably the entire rest of staff combined, about 15, and I'm still here. Hopefully there will be no more before I retire.

When I got my W2 Form, Brooke and I were in the middle of the divorce, but she was still helping me out with the taxes. She asked, "What's this mean on your W2?" "I don't know, but I'll call my friend Miki in payroll and ask." Miki and I had always been very friendly, but I got her answering machine. I don't know why I did it, maybe because it was about two days before April Fools Day, but I thought, "I'll mess with Miki." So after her greeting I said, (in a phony, falsetto voice) "Oh, hello Miki. This is Ms. Lemmon. You remember me? I am a consultant for Manager S. Ranger Carlson may be calling you soon. Please help him out financially in any way possible. You can call him back at...," and I left my actual phone number. I assumed that Miki would recognize that it was me, because we'd played jokes like this on each other before, and I had left her my own, real phone number. I expected that she'd call me, and I could sort out the W2 problem.

The rest of the day went by and another day and I ended up showing the form to someone else and he was able to explain the issue. Then I realized, "Oh shit. I never heard back from Miki. I better call her up." So I called her up, all unsuspecting, and when she answered, I told her she could just disregard the question about my W2. She said, "What are you talking about? I don't think you even called me." I was like, (in a phony, falsetto voice) "Hello? It's Ms. Lemmon."

There was a long pause and then Miki said, "Oh my God. You're going to kill me. There is a huge investigation going on down here. This is a really big deal." I was like, "But you must have recognized me. That's my phone number." She said, "I never thought of that. Right now they have all the IT people working on this. Because you said, 'Help him out financially,' they think it's a phishing scheme to extort money from the District." I said, "I'm so ignorant of computers, I couldn't do a phishing scheme if my life depended on it." Miki said, "It's even worse than that. They called Ms. Lemmon and she said, 'That's not me. That's just somebody faking me.'" I said, "This is all so stupid. Why didn't anyone just call the number? It's my phone." Miki said, "They thought if they called the number, it would launch a computer virus." I was like, "Miki, I'm done for. I'm going to get in so much trouble." But I couldn't blame her, or be mad at her, since I did it. I started it. I understood that, even if it sucked. I told her to go do whatever she could to stop this from going any further. She said she would clear it all up. She would explain that it was meant as a joke, and try to make it all go away.

A couple weeks later I got the notice that I was again the subject of an internal affairs investigation. This was familiar ground for me. So I meet with a couple of the area superintendents and they asked me all the expected questions. Did you call Miki? Did you use a fake voice? Were you trying to extort money from the District? They also interviewed Miki, who, fortunately, was my friend, and asked her how she felt about it. Was she offended by my behavior? No, she wasn't. But I was regarded as having made fun of a manager's consultant, which they didn't think was funny at all. In the end, they found me not guilty of trying to get money out of the District, but guilty of violating the District's discrimination policy. I still kind of take issue with that. I imitate people's voices all the time and don't mean anything by it. I lost my longevity pay and I had to meet with the attorney who teaches the discrimination training.

~~~

There is a newspaper article from '95 or '96 about the history of the Tripp House at Bear Creek Redwoods, inside Gate BC01, where Maury Tripp once lived. Maury Tripp had his demons, but he was good with bloodhounds. One of their names was Sasha; I can't remember the other one's name. The house is just foundations now, but there used to be an abandoned house you could go into. He never owned it. The Jesuits just let him live there, and he trained his dogs out there in the meadow. Megan Robinson, who works for the Open Space Authority had a horse at the Bear Creek Stables and she and Maury used to get the kids from the stables to go hide for his dogs. He'd get an article of their clothing and he'd have the bloodhounds go find the kids. It was the perfect place, 1,000 acres to go train in.

He didn't just do the one rescue in the newspaper article where the dogs found a lost hiker after nine days in the Santa Cruz Mountains. Maury was friends with a sheriff's deputy named Paul Jones, who worked in the Santa Cruz Mountains. That was his in with the sheriff's department. He did have some issues, like he drank too much. Earlier in his life, he'd been a California state diving star from Los Gatos High School, an Olympic quality guy, when he was younger. I met him; I knew him, but not super well.

They were having all these burglaries of expensive jewelry and other valuables in Los Altos Hills. The guy was like a cat burglar, and they called him the Open Space Burglar because he would go into houses that were on the backside of Rancho San Antonio. He also burglarized rich homes up by Blackhawk, in the East Bay, which also have parkland surrounding them. He would break into the homes, even when people were there, and then take off through the open space land to get away. We had heard a little bit about it, but, like usual, the sheriff's office didn't tell us much.

Photo used by permission of MROSD
**Tom Lauston, Supervising Ranger
and Area Manager**

So one night when I was working late shift, I drove up to the Mora Gate on my way back to the office at Rancho and I saw a vehicle parked there and thought, "Oh, it's probably some kids going to sneak up to the water tank." It turned out to be this plain-clothes sheriff's deputy who was all excited. He asked me, "Did you see him? Did you see him? He ran this way. He's got a briefcase." Tom Lauston was also on this call, but at this point I think it was just me. The deputy told me that the only reason he happened to see the guy was that he was sitting up there at the gate in his car—like deputies do-- and had to take a leak. He had gotten out and walked into the preserve a little ways, and here came this guy running past him. Well, unbeknownst to Midpen, the sheriff's office had been planning for this, and had units positioned to try to catch the Open Space Burglar. This had been going on for a while and they were getting a lot of pressure from Los Altos Hills residents.

Tom and I and these deputies had a quick huddle. Tom and I told the sergeant, "Look, here's the deal: Rancho is like a big funnel. If he went up into the preserve, the signboard is a great place for somebody to sit, because most of the trails converge right here." "Well, that sounds good, but I don't have anybody." We insisted that it was an important spot. We said that he should also station somebody over by the PG&E Road. This cat burglar's car could be anywhere, because he was a runner. I remember they had the undercover cars at Mora, and at the St Joseph's Avenue freeway undercrossing. Finally the sergeant said, "Well, why don't you two take the signboard spot?"

So Tom and I got the signboard. We hid the patrol trucks somewhere, and we were just sitting there on the ground, in the dark, leaning against the signboard. I said, "Tom, I'm not sure what we should do if this guy does come by because reportedly he's carrying a gun. Should we try to stop him?" Tom was like, "It doesn't make sense. They should have given us a deputy." So we were trying to decide what to do, and we figured that probably nothing would happen and we could just sit there. So we sat there and sat there, in the dark.

Then we heard the, "Aarrrowh, aarrowh, aarrowh!" of distant bloodhounds. They had said that they had Maury Tripp on stand-by, so they must have called him in, and now he was out there running the hounds in the preserve. It sounded to us like they were heading up Wildcat Canyon, so we were thinking that the burglar guy had turned up Wildcat. We thought that was great that they had called in the dogs, because they'd be able to follow him.

Then Tom asked me, "Do you hear that?" Yeah, I heard it too. It was this like, sort of quiet, puffing, wheezing sound from behind us in the front meadow. I whispered back, "I think it's a doe that has scented us," because they'll do that. They make a noise like that. People that don't spend much time in the woods don't realize that. Tom was like, "Or, it could be the Open Space Burglar," but I was like, "Right, Tom." Then we heard it again, and I thought, "Probably a deer." And that's the last we heard of it. We were still sitting there, because we hadn't been cleared to leave.

Well, 30 minutes later, here came Maury Tripp with his bloodhounds, and he yelled at us, "The guy passed right through here." Tom and I realized then that the weird puffing sound was the burglar's breathing as he went past us. It was pitch black, and of course, we didn't have any lights on, but it was weird that all we had heard was the puffing. Probably just as well we hadn't realized it was him and we hadn't tried to stop him because we might have gotten shot. So, Maury yelled for us to follow the dogs with him, so we all took off running down St. Joseph's Avenue, and actually out into the neighborhood. The deputy at the underpass, who joined us, said he hadn't seen the guy come past, and about then the dogs lost the scent, so we started back toward the signboard. The burglar must have spotted the undercover car because the dogs then found his scent where he had climbed over the fence and gone up the embankment onto Highway 280, and got away.

Later on they finally did catch the guy over in Danville somewhere. He was a former high school track coach. Yep, we might have caught him, but he ran right past us in the dark, and I told Tom it was a deer.

~~~

When I drive past the Soquel Demonstration Forest it reminds me of the time when I took this employee brand new to their position on a tour of the south area. We went south along Loma Prieta Ridge, then down Ormsby and back up Highland Way. Then we went into the Soquel Demonstration Forest, across the bridge into the parking area. My truck was brand new at the time and there in the parking lot I backed up to turn around and—you guessed it—hit a tree. The back bumper got a pretty obvious dent. I was already in trouble for something else, so I was upset. This was not good. But then this guy says, "I'm going to be in a lot of trouble too because I should have been out of the truck spotting for you while you were backing up. I'm still on probation, so this is no good for me either. It's bad for us both." What could I say? It was an accident. We drove around some more, but they had to get back for some meeting or training that afternoon. Then I suggested, "How about I drop you off at the training, and later on, if the bumper doesn't look so bad, we both just forget about it?" "I don't know. I don't want to lie about it. But, I guess if it's all fixed...I guess so." I dropped them off, and then went to Ace Hardware for some sandpaper. Using the tow chain and a small sledgehammer I got rid of most of the dent. I sanded it down and re-painted it using a can of "appliance white" paint from the paint shed. The problem dent was hardly noticeable by this point. Neither of us ever got in trouble, and neither of us ever brought it up again.

~~~

When I drive pass by the intersection of Summit Road and Old Santa Cruz Highway, I am reminded of this neat woman who lived about two houses away from here. Years ago I was driving through Sierra Azul, way up on the Limekiln Trail, and I came upon this woman hiking along, alone. I thought that was cool, and she was good-looking, too. I got out and started talking to her. The usual, "Oh it's great to see a ranger out here," etc. I said it looked like maybe she was preparing for a backpack trip and she said she was going trekking to some foreign country. We were looking at something over toward Soda Springs Road and I had out my binoculars, and had set them on the utility box. She said her nickname, or trail name, was "Lost Girl," which I also thought was kind of cool. It was a nice contact, and I went on my way, thinking about Lost Girl.

At some point, hours later, I realize that I had never retrieved my binoculars from the top of the utility box, and now they were gone, and I was not ready to go drive all the way back out there to look for them. Three or four hours after that, toward the end of my shift, Dispatch came up on the air looking for any ranger who had lost their binoculars. That was kind of embarrassing. I called the number and it was Lost Girl, and she had my binoculars at her house, there near the junction of Summit and Old Santa Cruz. When I went by to get them, she was out in the yard with her husband. I was sort of sorry to see him.

They invited me to have a glass of wine, which I had to refuse, of course, but I did get out and talk to them for a while. When she handed me the binoculars I noticed that they looked like they had been professionally cleaned. She said, "I noticed that your binoculars weren't very well kept. They were extremely dirty, so I cleaned them up for you." It was the nicest my binoculars had ever looked since when they were brand new. This was all about seven years ago. Then, just the other day, I was at the Summit Store getting a sandwich and I saw this woman standing outside her car, and it was like the same thing. "Huh," I thought, "that woman looks well taken care of. She's kind of attractive." But there was something more, and I was looking at her, trying to see if maybe it was one of my friends. She saw that I was looking at her, and she goes, "I think you're the ranger that lost some binoculars years ago." I said, "I don't remember your name, but I know you are Lost Girl." She started laughing and said, "Oh, you do remember." I was like, "Oh yeah, I remember."

Photo by Frances Reneau
Kerry Carlson in old madrone in Bear Creek

Thank you, Kerry

Kerry had not yet retired when I interviewed him in 2017

While serving as Foothills Area Superintendent Michael Newburn went back to school and finished his BA in park management. His job counted as his internship.

The sandstone rock pictured, about 3 'X 2', was made by Jimmy Rapley's longtime caregiver, Hildegard, to honor his memory. It has now been placed at the base of the big redwood tree near his old home, the Rapley Ranch at Russian Ridge OSP. Long after the house and barn have fallen down and rotted, and the etching on this stone has weathered away, the tree he planted and the land he loved will be protected.

Ranger Frances:
Thornewood in my Side

Many of Kerry's stories are about conflict, and not just with difficult visitors such as the equestrian and her dog on the Black Mountain Trail or the mountain bikers in Stevens Canyon. He also had a propensity for trouble with supervisors and management. As much as he may disclaim any great interest in his law enforcement role, and profess that he would rather just work with the crew, Kerry was a very good ranger, an attentive listener and not easily intimidated. I always admired his willingness to take on the status quo and argue against policies he felt were stupid, or in favor of changes he felt were needed. I think he admired me for the same reason. I too could try my supervisor's patience as I tried to understand why my suggestion or request had been ignored or denied, as so often seemed to happen.

~~~

Tiny 167-acre Thornewood Open Space Preserve is one of the smallest of District Preserves. Secluded halfway up Woodside Road, it hides behind unmarked brick walls framing the entrance. A second entrance, off Old La Honda Road at the crossing of Dennis Martin Creek was until recently completely unmarked and was used only by in-the-know neighbors. The preserve is largely forested in second-growth redwoods, but also features a small and shrinking ornamental pond ("Schilling Lake"), and other odd remnants of the Schillings, the former property owners. Small and secluded as it is, it has some frustrating management issues, one of which, the old route up Dennis Martin Creek, kept me periodically engaged for many years. I so often bugged Area Superintendent Brian with questions and complaints, and wrote so many reports about misuse of the area, that he laughingly quipped, "You're becoming a Thornewood in my side."

Photo used by permission of MROSD
Brian Malone, Supervising Ranger, Area Superintendent, Land and Facilities Manager

If you look at the public map of Thornewood, you will easily spot the Bridle Trail going from the turnout on Old La Honda Road up to meet the Schilling Lake Trail near the pond. But on no map will you find marked the wide, welcoming, but supposedly unmaintained use-trail up Dennis Martin Creek. As you start up the Bridle Trail from the parking turnout, you can't miss the start of this unofficial trail, branching off to the left about a quarter mile up from the crossing of Dennis Martin Creek, even though there are no signs there marking this trail junction. There is nothing saying, "Not a Trail," or "Closed Area," or "Unmaintained Trail." Visitors arriving at this spot must surely wonder why this trail is unmarked, as though it didn't exist. This has always seemed unacceptable to me, and I tried to get it rectified. I wanted this awful old use trail closed down. After all, hadn't we recently built the nice new Bridle Trial covering the same route, just up on the hillside, out of the creekbed?   Why was this old DMC (Dennis Martin Creek) Trail allowed to persist? Here's the story:

Journal entry 11/25/14: It turns out that the icky old trail up Dennis Martin Creek is actually "an informal neighborhood hiking trail," permitted by an "Amendment to the Thornewood Use and Management Plan" dated July 25, 2007. Unbelievable but true. Superintendent Brian, in response to my recent photos of the erosion and trampling going on in the DMC trail corridor, sent me a copy of this Amendment, written by Meredith, one of the planners. It specifies that, in addition to building the new Bridle Trail, the Board has agreed to allow for a "narrow footpath" to allow neighbors "access into the preserve through their private properties." According to this document, there were two public meetings to which stakeholders were sent invitations. Had I known what was up, I would certainly have gone.

Journal entry 12/1/14: Talked briefly with Brian about the DMC issue. I got the impression he isn't entirely happy about the situation either, but he feels that it is hopeless, that we have to accommodate the neighbors' rights, granted by the Board, to walk the route. My desire to close it down, in his words, "isn't going to happen." So then I pressed him for why we can't simply treat it like a genuine trail, if it supposedly is one? Let's choose the least offensive option of the various braided, trampled pathways, and sign it and maintain it and put it on the visitor map. His answer? "Because we are trying to restrict use as it is an erosion and landslide prone area, and publicly recognizing it would lead to more use." I think not. There could hardly be more use on the web of muddy unmaintained paths. My suggestion seems like the better option.

Reading back through the aforementioned Amendment, I find bitter irony in the words of the fourth paragraph under

Drainage Improvements/Restoration. "Staff recommends leaving a minimal trail open as an informal route available to hikers per District policy that allows hikers to explore off trail. The route will not be formalized or advertised on trail map brochures, trail signage, or the District website, and the intersection will be vegetated and largely hidden from the designated trail system." This might have been the starry-eyed vision of the planners, but it is not what has taken place on the ground in the meantime. The number of visitors using the DMC turnout on Old La Honda Road increased dramatically after the new Bridle Trail was constructed, and the formerly daunting crossing of Dennis Martin Creek reworked. Visitors naturally are using the old DMC route, in conjunction with the new Bridle Trail, to make a fun and pleasant hiking loop, and their impact on the riparian corridor is not at all "minimal" or "hidden." Since the Amendment doesn't specify whether this "neighbor trail" should or should not receive any District maintenance, yet does seem to call for its continued existence, some neighbors appear to have taken on the upkeep themselves.

Journal entry 11/29/15: Walked the DMC today, and on my way back up, on the route closest to the creek, found four places where someone has taken a chainsaw to some of the trees fallen across the trail, in one case cutting little notched steps into a three-foot fallen trunk. I left my business card stuck in the bark with a note asking the responsible party to call the office. I understand from my last go-round with Brian that we won't be clearing the DMC anymore, but that no one else is supposed to, either. I hope this winter's storms bring some huge landslides and tree falls to put an end to this headache. Already wrote the "Illegal Maintenance" report. Even managed to get the photos in the clumsy computerized IR form.

Journal entry 12/12/15: Ended up having to write a big email to Brian after he ordered me to redact the report. He seems to feel that the neighbors have some "right" to keep "their" trail open. Then, today got another email saying to reinstate the report. Maybe he had second thoughts about allowing the public to wield chainsaws in the preserve. Partial victory.

Having the wind punched out of my sails in my efforts to kill the DMC trail, I sat becalmed in the Great Sea of Ranger Futility and Frustration. A simple ranger has very little political power in the District hierarchy, and very little wiggle room when up against our superiors in the chain of command. We can feel completely thwarted and stymied in our efforts to address issues we really care about. Some rangers, for example, care deeply about off-site law enforcement issues. We are unable to deal with speeders or drunk drivers on the highway, or kids selling drugs or drinking at the Caltrans Vista Point. Others are frustrated by the strictures imposed by the District on our emergency medical response, where we can't use any sort of medication on visitors, not aspirin, not epinephrine, not even antiseptic wipes. The law enforcement and medical limitations don't bother me as much as my total lack of say-so on resource management issues, and the DMC trampling hit home, squarely in my pet peeve sweet spot: people loving the preserve to death. I had tried, but failed.

Then a new DMC trail issue cropped up to rouse my ire, and again with a resource management edge to it.

Journal entry 5/24/16: Last week Wednesday I went up DMC from the turnout and was highly annoyed to find that someone, or more likely a team of someones, had cleared a long stretch of the creek and trail area of all fallen sticks and branches larger than about a one-inch diameter, and neatly cut and stacked them in enormous but tidy piles leaning up against the redwood trees. There were about ten such piles, each about 15' long by 6' high.   It was an incredible amount of work, and will be a lot of work tearing apart the piles and redistributing the sticks and limbs.   I also found a sturdily constructed shelter, of the kind we used to make with the kids when I was teaching for San Mateo Outdoor Ed.   Could this be the same perpetrator?   The cutting and stacking looks more like an adult crew of paid workers, whereas the hut looks more like kids playing, but once again, neat and tidy with the bottom ringed with pale stones.

I called Ranger Heimer to come and see all of this in the hope that he might put up a trail camera to catch the culprits in action, but he pointed out that we would need to have a video of someone actually collecting material and adding it to the pile, and "which pile are you going to film?"   Maybe they are all done with whatever they are up to.   What exactly is that, anyway?   Fire clearance came immediately to mind, especially as I suspect a neighbor is responsible, and I even have a particular neighbor in mind.   Near one of the higher creek crossings--bridged quite unsafely with a 10" plank, which I (once again) threw into the creek—a secondary trail leads steeply uphill into private property. The denuded area and stick piles continue up either side of this secondary trail, leading to whose house?

What the hell are they thinking? Do they want to "prettify" the woods, and have the money to hire laborers to make it happen? Don't they understand that all that fallen material needs to remain, to become soil and serve as homes for critters who live in fallen, rotting vegetation?   They have no understanding of the importance of forest "litter," or its role in the overall health of the forest. I wrote an incident report and hope to bring Chris, the new SFO superintendent, out here tomorrow. I'll probably forward the whole mess to the encroachment team downtown.

Photo by Frances Reneau
Hut in the redwoods, Thornewood OSP

No one downtown had the slightest interest in my stick piles. I couldn't get permission to pursue an investigation of the suspected neighbor. (I so wanted to walk up that trail and see where it led.) The only staff member who seemed as outraged as I was Ellen, the Volunteer Program Lead, who had worked in resource management on slender false brome eradication in Thornewood and knew many of the neighbors. She arranged for a crew of teenaged volunteers to spend part of a day scattering the piles. I got to come help, and enjoyed working with the young people doing something worthwhile. Trying to explain to these low-income, mostly minority youths why the piles were a problem was a fun challenge, as they had probably even less understanding of forest ecology than the know-nothing neighbor who did this. The kids did enjoy hurling the cut branches like lances and having marksmanship competitions. We missed one pile; I think we ran out of time or motivation, and it is still sitting there waiting for me. Somebody recently piled more sticks on top, but no new piles have appeared, so it seems to have been a one-time event.

How can I reconcile myself to my failure on this issue so dear to me? I was explaining the problem to my friend Emma, and she blithely admitted that she regularly hikes the DMC trail, climbing over fallen trees, edging around steep embankments, and wading through the creek. (She refuses to balance across the 10" planks.) "I love to explore up there. It's fun and adventurous." Aack! Even my well-educated, environmentally conscientious friend doesn't see the problem in allowing this free-for-all up the creek. It's unbelievable. What's going on? Perhaps we are all so starved for any sense of adventure when walking standard preserve trails, that we are irresistibly drawn to the magnet of an "unofficial trail." Every children's nature camp (like Hidden Villa, where I volunteer) has at least one "sacrificial zone," a lakeside, or a creek embankment, or a bouldering area that has been destroyed by the rampaging of little feet. The destruction is so thorough that it would take great effort to rehabilitate the area, so the camp has given up. They have decided to let the area serve the interests of free nature play, unhindered by concerns about the great damage the kids are causing to the homes of the creatures who might otherwise live there. I guess DMC is our sacrificial zone, an adult playground for off-the-grid travel, also available for unauthorized maintenance and bridge and hut construction. Have at it.

Photo used by permission of MROSD

Loro Paterson, Ranger

I've always been interested in parks. When I was a kid and we went camping, I'd follow the park aides around and help clean out the campfire pits. I grew up in Marin, so we went to Samuel P. Taylor State Park. When I was in high school, my first real job was working with the Youth Conservation Corp on Mt. Tamalpais re-routing the Dipsea Trail. That was really neat, and got me interested. For six hours a day we'd work on the trail, and for two hours we got environmental education. We got to go on a ride-along with a park aide, which I thought was great. In college, I took natural science courses. I went to Indian Valley Community College, then transferred to Sonoma State. I got a natural science degree from Indian Valley, and then majored in geography with an earth science emphasis, and a minor in geology at Sonoma State. The math was too much for me in geology. I liked the landforms and the meteorology. I still collect rocks.

~~~

When I was getting close to graduating from college, I sent out inquiry letters to a bunch of park districts. I was already working seasonally at Mt. Tamalpais State Park. I sent a letter to the Open Space District, because one of the guys I worked with had gone to a trails conference and had told me, "The rangers there actually do trail work. You might be interested." I graduated in 1987, and was hired by the District in '88, on 8/8/88, to be exact. To my great surprise, I got the full time, permanent job with the District. I think there were 120 applicants, and I was one of two hired. The other guy, Don Somebody, didn't last long.

I started working at Rancho San Antonio. Tom Lauston, Michael Newburn, Kerry Carlson, Craig Beckman, Dennis Danielson, David Topley and Sango were all rangers at the time. Sango was actually my first boss. We did a lot of maintenance because rangers would rotate for a couple months at a time onto crew. That almost ended my career with the District, because there was so much poison oak at Rancho. I called it the poison oak preserve. When you look in the fall, half of it is red, and I get poison oak pretty bad. I got the worst poison oak on a project that never even became a trail, which was extra annoying. It was out there in the front meadow, before you get to the split for the office. It was August and over 100 degrees, and we got sent out with chain saws. I still didn't have a uniform and was wearing my own clothes, which got poison oak stains on them. It took forever to get a uniform because they didn't have the right size and they were just dragging their feet. We all got poison oak so bad. John Kowaleski—he was the crew supervisor—couldn't go to this concert where he was supposed to play banjo. He couldn't play because his hands were so swollen. I got it just royally. I thought, "No way I'm going to live with this," and I thought about moving to the desert or the Sierras.

After about a year, I got to go for a ride-along with John Escobar who took me up to Skyline. He said, "Working on Skyline is like a regular parks job. People come up here and have questions. You're not just dealing with a bunch of neighbors. I think you'd really like it," and I did. It's more of a destination, and a lot less people. It's greener and prettier too. I was living in a travel trailer I had bought when I was working for state parks. State parks had a lot of housing where they would let you camp if you had a trailer. I figured I might be working seasonally for a long time, maybe for the NPS (National Parks Service), and they mostly have places where they'll let you camp in an RV. So, I had this little travel trailer that I could tow with my pickup. I was living in a trailer park because the District didn't allow you to live on District land. They'd let caretakers live in trailers on District land, but not employees. There was only one crew at the time and they worked out of Rancho. Kerry, who was stationed on Skyline, was rotating into his ranger-on-crew time, so there was a temporary ranger spot on Skyline, for two months, which I got. I commuted from the trailer park to Skyline for a short time, and then Kerry decided he was going to stay down at Foothills, because it was an easier commute for him.

~~~

Meanwhile John Escobar had been promoted, and so he was moving out of the Skyline house near the SFO. Dennis Danielson then moved from the house at Purisima to the Skyline house. Matt Ken was working for the District then, and he was going to move from the Monte Bello cabin into the Purisima house as soon as Dennis was out of it. I was then supposed to then get the Monte Bello cabin. This whole three-way move was pending, pending, pending and Matt and I were both anxious to move. Dennis had already moved, but still had his stuff at the Purisima house.

It was kind of neat that in those days we all did DTs (defensive tactics) together. We all got together for that, and for the first aid trainings. DTs went all day and the big boss, the ops manager, would still come, meaning John Escobar was there. So, we were all at DTs together working on compliance techniques and come-alongs and that kind of stuff. Matt was on one side of John Escobar and I was on the other, and we were trying to convince him, "Hey, can you give us a date for the housing? I have to give 30 days' notice to the trailer park." We were both holding John like this and he said, "Oh, pretty soon," at which point Matt and I both cranked up the pain and he started literally dancing. I said, "John, can you give us a date?" and he said, "How about April 10th?" and then we relaxed. That was so funny. He actually kind of respected us for that. He might have fired us, or something, because we were torturing him to give us a date. He just laughed about it, and didn't hold it against us.

Photo used by permission of MROSD
Christmas party potluck spread below the tool wall at FFO

I knew Escobar really well, of course. The whole District was much more friendly then. More people would have parties and invite everybody because there were less people, and not that many people were married or had kids, so we would hang out together. We would all go to The Cats in Los Gatos. People hosted barbeques and other functions. Later on, when Craig Britton was the general manager, his secretary, Susan, was a fun person. Her nickname was Captain Fun. She'd set up dates and we'd go bowling, off duty of course. Everybody would go. They went to ball games, and went golfing. I only went bowling, because I'm not a sports fan. The whole staff had fun together. You knew people better then. Plus all the trainings where you'd see people at break times and lunch time.   There was more camaraderie, and I think that slowly changed. It's partly just size, but partly now the mentality is that they want to divide and conquer and keep people separated.   When I started, most people, even those who'd been there awhile, had started their careers at the District. Kerry and Michael and Craig had all been there several years, and they're still there. It was a career; people didn't leave. When suddenly people started leaving left and right, it was like, "What's going on?" I always looked at it as a career, and was happy to stay.

~~~

I was in the process of getting hired by state parks when the District hired me. The states parks process took so long that about a year into my District job, I got called in for the state parks interview.   My deciding point was when the District housing came through, because I was in the final process to become a state park ranger, which had been my original goal. Two reasons I didn't take it were because I didn't want to move, and I didn't want to go to one of the problem parks down in Southern California. You usually had to start at one of the no-fun parks where they had 24-hour shifts and practically riots. I knew someone who used their baton on people at the beach down there and I really didn't want to do that. We made more money, too. Matt was in the same process and he was the math whiz. He said, "It's going to be about a third pay cut." They had just coughed up my housing, so I decided to stay. Being a resident ranger involved more of a commitment. Maybe that's why I bought this retirement cabin: I needed a place to get away. When you're in housing, you're never off duty, and when you retire, you become homeless. I was hired in '88 and bought my house in '95. There are no call-outs up here, and I can't hear any motorcycles. I heard enough of them over the years. I like the peace and quiet. But Skyline was beautiful, and even Rancho.

When the District bought the Monte Bello cabin, Dennis Danielson became the first resident. He lived there about five years, then Michael Newburn and Jill had it, but only for a short time, when they were first married. He was way too tall for it, first of all. He had to bend over just to get in the front door, as well as the door into the bathroom, and it's too small for two people. Matt Ken lived there for three years. I was there for 25 years, a long time.

~~~

We had to work a lot of maintenance early on. On your patrol log you were supposed to show that you had worked at least two and a half hours each day doing maintenance. Luckily, during the time I was assigned to crew, they were building the trail around Horseshoe Lake at Skyline Ridge. They let me just report to the worksite, rather than down the hill at Rancho. I'd continue working after crew left for the day, just doing some finishing work, and then start again before they got there in the morning.

You didn't used to get to take your patrol truck home at the end of the day as a resident ranger. It was crazy. Also, when you were assigned to ranger-on-crew, you lost your patrol truck assignment. What changed all that was the Russian Ridge Fire in

1990. Dennis was on vacation and I didn't have an assigned patrol truck and Craig Beckman, who was a ranger at the time and was living at the Corte Madera house, didn't have an assigned truck either. They only assigned take-home trucks to some people. I thought it was silly. I should have a truck for emergency calls. Instead I had to first drive to the office to get a truck. That took time, of course, and maybe the call was actually in the opposite direction.

Photo provided by and used by permission of Patrick Congdon
Pat Congdon leading a fire training with CDF

Pat Congdon was a volunteer firefighter--I think a fire chief--as well as a resident ranger. Major after-hours incidents would usually involve calling out the volunteer firefighters, so he would get paged out. He would then have Bunny, his wife, call up the other resident rangers. Bunny later worked as the payroll person for the District. It was nice to have a friendly, familiar voice saying, "Pat's out on this call. Can you go out and help?"

Pat worked 24 hours a day, a total go-getter. He was also interested in Skyline history and started the binders on the bookshelf at SFO. He took on saving the little Sunny Jim shed, and the old farm equipment. He was also super knowledgeable about Native American things, and an expert on fire stuff.

So on the Russian Ridge Fire, Bunny called me and said, "There's a fire at Russian Ridge and Pat's responding." We had radios at home, but she'd usually call on the phone. "Okay," I said, "but I'll have to go and get a truck first." Luckily, because Dennis was on vacation, I had been using his truck. Not everybody even had a personally assigned truck then, especially the new people. We shared trucks. We didn't have our own assigned radios either, except for resident rangers. Anyway, I still had the keys to Dennis' truck on my belt, which was good. I had to hop in my personal vehicle, unlock and get through the gates up to the Skyline Office to get Dennis' truck, but because I already had his keys, at least I didn't have to disarm the office alarm and go inside to get the truck keys. I just jumped in his truck and went to the fire. Pat was already there. Woodside Fire was on scene, and it was burning pretty good. I fought fire all night, right there at the flames.

The fire had started not too far inside Gate RR01, probably by somebody smoking on the rocks there. It was August, and I remember that at 4:00 in the morning it was 90 degrees, one of those hot, dry nights when it's hard to sleep. I had just gotten to sleep when the phone rang. The fire started around midnight, and we were out working it all night. I just parked my patrol truck when I got on scene and got hooked up with a Woodside Fire unit. They didn't know where they were going. We did a hose lay and then we started some mobile attack behind a dozer. Pat was out with a backpack pumper, walking along the dozer line.

This was before there was any prohibition against riding on the back of trucks, so I was on the back of this brush rig with its little pumper, and we were following the dozer down that steep front face of Russian Ridge. We were going down, and it was getting steep. I was sitting on the side of the truck just squirting out the fire as it came up to the line the dozer was creating. We were doing good at getting some fire put out. Then the truck ran into a rock and it tipped up, and I jumped off. Pat yelled, "Jump!" but I was already off, because it was starting to roll onto my side. I leaped off and landed safely on the ground, and the truck didn't roll. It just came back down. "Okay, I guess we're done with this flank," I thought, as soon as my heart was back in my chest. It wasn't pitch black out, but it was before we had good headlights for our helmets. Our fire gear was questionable. I thought, "I can see why three times more firefighters are killed than police officers." That's changed around now.

It turned out that the fire had gotten all the way down onto the True Ranch. It was being pushed by hot, dry, easterly winds. It was the biggest fire in San Mateo County in ten years. I forget how many acres burned, but it was big. At about 6:00 in the morning the District staff got released. Sango was on by then; he'd gotten called out and was at the IC. He told me, "Yeah, you can go home and sleep a couple hours," because I had an early shift that day. "You can come in a little later." Of course, I was wide-awake after all that. I couldn't even talk because I'd inhaled so much smoke. I'd say like three words, then start coughing. I called my parents, "Hey, watch the news," because there had been news helicopters out there. I still had to work the rest of the day.

That night, the next night after the fire, they said, "Take the truck home." They changed that dumb policy. When Dennis came home from vacation, he could smell in his truck that it had been on the fire, and he had missed it. I had left the truck running with all the lights on, and it had run all night. It had burned a quarter tank of gas just sitting chugging away for six hours. But Craig and Pat used their District truck's pumper. They were smaller units then, only 100 gallons, and the hose was like an inch-and-a-half garden hose. Craig and Pat were on the Alder Springs Cutover Trail and we'd gone down to help them. It was so dark and smoky that you couldn't tell that the fire had already jumped the Cutover, so they were still trying to hold it there. I remember watching Craig standing on the side of the truck on his tippy toes. He was just tall enough to hit this little tree that was on fire. Hey, he saved the tree. Later we saw that the fire was already clear down the hill.

Some resident rangers had already been able to take trucks home. Matt Ken had a truck at the Purisima house. He was crew-supervising ranger at the time, and had a Ford Ranger truck without a pumper. Rangers rotated into the position of ranger-on-crew, and when there, they sometimes acted as the supervisor, not always. Sometimes there was more than one ranger on crew. Eventually Pat became crew supervisor, and rangers no longer rotated into that position. I never got rotated into crew supervisor because I didn't have great maintenance skills. I could run a chainsaw and had done a fair amount of construction work with my uncle, so I had some skills, but not the heavy equipment. That has definitely changed for the better. Specialization is good, but it's good to have some general knowledge. I worked with one new ranger a few years ago who didn't know how to use a shovel. It was a guy, too. I couldn't believe that he didn't have a clue how to shovel. Another new guy had never run an electric drill. Drills have a forward and a reverse, and he got really huffy when I pointed out that he had it in reverse. Another guy had never used a socket set and didn't know how to release the ratchet. If you've done that stuff, you just take it for granted. A recent ranger didn't know that you have to lock the hubs on the patrol trucks to use the four-wheel drive, although some trucks like the Chevys have automatic locking hubs.

~~~

When I was hired, I didn't go to the ranger academy for about six months. I just did a ride-along with each of the rangers, a few days a piece, and then I was sent out on my own. "Here's a truck and here's a map book. Have at it." Because I'd already had the PC 832 class, I could already write tickets. I had maybe two months of training, and part of that time I was rotated onto crew. I remember that Tom Lauston told me that the first time he wrote a ticket, his hands were shaking, so not to worry about it; it was normal.

I think the first paper I cut for something was just a written warning, a lady with a dog down by the Mora Gate at Rancho when I was out on foot. Rangers also got assigned all-day foot patrol, because there weren't enough trucks. When I caught this lady, I didn't have my truck there to use as a desk, so I used the fence as I started filling out the cite form. I hadn't been told anything except casual mentions from other rangers about officer safety. Tom filled for me from the Mora water tank, and after I'd finished up with this woman, and she'd gone off, Tom said, "I just want to say: you should never turn your back on a suspect. You didn't do wrong, just keep it in mind." Mostly my ranger training fell de facto on Tom, who was just another ranger at the time who worked the same shift. He was a great trainer, a natural supervisor, always really nice.

Tom would tell you what you're supposed to do by the book, and what you really do. For example, he talked about when you're sneaking up on people at the Mora water tank. At the time they were real strict about the Smokey the Bear hat. I never wore my hat too much. You were supposed to wear it on foot patrol and on law enforcement contacts. Tom said, "When you're walking up there, you might want to carry it against your chest so you're not silhouetted against the sky, with your hat profiled. They'll think you're just another kid." Then you had a chance to see if it was even safe to approach the people. You could check on how many kids there were, if they were impaired, or if there were any weapons. You might not even want to approach. He said it was safer to just sneak up on them, and you can't sneak up so well wearing the ranger hat. We had our hats, but he didn't say we had to wear them!

~~~

We were still wearing the brown pants. People would think we worked for PG&E. And if we went to a Shell gas station, the attendants there wore exactly the same color uniform, and we went to the Shell station for vehicle repairs. People would ask you to pump their gas for them. We still had the dope leaf logos then, on the door of the truck and on our uniforms, so people would ask whether we used the pumpers for watering the marijuana. We had leather belts and the old radios which were about the size of a Kleenex box. You could probably have used them in self-defense. It was bigger than a brick and it hurt your back. The new duty belts helped distribute the weight better. It was so nice when we got the new duty belts, although you were supposed to wear the equipment on the new belts in exactly the prescribed spots. All the tools had to be behind your back, so they would all stick in your back when you sat down. We didn't have batons. We had pepper spray, cuffs, the radio, and a flashlight. Since we didn't have batons, we were given training on how to hit people with the flashlight. Eventually there was case law from other agencies being sued for this use of the flashlight. When we changed DT instructors, the new guys said it wasn't a good idea.

All the rangers went to a Board meeting where we gave a presentation asking for all this defensive equipment: shoulder mics, batons, body armor, and even guns. We got three out of four. They wouldn't go for the guns. I actually got up and spoke at the presentation, one of only two times I spoke to the Board. I don't like pubic speaking. I told them about the time I was shot at.

That was up on Monte Bello Ridge. I never saw the gun, but I heard the whiz of the bullet past my ear, and I heard the bang. Ranger Warren and I were working the late shift, and from Skyline Boulevard we could see lights flashing up on Black Mountain. We thought it was after-hours bikers or hikers, so I went sneaking up Monte Bello Road blacked out. We were allowed to drive without our lights. I was past the towers, driving along. Warren was still down by my residence gate looking up across Stevens Canyon and reporting where the lights were. I had the truck windows down and suddenly I heard this "BANG," and this "TZING." I called the Dispatch, "I think I've just been shot at." I remembered that we had some suspected poachers up there at the time, who would come up and enter the preserve from the other end of Monte Bello Road at the south gate, so I thought probably that's who it was. Later I learned that you can't sneak up on people on a gravel road. Half a mile away you can hear the crunching. If somebody was out there creeping around looking for deer, they would have heard me coming. That wouldn't be a good time to poach a deer. I think they were shooting at the vehicle.

I didn't know where the shot came from, but I quickly drove out into a big clearing, where I could at least see around. Palo Alto police were started my way, because it's their jurisdiction, and in theory they could be up there the fastest. Kerry, who was the other late shift ranger, said we should also start Santa Clara County Sheriff. Okay. Good call, Kerry. Warren came around to meet Palo Alto at the Monte Bello gate, but they went flying past him, on up Page Mill Road, so he had to go chase them down. Meanwhile, I sat there for a long time. The first officer to arrive was a Santa Clara County SO (Sheriff's Officer) from the south side and that was 44 minutes, the longest 44 minutes of my life! Were they going to try to come and get me? Should I go forward, or back out? There was a good moon out that night, so I could see around, but it was creepy, and I didn't like it. They never found anybody, but, all the same, I was shot at.

So, back at the Board meeting, I got up and told my story, and why I thought we should have weapons. We are sent out alone in the dark and have no way to defend ourselves. We didn't even have pepper spray then, or batons. They're no good against a bullet anyway. After the presentation, right that same evening, the Board voted to go forward with everything except the firearms. I heard later that part of the reason we got the shoulder mics is that Craig Britton, the GM, had gone on a ride-along with me. When I had heard that he was going to ride with me, I'd thought, "Oh, what did I do?" That was probably a couple months before this presentation. He'd watched when I'd stopped somebody for not having a helmet. There was a guy and a gal, and the gal was the one without the helmet, but the guy was the one giving me crap, "Get a real job. Go find real criminals," the whole spiel. He was moderately hostile, not like he was going to take a swing at me, but they weren't happy campers. He'd lied, "It's her birthday," but when she gave her DOB (date of birth) no, it was a couple days off. Craig said, "You handled that really well." He saw how I'd had to shout into my radio since I had to hold it up way over my head to get reception and how having shoulder mics would solve this problem. Later, I heard from another person who's now a supervisor, that in the discussion behind the scenes, Craig had argued for them. They are handy in noisy conditions, too.

I was impressed that John Escobar got up and did part of the presentation. At the end of it, when the Board was questioning, "Well, what does body armor look like?" for the public image and all, Escobar said, "I'm wearing it right now." You couldn't even tell. I thought that was really smart of him to go in and just make his whole presentation and not bring it up. I think a good part of the reason the District rangers have never gotten guns is just the public image, the look, which is so important to the Board. That was all a long time ago. The duty belt helped carry the weight better, so I was happy about that. One of my injuries was presumptive, from the duty belt. If you got a back injury, and you wore a duty belt, it was a presumptive thing; they had to prove it wasn't. That was a new law then. For my first bad back injury that law helped me because they were saying, "Well, we don't really know it was the duty belt."

~~~

So, back to call-outs, the middle-of-the-night kind of stuff. I was called out late at night for another scary time in Monte Bello. Someone had broken into the radio station up there, the little college station. It was down the dead-end road like you were going to go down to Black Mountain Trail, except you kept going past the trail junction. There was a radio station there, a low-power college station. I forget the call sign; I think the numbers are 88.something. I got a call that somebody had broken in, and they were broadcasting over it, which was a major crime.

Most of my after-hours call-outs were with Dennis, because he was the closest other ranger. If it was big enough, they wouldtwo of us. We met with two Palo Alto police officers and a person from the college. The college guy said it would have to be somebody who knew how to run this thing. A hiker or bike rider couldn't have just figured it out. They had tried to disable it from the main station down at the college, but he said the manual override switch had been turned off or something, so it had to be someone who knew exactly what they were doing. The station had a disgruntled employee at the time, someone who was mad about being fired. The suspect was reportedly broadcasting "cop killer" music. Sure enough, if you tuned into this 88.something, it was music from some movie I'd never hear of, where there were sounds of automatic weapon fire and a voice saying, "Kill the cops! Kill the cops!" It was creepy driving up there thinking that this nut, playing this gunfire music, was up there, and might be a disgruntled employee, and might have brought their gun with them. A good day for body armor.

We all went down towards this radio station together, and then they said, "Loro, you wait here with the RP, the college guy, and when the building is clear we'll call you." So I was left with the RP, and I was thinking, "Well, if the person's not in the building, maybe they are out here somewhere, and if they don't like the person I'm sitting with, then this is not a good situation." But nothing bad happened. We never found anyone. It was unsolved.

~~~

This next was a self-initiated call-out. My phone was down, my landline, but I had my District radio, and I had left it on all night, just on our frequency, not scanning everybody else, so if they needed me they could still call. I had fallen asleep on the couch, and then I heard Dennis' whispering voice saying, "Yeah, I can still hear the banging down there." I woke up and turned the radio up and called Mt. View Dispatch and then Dennis, and asked, "Do you want me to come out?" He answered, "Please do, but be careful because I think somebody is trying to break into the office. From my residence I can hear these banging sounds from the buildings." Dispatch said that SO was responding with the closest unit coming from La Honda, so that wouldn't be too long. Dennis said, "Don't go up to the office. Just drive by on Skyline Boulevard and see if there are any associated vehicles."

As I was approaching the office driveway on Skyline, I saw these two cars at the Page Mill Road intersection, one with the hood up, like trying to jumpstart it. I thought maybe they were associated, but I wasn't sure. There was a Monte Carlo and a pickup. I slowed down a little and tried to get the plate, and the people looked over at me as I went by. I then was waiting for SO a little ways up Skyline when the pickup drove past me, going north. I reported this on the radio, and gave a description of the truck, occupied by two. When the SO got to me, he said he would go up to the office to check on things there and would let his second unit know about the pickup. I went north on Skyline and found the second SO unit now had the truck pulled over, the same truck. There was a sleeping bag or a tarp in the back covering something, and they were talking to the occupants. I was just watching. Then the pickup drove off. I asked, "What was under the tarp in the back?" and the SO said, "I don't know." He hadn't even looked. I thought, "You're kidding me!" He didn't even ask the driver what was in the back. I thought, "That's so dumb."

Then we went up to the office. The SO said, "We're not sure whether they broke in. The other officer hasn't found any evidence of a break-in." We found one of our patrol truck's side boxes was open and there was stuff spread out like someone had been rummaging through. They had tried to open another truck, too. We could see nice fingerprints and I said, "Get these, at least." Dennis had to really lean on them to get fingerprints, which they finally did. We never saw which way the Monte Carlo went, and I hadn't been able to get the plate off it, either. They had looked suspicious enough that I figured I shouldn't just be stopping to say, "Hi guys." They probably were the suspects. SO never even went to the associated house in Half Moon Bay until a day later. SO should have looked under the tarp. They didn't even ID the passenger. They didn't do anything! The whole thing was frustrating. We did lose several hundred dollars' worth of tools from those side boxes. Following this incident, the memo came out again, "Keep the side boxes locked when you're not with your truck." Water under the bridge. Dennis said he had just gone out to get firewood when he heard this clinking sound coming from the office. When you're dependent upon another agency to do your work, you get a variety of people. There were some great officers who were real go-getters and very helpful, and others who, when they had somebody red-handed didn't follow up. Those were some frustrating times.

~~~

This was a more recent story. I was driving home and I believe it was a Wednesday because everyone was at the office after the staff meeting. When I got to my gate, there was a Ford Explorer parked outside the other gate of the double gates into the tree farm. It was not totally blocking my gate, so I was able to jockey through. At the split, where my driveway goes down to the right to my cabin, I saw this person. It was late afternoon by then, and kind of cool-ish, not warm weather, but she was dressed in this gauzy dress-thing, and had no shoes. The tree farm loop is open to the public, so that wasn't an issue. She was standing there and a couple other people were there sitting on a blanket and they were all staring at this big oak tree.

I said, to make consensual contact, "Hi. How's it going?" She was either a space cadet or flying on something and said, "Oh, isn't this tree beautiful? It's talking to me," and I was like, "What are you guys doing here?" "Oh, we're just picnicking." I asked if that was their Explorer out at the gate. "Oh yeah." I thought all this seemed weird, so I called for a fill, and I think Greg was the first to arrive, and we started walking them back up to their vehicle. You could tell that they were just out of it. We started police of some sort toward our location. I think I called for the wrong county because the gate is actually right on the Santa Clara/San Mateo County line, so technically I had the wrong county. I believe it was Santa Clara that came, and they eventually arrested this gal. She had a scale and baggies, and other drug stuff for some kind of drug sales, not just personal use. This woman was so out of it, and the other people were weird too, three very odd folks associated with this vehicle. At least the woman got taken to jail. She had this little powdery substance. I don't remember what it was called. We looked it up on-line and even the deputies hadn't heard of it, but it was supposed to be stronger than LSD. I heard later that she attacked an officer at booking and tried to choke him out. She went from being a total space cadet to being violent. The other two, I think, were just let go, or they were cited for some minor drug things. That was a weird thing to happen when I was just trying to get home.

~~~

Speaking of the gate: one time when I was coming home from a weekend off, I found there was a dome tent set up just inside my gate. There was a car there too, but there were often cars outside the gate, and it wasn't blocking the gate. Rather than going in, I drove to the office. It was late, about when the late shift was getting off, so maybe 10:00 or 10:30. Warren was an acting ranger at the time. He was an OST, but one of the rangers was out for an extended time for a medical condition, and because Warren had been to the ranger academy, had his PC 832, and had been a law enforcement ranger in Yellowstone, they let him work temporarily as a ranger. Maybe, by this point, he had already been hired as a real ranger, but, anyway, he had not been a ranger for the District for long.

I went to the office, and I explained that there was this tent inside the gate and he needed to go check it out. I went back in the truck with him. I thought I better go too, since he was new. I was just dressed in jeans and a plaid shirt. We got back there, and the guy came out of the tent and he was pretty mad and somewhat in our faces and one of his comments was even, "If I had a gun, I could shoot you." He said this quite casually. Warren was just going to give this guy a written warning, but I said, "Excuse me a minute," and I called Warren away. I had been trying not to say too much, but I told him, "Warren, this guy deserves more. He's not going with the program. He's not just packing up his tent and leaving. He needs a ticket." "Well, I don't know." "This guy is not going to learn his lesson with a written warning. He needs to get some real reason to not come back here. You can cut him a break on one, but he needs a ticket either for the camping or for the afterhours." So Warren got the guy's info. The guy looked at me and said, "I know you're the one making him write that ticket." The guy took his ticket and left, and Warren admitted, "Yeah, I think you were right." "Warren, this guy said he would have shot us if he had a gun. He was not just saying, 'Yeah, sorry. I shouldn't have been here.'"

~~~

I usually didn't second-guess other rangers too much if the other ranger wanted to just write someone a written warning, or just say, "Hey, you're not supposed to be here. You're out of here." Especially since I was off duty, I wouldn't have argued with it. I used to try to figure out if the person knew that it was a violation, unless it was something obvious, like a roaring campfire in the middle of August. In that case, who cares if they didn't know. Who wouldn't know they were not supposed to have a campfire? They're getting a ticket. If they really didn't know that they were supposed to wear a helmet, or that dogs weren't allowed or something, then, no. Yeah, they walked by a sign, but it's possible to walk by a sign. Also, how are they taking it? Are they apologetic? "Oh. Okay. Sorry." Sometimes it seems like just a warning isn't going to make the point. You are supposed to be a generic ranger, and you should all act the same under the same circumstances, but we are humans and so we can't. There are certain violations that some people think are no biggie, and are somebody else's pet peeve. It's just their little thing they are always going to ticket for, no matter what. I was told that I should try to come up with my own standards that I was going to use, and to try to be consistent about that.

They say that attitude shouldn't be the deciding factor. You shouldn't just give them a ticket because they are rude to you, but if it doesn't seem like they are going to take a simple warning to heart, then attitude should matter. If you catch somebody doing whatever and they say, "Oh yeah, I shouldn't have my dog here," they've admitted they knew. But why would you necessarily ticket them, and not the person who throws a crying fit? That's where I tried to be consistent, even if the suspect went into meltdown mode. If I was going to ticket them in the first place, they were still getting the ticket. Why should the weeping, crying person get off the hook, while the person who owns up to their behavior got a ticket? I'm sure there were times when I was probably softer on somebody one day than the next. I kind of miss being able to cite people now, but only for the more egregious things, not for the stuff I thought was kind of piddly. I'm glad I don't have to do that anymore. For people who are really tearing things up, doing damage, vandalism, or letting their dog chase after animals: these are the things I wish I could still take action on. The piddly stuff, like it's ten minutes after sunset and they are still there, just looking at the stars? No. That kind of stuff I'm just as happy not to have to be the enforcer.

I miss the interaction with visitors. I don't miss being cursed at, and all the crap that we had to take. I'm sure rangers take a lot more crap than the average police officer. When people get stopped for speeding, I don't think the cops are hearing, "Get a real job." I think suspects are not happy to be stopped and they still have some comments about their situation, but they don't instantly spout the disrespect that rangers get. "You don't even have the right to talk to me. Who gives you the authority? You can't stop me." I don't think they would tell a regular officer that. If they give them too much crap, they are really asking for trouble, and not waiting an hour for an officer to arrive. The rangers have to take more BS.

~~~

I was once working radar with John Lloyd on the Canyon Trail late in the afternoon, but well before dark, radaring the after-work crowd. Some bikers came just flying down, a whole group of four or five. We stopped them, and they all stopped, but the lead guy was instantly cocky. They were going plenty fast enough, mid-to upper twenties, definitely in ticket range. I started asking the guy for ID. "I don't have any on me," he said and gave me some verbal info, and I just knew he was lying. He was squirrelling around and his lies were not coming back with a match from Dispatch and it was getting late. We called for Tom, the supervisor, and he started coming up from the Foothills. I wanted to call for Palo Alto police; it was their jurisdiction. The guy was just so obviously providing false info, but Tom said, "Let's get a thumb print, and just let him go." Both John and I didn't like it, but we did. We let him go. He was all happy. Later John realized, "This isn't even the right zip code." So, we looked it up and the zip code he had given us was for somewhere else. Then we tried calling the city the zip code came back to--I think it was Seaside--and asked, "Do you know this person?" They said, "Oh yeah," and they gave us his real name and a picture that matched. We sent them the thumbprint, but it was no good. They didn't have a match. If you have a criminal history it works, but not otherwise.

It was funny then when the next day, Tom called us up, "I couldn't get to sleep last night. I was sorry that I didn't let you guys call Palo Alto police." He had this remorse. I didn't lose sleep over it. I was able to find out who the biker was, and we met with a deputy DA for Santa Clara County. They pursued the False Information to a Peace Officer misdemeanor, and he was convicted. This all was from piecing together the bits and pieces of information that all fit together. He had been stopped before for speeding in Seaside. Tom was like, "That was great investigative work." We got the last laugh even though he had ridden off literally laughing at us. He got like six months of probation and a fine and a criminal history. We never saw him again. He lived off of Kings Mountain Road, but he had once lived in Seaside, so that's how he knew enough to fake it. It felt good knowing that liars don't always get away with it.

With the burglary thing and again with this case, it felt like a frustrated investigation. Why can't we just call? Why can't we just follow up? Why can't we go to the house? I didn't like that. The same thing on the couple of drunk driving cases I was involved in. They didn't want us doing that stuff, but for me, that was the important stuff. Get somebody off the road who's going to kill somebody. You could literally be saving a life. But the couple of times I did, it was pushing the edge of District policy. I had to think, "I also have to live with myself. Even if I get in trouble for this, I'm not letting this guy go off and kill somebody." I never totally violated policy, but I probably pushed the envelope a little. Same with stopping juveniles and all the overtime waiting for parents to come get them, rather than letting them drive their friends with just a provisional license. They'd be begging us, "Couldn't you just let us go?" "No. You've got to be safe." The same thing when you find people out stoned. You can't just say, "Well, don't drive off," and leave them there. I mean, you can, and that's what the stoners want you to do, but you know what's going to happen. "Just clear. You've done your job." No. You are a public safety officer.

~~~

My first CPR case was a big one. I was first on scene. I had lots of medicals, but luckily they don't stick in my mind as much. I was at the Skyline Office as was Dennis, but he was parked facing the other direction. I was parked facing out, when we heard on the Palo Alto frequency a dispatch for a vehicle into a power pole on Highway 35 south of Page Mill. Okay, we're probably going to be first on scene. We both responded, but I beat Dennis by like a minute. I came around the corner and there were all these people standing around right across from our circle lot at Skyline Ridge. A telephone pole was right by the gate that accesses Skid Road into Monte Bello. A motorcycle had hit it and had exploded, and the pole was on fire for about two-thirds of its height. A guy was lying on the road near it, covered by a blanket up over his head and people were standing around doing nothing. So I rolled up and grabbed my fire extinguisher. The neighbors who lived at the house there, the Sherills, were there, so I handed him the fire extinguisher. I said, "If you could carefully, safely, put out this fire, the part closest to us?" He said, "I think he's dead." By the time Dennis rolled up, I had called back Palo Alto to say I was on scene and to give a report, "The pole is on fire; the patient is down, looks unresponsive. Keep everything coming Code Three." Dennis was like, "Oh crap."

We got the guy's helmet off and the blanket, and Dennis started doing breaths with the mask, and I started doing compressions. Dennis had actually told me as I was pulling out of the office, "Be careful. If they hit the pole, they might have broken it." I looked and the pole was there. It was okay, but I hadn't noticed that the cross member had broken, so electric lines were hanging down. I told this crowd of bystanders to get back, to get out of the way. We were in the middle of the road, but it was blocked with our trucks, anyway. We did CPR for a while before this doctor came up to us, a pathologist I think. Dennis made him actually show ID before he pronounced.

Cal Fire came in maybe ten minutes from the Saratoga Summit station, and they took over the breaths part, so Dennis took over compressions. They used the "on-demand" breathing machine they had at the time. I recall that we could tell Dennis' compressions were good because fluids were exuding out places they shouldn't have been. The ears had cerebral spinal fluid coming out, and also blood coming out the whole crotch area because of where the motorcycle hit. He was obviously not coming back, but we did CPR because that's what you do. When Dennis took over compressions, I went to set up the landing zone for Life Flight. As I got over there, just as Life Flight was about to get on the ground, they pronounced.

As I was coming back, after they cancelled Life Flight, someone came up to me and said, "This person has broken his arm." There was this second medical aid, a bicyclist down with a broken arm. So I called it in, "We've got another medical." I was trying to clear from the motorcyclist medical when this other guy came over and asked, "Why is the helicopter leaving?" I said, "Because the guy didn't make it." It turned out that this guy was the motorcyclist's brother. We didn't have any training in how to handle things like that. He said, "This was his first ride on Skyline. He was only 22." It was a lot for my first fatal medical to have all this stuff going on. We found the guy with the broken arm, and it was just a broken arm.

One of the Cal Fire guys said, "You guys should come to this critical incident debriefing. It was set up for an accident last week down on Highway 9. Why don't you guys come as soon as we're done with this?" It was good, and I'm glad that we had it right away. I'd never before been involved in a fatality, especially with the fire and so many bystanders. What else could go wrong? I think we changed our CPR training after this incident. We used to remove the little one-way valves for the CPR masks during trainings. They cost 25 cents, literally, to replace, so we would train without them. Dennis realized he had never put the valve back on, and I hadn't noticed either. I guess he noticed halfway through. The person was so bloody! I didn't get any blood on my skin, but I got blood on my boots, as did Dennis, so I took bleach and scrubbed everything up. It was kind of yucky.

When I first started as a ranger there wasn't the helmet law for motorcyclists. People didn't always wear helmets. At least they don't get killed instantly at the scene so often anymore. This guy had a helmet on. I felt better after the CHP report came out and they gave the estimated speed as 86 mph. For your first ride on Skyline Boulevard, the guy almost committed suicide. That's a logical consequence if you're going to go racing as a new motorcyclist on Skyline, and you don't know the road. There were so many bad accidents at that spot that they finally moved the pole. We had had six or eight or so in a couple years. The

Sherills were tired of it too, having to be first on scene, and having injured people coming up to their door. They lobbied PG&E and got the pole moved. The very next week after they moved it, there was another crash, and the skid marks went right over the same spot. It was good that it was moved because just going over the edge is better. It slows down your rate of descent.

~~~

I responded on the guy who hung himself in Purisima from the big fir tree at the intersection of the Harkins Cutover and Harkins Road. There was a car in the Northridge lot with a note and the guy had a history of mental trouble. He had gone missing at Thanksgiving, and I was involved for two or three days on this search but we never found him. Then, during Christmas vacation, right after News Year's, someone was out hiking and they looked up and saw some blue jeans hanging in this tree. It was our guy, who had been hanging there that whole time. It was an area we had searched, but he was way up the tree, and unless you stood at the right spot, you wouldn't notice. I was on duty when the dispatch came in for a person hanging in a tree, and I immediately wondered if it was him. The volunteer firefighters climbed up the tree and determined that this was an old case. The next day, I was assigned to go out on the recovery. Because the guy had been hanging there so long, his body was going to come apart, so they had extra people to climb up and wrap him up, to kind of mummify him. We had tarps set up below, but I stood way back, because I thought, "I don't want to see pieces coming down." It was wet in there because it was winter, but we had to get the body out. The search and rescue volunteers had come in with a two-wheel drive truck and had gotten it royally stuck. I was able to carefully, carefully back down far enough to get the corpse out in the bed of the patrol truck, rather than having to hand carry it out. It wasn't that gross. The skin looked like leather, like a mummy, but it wasn't pleasant. The rope was way into the neck. It had gotten kind of incorporated into the body, so you couldn't detach it. I don't think about the suicides too often, although I've been on a number of them.

"The One that Lived" was this woman who had parked her car at the Clouds Rest Vista, and they thought she might be out trying to kill herself in Russian Ridge. Maybe there was a note. There was a daylong search, which I think was during my days off, so I wasn't part of that, but they called me when I got home that night. The next morning the search would be starting again at 6:00, so they wanted me to come in early. Pat and Sango had been on the search the day before, and they had agreed to meet at first light on a premonition. I got called out early that morning to come out and help them because Sango had found the woman. She was very hypothermic. I was to come right away and bring more blankets and heat pack stuff. She was near the junction with the Ancient Oaks Trail, a strange place to be, without a good view or anything. Sango told me he just got the idea she might be out there.

When he found her, he had thought she was dead, because when you're super cold, the pulse is really slow. She had taken a bunch of pills. There were pills there at hand, and vodka, and the combination had slowed her whole system down enough that it probably saved her. We asked, "Are you sure she is breathing?" "Oh yeah, but barely." Sango had put his big Filson Cruiser jacket on her, and I think I brought a down vest and we put heat packs on her. As soon as she started to warm up, she started to come back. It was interesting to watch somebody go from "out" to "back." We had to carry her for a ways, and she was kind of heavy, down to the Ancient Oaks LZ. Tom Karnofel had been called up from his early shift at Rancho to help with the hand carry. They flew her out. They said her core temperature was down to 86, and I think you lose consciousness at 95. I guess she lived for a while after that. You never knew whether these people didn't just turn around and try again. I'd guess she was in her 50's.

Another Bunny call-out was at like 2:00 in the morning. I believe it was summer, but it was foggy. Maybe because of all the big parties, there were also a lot of falls in Devils Canyon. The report was of a person who had fallen over the waterfall and needed a rescue and carryout. At that time, Devils Canyon still wasn't ours, but Bunny said Pat was already on the call, and I should go, too. This was before there were necessarily supervisors on duty all the time. It was vague whether you were supposed to let your supervisor know about a call-out, whether you were supposed to wake them up to tell them. Then the policy became that there were always supposed to be two rangers called out, so then was I supposed to go even if no one else was coming? It was not always clear, and it was left up to my best judgment. I called Sango one time; I woke him up. I called Brian in the middle of the night too, just to let him know what was going on.

I assumed that since Pat was already on the call that the District already knew about it. By the time we got there, they had the person already up out of the canyon, the victim of a severe fall, with a head injury. They were on their way out, with him in the basket; it wouldn't be too long. Life Flight was en route, and they were going to try to land at the Portola Heights gate, but it was so foggy that they had to move the LZ to the Skyline Ridge lot. When I saw the victim, just while helping to load him from the ambulance to the helicopter, he had no face. It was just gone. You could see the eyes, but no nose, just two holes, no mouth, no chin. That was all missing. I had the guy's dad with me in the truck at that point and dad was covered in blood. Dad had gone to Devils Canyon because his son was missing, and he had gone looking for him, then called to say he had found his son who fallen in Devils Canyon. The dad was an emergency room doctor from Stanford. He was embarrassed that he couldn't carry the kid out alone. He had gone to the Saratoga Summit Fire station and said, "My kid fell and I can't get him out." Fire, seeing him covered in blood, had asked, "Should we call for an air ambulance?" "No. I just need help getting him out." They immediately called for an air ambulance anyway.

When the Life Flight nurse saw the victim, she said that this could be an attempted suicide. It looked like the victim of a gunshot wound. When I asked the dad, he said, "Uh, yeah." He had tried to blow his head off with a shotgun and flinched, which the Life Flight nurse said often happens. He was an 18 or 19-year-old kid. It was interesting that the firefighters hadn't recognized it, and I had never seen that kind of a wound before. At that point, I didn't know all the details. He was overdue coming home and dad found the shotgun missing, and went out to look for him. He had tried to carry the kid out himself. The kid hadn't gone over the falls at all; he was just down in this cave, and it wasn't a fall on his face. There is a little set of caves in the Tafoni Sandstone if you walk the ridgeline between Eagle Rock and Mary Jane Cave. This was a little cave that you could get up into, just big enough for three or four people.

Later we wondered, "So, where is the gun now?" It was still back in the cave. Dad couldn't carry both the kid and the gun. Pat said, "I know where the cave is. Let's go get it," but the sheriff deputies wouldn't go with him. They just absolutely wouldn't go. Pat ended up hiking down at 3 o'clock in the morning by himself to retrieve the gun. I don't know if the deputies were scared or what, but they wouldn't go out into the dark, scary woods. Pat went and got the gun because he didn't want anyone else to find it. When you got inside that cave and looked up, there were pieces of flesh and bone stuck to the ceiling. They're no longer there. If you're around long enough, you have pieces of the preserve that bring back not-so-fond memories. Following this incident, we called it shotgun cave for a long time.

Photo by Frances Reneau
Mary Jane Cave graffiti in 2016

Before Devils Canyon was ours, there was a lot more partying down there. People would have these giant parties down at Mary Jane Cave. The whole inside was painted psychedelic. One of the OSTs was on his way home one time and called to say that there was obviously a party staging to go down into Devils Canyon. This must have been wintertime because it got dark before this whole thing got too far, because the OSTs get off at 4:30. I was assigned a middle shift, back in the days of middle shifts, and before we had assigned trucks. Matt was on, and Kerry and I were sharing a truck for some reason. His flashlight was broken, so he had no flashlight, but we were both middle shifts, so we weren't concerned. I didn't have a flashlight either. Anyway, between the three of us we had only one working mini-mag light. It was still daylight when this started, but it went on so long that it got dark.

We found these people before they reached the cave with their guitar and a bunch of alcohol, and we were trying to deal with them and get them out of there, but from the direction of the cave we could see little embers flying up, and we could hear voices. So, Matt went around the top, where that last little trail leads across the creek, and I climbed up on the biggest rock there, not far from Matt. Kerry was going to come in from the trail by the creek. We could hear the people coming our way, and just as they came up to Matt, he turned on the mini-mag light and yelled, "Park Ranger. Stop." But I yelled, "Hand me your light! " and "Hand me your lantern, too." Now we had three working lights. The people turned out to be this couple with a little five-year-old, and they weren't impaired or anything. We went to check the fire, to make sure it's out, then started walking them back up to the road using the suspects' own lights. We were encountering more and more people as we went back up, because they all still thought the party was on, so we had to turn them all around. It was just funny having to depend on the confiscated lights.

~~~

A good happy-ending funny story was for a missing dog in Monte Bello, a neighbor's dog. Sango and I were both out looking because someone had reported barking. Sango had beaten me down there, and he called to me, "I've found the dog, and it's in a log." I guess this dog had tried to crawl inside, but had gotten stuck. The dog was about up to its shoulders inside this log, with its butt end sticking out. We got out our hammers and screwdrivers and we were trying chip off pieces because it was kind of a rotten log. The other end of this log was open too and some visitors had come by and they were talking to the dog from the other end. They were trying to console it from the head end, while we were trying to excavate from the rear. Sango may have a different version of it. We did get it chiseled out before too long. It had been missing for about three days, but probably not stuck in the log that whole time. This was on the Canyon Trail, where the single track comes down from the parking lot, in the walnut orchard area, and only about four feet off the trail, so it couldn't have been there four days. Someone would have seen it and reported it. I think it was an Australian Shepard, something pretty furry. It was scared. It must have been noisy when we were chiseling around its head. We pulled it out carefully and the dog was happy to be out, and it wasn't badly dehydrated, but it was a funny thing to see the dog in the log. We still talk about it.

Another funny dog story from Purisima happened not that long ago. I was sitting in the lot on a Sunday watching the people coming up the trail into the lot. This one guy had a big pack on, but I saw a leash dangling out of the pack. The dog was tucked in there so well that I couldn't even see it, just the leash hanging out. I stopped him and I was talking to him, and then I noticed a little movement in the pack, but he was like, "Dog? No, I don't have a dog. What do you mean?" "Well, what about this leash hanging out of your pack?" "Uh, leash?"

~~~

I learned a little bit about The Land from Brian and Vicki, who lived in Portola Heights. Brian was a District volunteer for a long time, and Vicki was a volunteer firefighter. One time when my volunteer flaked out at the last minute for deer surveys, Vicki came and helped me out. We had worked other calls together, searches and medicals and such, but we had never had a chance to chat. A deer survey is perfect for chatting. She told me that, back in the time of The Land, she and Brian would do this summer camp out there. She told me about the oven that's still there. Brian had been a middle school science teacher, and he and Vicky did a summer science camp using some of The Land's residential area. I had always heard about the District's clearing out The Land. That is, I heard the District's side. I mean, it was our land, but I guess the District just went in with a bulldozer with hardly any warning, in the early morning. They didn't want people to chain themselves to the buildings or something. They went in and just demoed stuff, like they do homeless encampments. That's what I heard. I heard Joan Baez lived there for a while even. It's a real bit of Skyline history.

The Jikoji property was an alternative high school; that's why there is School Road there in Long Ridge. Jikoji's main building used to be the school building. I once met someone who went there.

~~~

Some of the Portola Heights people I ticketed I think realized that I was just doing my job. I didn't have some grudge or agenda and just hate them all. For a while it was certainly an "us against them" thing. And then, over time, the District became a better neighbor, like when Doug's house burned down. That was maybe seven years ago, not super long ago. I was at home listening to the scanner. If I was home and awake, I always listened to the scanner because it really was 24-hours-a-day job. I would hear all this stuff that was probably related to us and I would call up the on-duty supervisor to report it. It was late at night, and I scanned a call on Long Ridge Road. I thought, "A lot of that is our land or close to ours, and if there is a fire in there, it's ours." I called up Dennis and he said, "I'll meet you at the gate." I called CDF Felton but they didn't know anything, and couldn't give me a good cross street. They were already cancelling units. Dennis and I found all these neighbors at the fire scene who had already put out the fire themselves. When they realized there was a fire, they had all come with their McClouds. We got some good credit though because we did check in and wanted to make sure everyone was okay. Word got around pretty well, "The District even came out. I saw District trucks." We got to be the good neighbor.

~~~

Most rangers took fitness time back when I started, because every quarter you had to do the timed run or else the timed walk, which they added just before I was hired. Now it's only once a year, but then it was quarterly. At first, ranger residents could take fitness time at their residences, just as they can now, but there were some 15 years when we couldn't. Only the ranger resident who lived up on Mt Umunhum was allowed to, because he lived so far from the office. There is so much other opportunity to cheat the system, but still they were afraid someone was going to go home early just to relax or take a nap or something, rather than actually doing fitness time. So, rather than wait to catch someone cheating, they just said, "No, you have to bring your running stuff to the office, and do it there." That made it inconvenient, so people wouldn't take it. I would still try to take it, but you had so many different things to bring, that if you forgot one item at home, it didn't work. It's so much nicer just to do it from home. They would trust you with people's lives out there on the road, but they won't trust that you're not cheating on the fitness time.

~~~

I never got to a Fort Ord fire training, where I heard they had big areas burning at once, and the fire would always escape. We used to go to UTC when they had the rocket fuel there. It was a scary time of the year to burn and they would say, "Well, try to keep it away from this high pressure fuel line." No kidding. The fun part was that rather than just lighting off with drip torches-- which was fun, too--we were taking lit road flares, and throwing them out into the brush. When Andrew finally got to go to a real fire training, he said how neat it was to have live fire, rather than just having to "envision this is on fire." It is invaluable to see how just a little breeze can perk up something that's just punking along. You can't simulate real fire. If rangers are going to be expected to fight fire, they need to keep sending us to those live fire trainings.

One time Matt and Frank and I went to a fire training at Laguna Seca. We were just doing the blacklining. It was like 104 degrees that day. You're about dying with all your fire gear on, much less cutting line. I thought, "Is this a good day to be playing with fire?" They started doing a little blacklining and something failed in one of the fire trucks they were using to support the blacklining. It started leaking diesel, which caught fire, and two people got burned. They brought in Life Flight, and they stopped the training. It was about noon, and it was supposed to be an all-day training, so what were we going to do now? We had picked Frank up on the way because he was living up on Loma Prieta somewhere. We had to take Frank home anyway, so we didn't go straight back the most expedient way.

Having been on some live fire trainings and on the Russian Ridge Fire, I knew something about how bad being on a fire line could get. It would be hot and uncomfortable, but I wasn't going to get burned unless I went out into the rough. But people who have no live fire experience don't understand that you can stay in an area that is burning. It would make more sense to get a couple real pumpers, but I also have to say that in the time I was there, the little dinky pumpers saved at least one big fire. Maybe that's only one in 26 years, but that could have been the one big one. Our little garden hose put it out.

Another fire story: someone was driving along Highway 84 throwing out lit flares, and all those little fires shortly overwhelmed the system. This was on the La Honda Road section, down toward Mindego. There were four fires, three along Woodside Road, and one on Old La Honda Road, which we responded to. When we got there, it wasn't yet too big, but it was running up the hill in the grass. We had to work as a team just to get access to the fire because the hillside was so steep. I remember we had just gotten these brand new fire pants, with the double-thick knees, which was nice when we were climbing through stuff that had just burned and was still glowing. We were dragging hose, and putting out fire, and we were able to get this little fire out, to stop it. It only burned a couple hundred feet, but it was getting ready to make a run, and it would have made it to Skyline Boulevard, at least. There were these three other fires going at the same time. There are people's houses around there, so we got a nice note from one of them, "You guys saved the day," because we probably did.

There were other fires, barbeques and stuff, when maybe we could have put it out without water, but not very well. One time Greg and I found some illegal campers at Foothills Preserve, not on the knob where they usually were, but off in the brush. They had cleared maybe three feet around it, but the brush was crunchy-dry and they had a big bonfire. We ended up using our litter buckets, after dumping the litter out. We pumped water from the pumpers and then had to carry the buckets up there. We had backed up as close as we could, but it wasn't hose distance. The campers were saying, "Oh, we were being safe." These peoples' ideas and safe were two different things."

~~~

We had just bought Stevens Canyon Ranch and Brendon was showing me and John the old-growth redwood tree there. We had hiked out to it, when Brendon got a call from Dispatch saying to call them, Code Three. He told them, "I've got no cell phone coverage. Just give us the info over the radio." So, Dispatch said, "10-91M at Freemont Older OSP," which means a mountain lion. He told them we were responding, but we were ten minutes out on foot. We started hustling back to the trucks. John turned on the scanner, and we copied on the County Fire channel that it was a nine-year-old attacked by a lion. Brendon said I should go with John, whose truck was a little closer, so I hopped in with him, and we got a little more info about where it was supposed to be. Tom was coming, as was a Santa Clara County deputy, and Fish and Game. Anthony had phoned up Fish and Game because he had the warden's personal number. Then

Dispatch reported, "County can't find a deputy for you. Their parks unit is tied up over at Grant Ranch." "We don't care if it's a parks unit. Just get us a beat deputy." This was all Tom's communication, not us. Fire units were UTL (unable to locate) at the reported location, so they sent John and me to check another road. They thought it might be on a single-track trail though, so Tom and somebody else were on foot checking that. I was thinking, "Are we even supposed to be here on foot if there is a mountain lion that has attacked someone?"

The whole thing turned out to be a bogus call. When Kyle, the Fish and Game warden, arrived, having come Code Three from Morgan Hill, he was like, "What? This is fake?" He had been coming at 90 mph on the freeway to get there for us. I thanked him for coming and apologized that it was fake. He said he was actually breaking policy coming to a mountain lion call by himself. "I'm armed and I still can't respond alone. What are you guys doing? I would recommend that at least someone on your field staff, a supervisor or someone, has a shotgun." I was pissed. What if this was a nine-year-old kid getting torn up? Are we supposed to just stand there and watch? I was told that it would be my own judgment whether I would want to get out and confront the lion. That's crazy, just dumb. You don't take pepper spray to a mountain lion call. We went round and round, but nothing ever happened about the shotgun, a piece of equipment we should have. John Maciel, who was operations manager at the time, cut the warden off and stomped away. He wouldn't listen to any of it. That was a frustrating day.

~~~

A few years ago at Rancho, we did have someone attacked by a crazy guy, up on the Wildcat Knoll. Someone called in that a visitor was being attacked. You get strange calls like that occasionally, but the Star One helicopter happened to be overhead and they said, "Yeah. Come quick. There's a person on the ground and there's another person over them beating them up." They kept it up, even with the helicopter overhead. We had lots of staff at Rancho, and Brendan was the supervisor and he told them, "Be careful. Use your own judgment," because the responding ranger had asked, "What should I do?" but then that ranger chose to just wait down at the bottom for armed officers. John Lloyd and I were together up on Skyline, and John made it down to the area even before the deputies did, and this other ranger was still just sitting there waiting. I thought, "Why not just go take a look?" Go blaring up there, lights and sirens. Use your command presence. I can understand not going toe-to-toe with the guy, but to not even go and see what's happening? Just that much might break it up. That was frustrating for me, and I assume to the supervisor too. I think Brendan even tried to coax the ranger to go on scene, but no.

I think most staff were more daring. You'd have to be holding them back. Most staff would be inclined to do too much, rather than to not do enough. I think the District tries to screen for, and hire people who want to do 110 percent. But the District is uncomfortable with law enforcement, maybe because there isn't anybody amongst the higher-ups who is a law enforcement expert. Even a former ranger is not a law enforcement expert. I was frustrated too at the unwillingness to pay for airtime, to fly our land. It costs like $2,000 an hour. Well, just pay whatever it is to get the information for our safety, and for the visitors too, so no one will just wander into marijuana grow. We shouldn't just bury our heads in the sand. Someone needs to go look.

~~~

One Sunday morning early, I was headed up to Purisima to open the lot, and as I passed by Corte Madera, I saw a pickup with the hood up, so I turned around, but the pickup was already pulling out, heading south, so I came up behind him. I don't know why I didn't have my headlights on already, but I turned on my headlights, not my red lights or anything, just headlights, and he pulled over. I pulled in behind him and got out and just went to ask him if he was okay and if there was a problem with his truck. He said it had been overheating, but it seemed to be okay now. He left and I left, but I went back to where I'd seen him parked before. I found these sticks, like tomato stakes, and a five gallon bucket and a jug of water, and I thought these might be associated with a marijuana grow.

I went back north to open the Purisima lot, and I was heading back south again when I again saw the truck, now parked at Skeggs Point. I was on my way to a POST (Peninsula Open Space Trust) kite day at Windy Hill, so I passed the information on to Matt, including the license plate. He must have called me back to the site, because we ended up going together down a deer path from where the stakes were. We started to hear the crunch, crunch, crunch of footsteps in the dry tanoak leaves, so we stopped and waited, unwilling to move because we were also crunching in the leaves. As the guy approached, I recognized him as the same guy associated with the truck. He was carrying two one-gallon jugs of water and something else I couldn't quite see under the sleeve of his jacket. When he got closer, we called out, "Park Ranger!" and he threw down the water jugs, but he held onto whatever was under his arm. I thought it was a weapon, so I grabbed the jacket and yanked it off. Matt and I looked at each other, without speaking, then I told the guy to turn around and Matt handcuffed him. We still thought there might be a dropped weapon where he had dropped the water. He said he was growing marijuana. We called for the sheriff, who arrested the guy for cultivation. Because of our use of the handcuffs—the first use in many, many years by a District ranger—we were both called in separately and questioned extensively. We both said we had done it for our own safety, for officer safety. We didn't know what he might have just dumped in the leaves. We didn't have any kind of pow-wow beforehand because we didn't know we were in for such a grilling. We both had to write extra reports for the incident. This was before there was a policy saying you had to do a special report for using defensive equipment. .

Then, about six months later, I heard there still might be some further investigation because we had actually caught a marijuana grower. We are not supposed to do that, even though we hadn't gone off stomping through the woods looking for trouble. I was just trying to show Matt the area where I had seen this guy. Probably because I didn't have a history of doing things like this, they said I wasn't going to be in trouble. Months later I heard that there was still discussion about whether I was going to be punished somehow. They were saying that we shouldn't have cuffed him, and that we should have just waited for the sheriff. Somehow we were guilty of putting ourselves into a position where we couldn't retreat safely. We knew we would be scrutinized because they don't really want rangers using their defensive equipment. You know that they will always try to find fault if you varied any little bit from policy, even if it was completely clean and reasonable.

~~~

While I'm thinking about going outside of the realm of what the District likes rangers to do, I remember this story. I was new to working on Skyline, and I was headed home. It was late enough that the then-crew-supervising ranger, Patrick Congdon, was also on his way home. He didn't get to take home a marked vehicle, but he had a radio, and he called me to report a drunk driver on Skyline. Pat wasn't in uniform, and was just wearing coveralls. This guy had almost hit him, and Patrick had turned around to follow him. He had already called for CHP, and he was providing a blow-by-blow description of what was happening. "He almost hit a pedestrian. He's taken out five Carsonite markers. He's going to kill somebody." I waited at the office driveway for him to pass. He was headed north and I pulled in behind him, no lights or siren or anything. The guy was all over the road. I had meanwhile called for a supervisor, "Are you copying the description that X4 (Pat Congdon) is giving?" No answer. Nothing. So I called again, "Give me some direction here, please." Again, dead silence. We were getting up to near the Clouds Rest Vista Point, so I thought, "Heck, I'm just going to turn on the lights and pull this guy over." So I lit him up, and he pulled over.

I went up to the vehicle window, and I could smell the alcohol. Pat was right behind me. I grabbed the keys out of the ignition and took them. I had the guy get out and go stand at the back of his car. He was really wasted. He kept trying to walk out into traffic and Pat and I were keeping him with his hands on the back of his car. He wasn't following instructions, but he was so drunk that he wasn't a real physical danger to us. This was back when the Honor Farm was still open down Alpine Road, and a deputy on his way to work in his personal vehicle pulled up to help us. He searched the guy and waited with us until CHP got there. This guy was way, way over the limit. He said he'd been drinking with his brother down in Portola Heights. Now, suddenly, there were all kinds of supervisors on the radio. I later heard (from Pat's wife Bunny) that at the AO they were all listening to the blow-by-blow Pat was calling out of what was happening and to me pulling him over. Evidently this crowd even included persons quite high up the chain. They were all there listening to the call, and they didn't offer any help when I was calling for it. Luckily they didn't say not to do anything, but they also didn't authorize my pulling him over. They offered no supervisorial input at all. I didn't get in any trouble for making the stop. They tried to figure out what they could do to me, but it says in the policy that if you go outside policy, you have to have a good justification. Yeah, we didn't generally go out and pull over drunk drivers, but I felt that it was an immediate public safety hazard, and I felt safe about doing it.

~~~

I never used either my pepper spray or baton, but I could have in this next case. Matt and Brendan were going somewhere together in one truck, and they saw this woman walk into the Windy Hill picnic tables' area from the Hamm's Gulch Trail side, where dogs were not allowed at that time. They called it in, and Brendan went in on foot from the tables after her as she continued north on the Anniversary Trail. Matt cut over to where you can go cross-country to the bench near the summit, and he cut her off by doing that. He was calling in the stop and you could just hear in the background the yelling of somebody completely out of control. I started their way from the office, and Dennis started too. I went to the picnic tables because Matt reported that she was headed back that way. She got around Brendan, so I chose a narrow spot where you'd have to go off the side of the hill to try to go around me, and I started yelling, "Park Ranger! Stop!" as soon as I saw her, but she just kept coming. Then she just plain ran into me, body-slammed me right in the chest. I started jogging backwards to keep ahead of her. Matt and Brendan were right there. I yelled, "Brendan, grab the dog," which was off leash as well as in a prohibited area. I figured she wasn't going to leave her dog. If we stopped the dog, she was going to stop. He grabbed the dog's collar. It's not a policy violation to touch the dog. As soon as he had the dog, she came to a halt. By this point, she was so pissed at all of us that she wasn't going to talk to us, but, when Dennis got there, she talked to him.

I think I got to write that ticket, for Dog off Leash and Dog Prohibited, and then released her. I could have cited her for Battery too because she had deliberately run into me, but we weren't sure about that. She left just before the SO got there. When he heard the story, he was like, "You let her go? I would have taken her to jail for Battery on an Officer. You can still file on that. You should do it." By then, my neck was starting to hurt. She was littler than me, tiny actually, but still she hit me pretty good. Dennis said I could pursue it if I wanted, but he didn't seem interested. Back home at the end of my shift, my neck was worse, so I did pursue it. I was able to add Battery on an Officer to the citation. We had cited her, correctly, into San Mateo County, but she mistakenly sent her lawyer to Santa Clara County to contest the first ticket, so she got a Failure to Appear in San Mateo, on top of the Battery on an Officer. When this came up as a $5,000 warrant, the police went to her house and arrested her at 7:00 am, and it happened to be her birthday. I heard through the grapevine that it took three Los Altos PD officers to drag her off to jail because she was such B-person with them, just like she'd been with us. She was arrested in Santa Clara County so they took her to the old icky Santa Clara County jail, but the warrant was actually out of San Mateo County. Maybe it was the weekend, because she was there a couple days, and by now the bail was up to $9,000. Maybe it just took her husband a couple days to post the bail. It turns out that he was one of our workers comp doctors. Sometime later, when I got hurt, I was like, "I'm not going to see Dr. So-and-So who's in bed with this suspect."

    In the end, they just dropped all the charges, but she'd been to jail, and I was perfectly happy about that. They dropped everything because they figured she'd already done time, and her lawyer had, in fact, appeared on the right date, just in the wrong place. I didn't care. When I heard she'd gone to jail, that made my day. Sometime after this, she started trying to gather petitions down at Windy Hill to have more trails open to dogs. That was fine, but she also went to a District Board meeting and was really nasty and rude about the rangers. They should have cut her off, but I heard they let her go on and on about how she was mistreated. That annoyed me. Later various supervisors pointed out that I could have used my pepper spray on her, that that would have been appropriate. They were happy I didn't, though. I had put myself in harm's way, so I kind of learned from that. Same with stopping bicyclists. Yeah, you want to stop them, but you want to give yourself an out. It's not worth getting run over.

~~~

One of my most hostile contacts, not many years before I retired, was with a doctor and his family in Purisima. I was hiking up the lower end of the Whittemore Gulch Trail and I could hear people down on that little side trail by the creek, so I was looking down there. I saw a stroller and kids, and then I saw this guy walk over and pee right into the creek! I went down to just educate him that that wasn't an okay thing to do, but he wouldn't even talk to me. He just yelled, "I'm leaving." I told him, "No. Park Ranger. You are being detained," but he just went stomping off. I called for deputies, and followed him back down toward my truck because he was heading out, refusing to stop. By the time we got to my truck, he was even more mad, just furious, but he did eventually give me his info. In the meantime, this had turned into a kind of sideshow for the whole preserve. Everyone was looking at us. The kids were crying, in total meltdown. Mom was yelling at me, too. These guys were just screaming at me, and I was trying to remain as quiet and calm as I could.

I told the suspect that the deputy was coming and he was like, "Fine. I want to talk to the deputy," but eventually he just signed the citation. The deputy had just arrived and we were all still in the parking lot. He just stomped right past the deputy, didn't stop and talk to him. The deputy later said, "He must have been fun to deal with. He sure looked mad." This was one of our regular Skyline deputies that I knew pretty well. He said, "I guess I was too big and black for him." He was like 6'5", just a really big guy. The suspect was this short, white guy. I just laughed. I thought that was a funny thing to say.

The suspect was eventually convicted on the misdemeanor 148 (Delaying a Peace Officer.) There was a visitor there who I think had come out of the bathroom, who came over to me later and said, "Wow! That guy's crazy! That guy's got problems. If you need anyone as a witness, here's a business card." His business was something about dealing with hostile people. I asked him whether he thought I had treated this guy disrespectfully or badly, and he said, "No. You were perfectly calm. You handled that better than most people would have. He did that all to himself." It was completely avoidable. There is a point where you've wasted the whole system. I mean, there are people out here with real emergencies that need dealing with. He was spoiling the afternoon for everyone, although maybe some visitors got a good story about "this ranger torturing this guy." He never even turned in a complaint about me, which I had thought was coming for sure.

I remember way back when I first started, the first complaint I had against me. It was another crazy person, this woman at the front gate at Rancho afterhours wrapped in a blanket. I only gave her a written warning, and she had a fit. Tom said he figured that rangers might not be doing their jobs if they never got a complaint. There are crazy people out there, and you're going to run into some of them, no matter what you do, so don't worry about it. If you get a whole bunch of complaints, then that's an issue, but don't worry about a complaint, or even a few. If you are so under the radar that no one ever gets mad enough to complain about you, you're probably not doing your job.

~~~

I wasn't the first female District ranger, just the first to retire. There had been Joan Ferguson, whom I met several times at functions. She was the first female ranger. Right before I was hired, somebody had been hurt. A tree had fallen on her, on the job, a tree being cut down by a fulltime staff member. She was still on probation at the time and the tree fell on her and she got a bad, career-ending, back injury. There was another woman too, but she failed the fitness test. She'd been hired, but then failed the fitness test. She became an OST, but then quit to become a county park ranger because they didn't have a fitness requirement. She was around for a long time. I knew her during her time with county parks.

For a long time I was the only female field staff except for one female seasonal OST, and definitely the only female ranger. I would have had my own locker room, if we had had locker rooms. This was at the original Foothills office. There was just one toilet and one shower, not male and female locker rooms. I had a locker, but not in the bathroom. Even at the original Skyline office, the bunkhouse, we had just one toilet, which all eight of us shared. It was also the shower room, so if someone was in the shower, you couldn't use the toilet. The guys treated me well. It was almost like, as we got more women, there was more discrimination than when I was the only one. I was just treated as one of the guys. I remember that Dennis pointed out to me something that I hadn't thought about. I was up on top of the pumper trying to get it started. This was before we had the electric starters. I was standing on the top of the sidebox, which was wet and slippery, as there was no diamond plating on top back then. He called up to me, "Be careful! Be careful! We have a hard time keeping female rangers. We don't want to lose you." It seemed to be true, but it was the only "sexist" thing I ever heard. The next female ranger was Jen, and there was Suzanna quite a while ago. Then, all of a sudden there were all kinds of female rangers. The other guys, when I got hired, hadn't been there that long either. They were all very nice, very friendly and helpful.

Photo by Frances Reneau
**Patrol truck P82 with the computer
("the lunch tray") installed.**

There were no computers except at the main office. Everybody shared the first computer on Skyline. I remember once somebody had left it on, and I didn't know how to turn it off, but Pat did, so I called him at home and he walked me through it. I remember learning to do the monthly update, which was a spreadsheet. Gordon came up to Skyline to teach me. He's a real good instructor; he has a knack for it. He would try to show me the easiest way to do stuff. Over the years, people would show me how to do stuff on the computer and I'd pick it up for a while and then lose it. I never had any interest in it, and that's something that rangers now have to know. It's on the hiring test. If it had been on my test, I wouldn't have been hired. Now I guess they're putting them in the trucks? It's bad enough people playing with their smart phones.

Even the radio, just the District radio, is a distraction. The only times I damaged a truck were when I was talking on the radio. Once I was down at Rancho shuttling the Suburban, and the radio was up so darn loud that it was breaking my ears, so I reached down to turn down the volume right as I was passing through the Deer Hollow Farm gate. I found the Deer Hollow Farm gate all right--with the side of the Suburban. I had to call Tom, and he was real nice about it. The other time was on my own driveway. I had been outside doing something, weed whacking maybe, and I had been listening to the truck radio turned up real loud. I had gotten in, to move up the driveway, and the radio was blasting, so I leaned over to turn it down. They used to mount the radios way down below the center console of the dash, which was convenient for the installer, but not so much for the operator. So I was reaching down into No Man's Land, and my driveway was a little soft because of recent rains, so I got a little off the side of the driveway, which gave way, and pitched the truck against a tree. The tree ran into me. I heard this excuse from another employee who claimed the tree fell in front of him, but I think what fell was the burrito he was eating!

Photo used by permission of MROSD
Loro

I had a lot of friends who were in public service and who had retired early, and I thought that was kind of neat. At the time I was hired, I was told that we would probably be getting safety retirement, like police and firefighters have, so I always thought that would allow me to retire by the time I was a little over 50. When we didn't get the big, cushy retirement, I thought, "Okay, I'm going to have to stay longer." I was trying to retire with like 80 percent of pay, but it turned out that, with the change in the sick leave policy, where we could no longer convert unused sick leave, I didn't quite make that. Work was interfering with my going on trips. I had the vacation time on the books, but they just wouldn't let me take it. They wouldn't let you make trades, or pay other rangers to take your shifts to try to make a trip work. I felt like I always gave 110 percent, and they wouldn't allow me, in some cases, just a few extra hours of time to make some trip possible. I also was trying to help out someone who was sick and I couldn't use family sick leave, because this person didn't fall on the short list of those who counted as family. That's not right. If you have the time, they should allow you to use it. It was becoming too annoying. The super-micro-managing, which always had been there, got really bad. Treating us like babies. Again, it's the contrast between the responsibility for others' lives, on the one hand, and not trusting us with simple decisions on the other. I had always put away a lot into deferred compensation, which the District only started when I asked about it right after being hired. I just figured it was time. As you get older, your priorities change. I'm getting 20 percent less but, at the same time, I'm no longer paying into my retirement. Yeah, I'm having a good time, but I've not gotten as much done on the house as I had hoped.

Thank you, Loro

Ranger Frances: Trio of Trouble

Loro's stories of a few of her memorable law enforcement contacts—the mountain biker in Stevens Canyon who gave false information, the irate dad in Purisima caught peeing in the creek, and the woman with her unpermitted dog in Windy Hill—fit right in with the unhappy customers in my three stories below. If anything, her suspects were even ruder and nastier.

Maybe at some point during these detentions, somewhere deep inside Loro was conflicted, suffering from self-doubt, and questioning her own judgment. Maybe she was just wishing the whole, awful contact were over and done with. Maybe, but if so, she never let on. I was on a couple of less-than-straight-forward contacts with Loro and she was cool-headed and clear-minded from beginning to end. Her concentration and control of the situation were unwavering. I was impressed. I also thought it was interesting that when I asked her what she missed now in retirement about being a ranger, she said she missed being able to cite for the violations she sees in the parks she visits, major egregious violations, not just "piddly stuff." I can believe that.

~~~

For most District visitors, getting caught by the ranger in an area where you are not supposed to be, or doing what you are not supposed to be doing, will really ruin your day. You are out enjoying a ride or a walk, having a good time, not too worried about a little bending of the rules, and the next thing you know, you're getting busted, ordered around, and ticketed by some narrow-minded, self-righteous ranger. How ridiculous! You will certainly want to give her a piece of your mind, let her know exactly how you feel about her, her job, and her employer.

I found dealing with these hostile suspects alone and far from help could be scary, and I dreaded nasty law enforcement contacts such as those in the three following stories. However, I also found that such contacts provoked a perverse element of challenge. Once a stop had started to go sour, could I hold it together, maintain my composure, and gain compliance from the belligerent, irate, out-of-control suspect? Having decided that I intended to cite them, could I stick to my guns and carry through my plan, despite ameliorating circumstances or frustrating delays? Could I continue to listen to them, and even have sympathy for their frustration, while also keeping myself safe and trying to expedite a resolution? Could I appear authoritative, assertive and calm when, all the while the better part of me just wanted the whole ugly scene to reach its conclusion as soon as possible? Of course, I also couldn't help thinking, somewhere in the back of my mind as each of these little dramas played out, "this is going to make a terrific story."

Photo by Frances Reneau
Neighbor's lawnmowers inside Miramontes Ridge OSP

Journal entry 3/12/16: I was coming back from lower Purisima, up Highway 92, and thought I'd go check the Highway 35 access to Miramontes Ridge (a district preserve not open to the public,) and maybe walk out to the little vista point. I parked outside the gate and climbed over (easier than dealing with the lock) then thought I would first go walk the little loop to the south that goes behind some neighbors' houses. I was out there walking along when I heard vehicles approaching and, around the bend in the bushes came two guys riding on motorized lawnmowers. Oh great, I know where they came from. Sure enough, it was the same neighbor whose house backs onto the preserve whom I'd contacted out here months ago. I'd given the dad a written warning for Dogs Prohibited. This time it wasn't the dad, but his caregiver accompanying Neal, the disabled son of the household, now 11 years old and mounted on the second lawnmower. "Stop! Park Ranger! Peace Officer! Get off your vehicles!" They were compliant at this point, and Neal was, as always, even quite friendly. We agreed to meet at their backyard gate, just a couple hundred yards away. I insisted that they park the mowers outside the gate for the duration of the contact, because I was concerned that they would just drive in and then shut the gate in my face, leaving me SOL. Neal happily stayed with me while suspect/babysitter went inside to get his license.

When he returned, Neal's mom came too, and she was not happy. She gave me an earful about how riding the mower was one of the few pleasures in her son's life, and how they had the right to mow the fire clearance behind their house and how they only rode on that, etc. She became more and more angry and uncooperative and insisted on moving the mowers into her yard. She was just to the point of slamming the gate in my face (at which point I told her I would call for the sheriff) when Supervisor Mike finally showed up. He was fresh meat for her attacks, but he got to play the "good cop," as opposed to my "bad," and kept her busy while I finished citing the caregiver for Vehicles Prohibited. A good "pinch" and kind of amusing with the suspects riding on lawnmowers.

Nothing is ever straightforward, never cut-and-dry in these difficult contacts. In the above story, I was torn about having to be so unyielding and unfriendly to Neal's caregiver. I had had multiple previous fun encounters with Neal and it hurt to have to play the bad cop right in front of him. I could appreciate that it would be a blow to deprive him of his outings on the lawnmower, and that I wasn't making life any easier for this family and their disabled child. On the other hand, it was obvious from the cut grass and tire tracks that they were indeed riding the entire little loop, not just the easement behind their house. My next stressful arrest had some of the same elements.

Journal entry 1/14/14: Had a memorable contact a couple days ago in Saratoga Gap OSP. I was driving down Redwood Gulch Road when I saw this kid pop out of the preserve onto the roadway carrying something, which proved to be an off-road skateboard. I stopped him, but he was so immediately ornery and uncooperative that I felt I couldn't trust him to hold still while I checked the map book to make sure he had been on District land, and in a closed area. I called for a fill, and Greg, who was acting supervisor at the time, showed up. In strolling past the kid's car, Greg did a double take when he smelled marijuana inside. Turned out this kid also had a bong, grinder, and bud with him in his backpack, so I added Possession of Marijuana to the written warning I was writing for the Closed Area violation, and we called for his father. When Dad got on scene, he and my suspect had quite a shouting match, and Dad told us to call the sheriff and have the kid arrested because he was sick and tired of dealing with him. Before SO got there, our suspect kid grabbed the bud, pipe, bong and grinder and ran off into the preserve. Damn it! We had lost control of the suspect and the evidence. I should have put him in handcuffs. At least Dad was there, and the kid returned in a few minutes, empty-handed. Kid got a chewing out from SO, who had arrived in the meantime, and I cited the kid for Littering and for PC148 (Obstruct, Delay a Peace Officer) and he got released back to his father.

Another family having a hard time of it. I felt bad for this kid who was so clearly unhappy and in trouble. I felt bad for the dad who, despite losing his temper and yelling at his son, clearly cared for him and was worried about him. I felt caught in the middle of this family dynamic. At some point I remember the kid crying to me that he hated his dad, saying that his dad didn't care about him. I replied that I thought he was lucky that his dad apparently did still care about him despite all the problems, and that not every kid was so lucky as to have a dad who stood by him. Maybe that was out of line, but that was my impression of the situation. It was not really my role as a ranger to assist people in relationship trouble, and yet law enforcement officers (more often cops) deal with such issues all the time. The finale of this trio is another story of a guy with problems beyond my help, but older and weirder.

Journal entry 8/8/15: The Blue Blossom Trail in Corte Madera is closed to all traffic and will be until next summer sometime when the recent trail work will have had time to solidify from the (hoped for) winter rains. It has five-foot-tall orange plastic mesh fencing at both ends as well as signs and barricades so anyone found out there on the trail really has no excuse for being there except naughtiness. I hiked it today fishing for a cite and caught one. It was a righteous cite in that the guy had chosen to climb over or go around the fencing with his bike. I should have relished nailing this guy, but he was so upset that I ended up feeling sorry for him. He was swearing "Fuck" over and over again, and stomping around and he even threw his backpack hard at the ground. He was crying and yelling about how he hated this country, hated his life and hated himself. He crumpled up his cite and stuffed it into his pants, "with my dick." Yes, he was a dick and I was so unnerved by his behavior that I totally forgot to run out his driver's license. I didn't even think of it until the contact was over. How embarrassing! At least it was a hard copy DL.

I looked him up in the database when I got back to the office to see if he'd been cited before. Three previous cites—Bike After Hours, Bike in a Closed Area and Trail Speed. A frequent flyer for sure. Then, a couple days later, Superintendent Brian told me that my suspect had called him to complain that Gate CM06, where he had entered, didn't have one of those laminated Temporary Trail Closure signs. True, and we'll fix that, but he still climbed over the orange plastic fencing. Brian also said that my suspect had called him a "fucking asshole," but that he hadn't make any direct complaint against me

Only a small fraction of suspects are quite this hostile, upset, and uncooperative. The gray area, the ameliorating circumstances, seem to be ever-present. Every suspect has reasons, excuses and stories for why they are in violation and it is easy for me to waiver in the face of a good excuse, but when suspects lose their temper and start stomping around shouting and swearing and throwing things, they have lost any chance of getting out of that ticket.

Dennis Danielson, Ranger and Supervising Ranger

My interest in being a ranger started on a family vacation to Lassen National Park. My sister and I had gone for a hike, had gone the wrong way, and gotten a little lost. We popped out not where our parents were expecting us, and the ranger gave us a ride back to our camp. I was 13 and my sister was five years older. Later on that same trip, we hiked up to the top of Mt. Lassen. When we got back down to the parking lot, there was a girl there about my age who had slid down a snow slope on an inner tube, gone into some rocks at the bottom, and gotten injured. The rangers did a lowering system and I got to help. She had a fractured vertebra and some other bad injuries. I had gotten to her at the same time as her father. He was upset that she had ruined the family vacation, and he was trying to grab her and pull her up. I told him, "No, no, no. She's injured." I think I'd had some basic first aid by that time, and Red Cross Junior Life Saving. I think that it was those experiences with the rangers in Lassen that got my curiosity going.

~~~

I grew up in Oakland, about two blocks from Lake Temescal, which was one of the original East Bay Regional Parks, but I went to Bellarmine High in San Jose. My dad was born in Montana and my mom on a homestead in South Dakota. Our family vacations were always going back to visit the relatives. I always joked that we had to drive 2,000 miles east to go Out West. My maternal grandfather and my uncle were true cowboys, out on the range. My grandmother lived through the Great Depression and the Dust Bowl. We used to go visit and go fishing in the creeks and riding horses, and they had cattle and a milking cow and all that kind of stuff. It's funny that, when we were driving across Nevada and Wyoming, my sister and I would want to camp out, but my parents were like, "We can afford to get a motel. Why would you want to camp?" One year we did bring some camping gear and camped a few places like Yellowstone and the Tetons.

Probably my first real backpacking trip was a trip with my friend Jane McClenehan to Point Reyes when I was in high school. She's still a good friend these 50 years later. We did everything wrong. I hiked in cowboy boots. I brought a cast iron frying pan, a heavy pot, and canned goods. We went from the Bear Valley Visitor Center out to Coast Camp. We had four rolls of toilet paper for just two days! But I liked it, despite all. I should have been working on my paper on Shakespeare, but went backpacking instead, which may have been the better choice. I misspelled Shakespeare 45 times and got an F.

As a kid I went to the City of Oakland summer camp a number of times at Lake Chabot. Then my friend Jimmy McDonald's family paid to host all his cousins and friends at this camp, (which is now the San Jose Family Camp) on the Tuolumne River outside of Yosemite. We could walk from the camp down to Rainbow Pool. We didn't go to Yosemite Valley even though we were less than an hour away. Another early influence was the Peaky family, these childhood family friends who belonged to the Sierra Club. At that point you had to be sponsored by somebody to join the Sierra Club, so the Peakys sponsored me. This would have been 1969 or 1970. I was still in high school, 16 or 17 years old.

The summer between my sophomore and junior years of high school, I signed up for a service trip with the Sierra Club that went to Evolution Valley. We camped in McClure Meadow close to the ranger station. We had packhorses to bring in the food and gear. We re-routed a section of trail in Evolution Basin away from the lakes, because the lakeshore was fragile, grassy, and marshy. On those service trips, you worked one day on, one day off. I was on the team with the trip leader, George Smith, and then the assistant leader had a second team. I think there were 20 people all together, ten to a team. George was a mountaineer, so we climbed Mt Darwin, Mt Mendel, and Mt. Huxley, all 13,000' to 14,000' peaks. That really did it for me. This was it. I also talked to the ranger at McClure Meadow and asked, "How do you get a job like yours?" which was a question people later asked me about a million times. I think he might have been the seasonal ranger who went missing 15 years later, the one in the book, "The Last Season." I'm not sure it was him. The following year I did another service trip to Granite Basin out of Cedar Grove where I was the assistant leader.

That next winter, my senior year in high school, I learned that the local Sierra Club chapter had this snow camping training. I signed up for that and ended up being involved for seven years. This was during the time when there was a transition from the old-school snowshoes to cross-country skis. For a few years we would snowshoe into camp, but carry our cross-country skis on our backs. Once we'd set up our snow camp, which was really fun because you got to build stuff out of snow and sleep in snow caves, then we would go cross-country skiing.

About 1973, the year I graduated from high school, I became a rafting guide for All Outdoors, which is now the largest outfitter in California. I guided for a number of years on weekends and in the summer. I did a lot of private trips with them too, including going down the Colorado River, the Rogue River, and the Salmon River. Along with the South Fork of the American, the Stanislaus was the mainstay before it was dammed.

During this time I also worked as an ambulance attendant in Oakland for about five months. We had some hot calls. I probably saw more action in one week there than in many years with Midpeninsula. Lots of shootings and stabbings, plus a lot of transfers between medical facilities, which were good too because you got to practice your skills under less stressful circumstances. There was a lot of lead in the air. I saw many gunshot wounds, including a shotgun wound to the chest. Not a lot of car accidents though, surprisingly. I saw more auto trauma working on Skyline. It was mostly poor people. Rich people drove themselves to the hospital. The patients had these little "POE" stickers provided by Medi-Cal to pay for the ambulance ride. This was before there were paramedics in ambulances. We had no gloves, no PPEs (Personal Protective Equipment) whatsoever. We wore white smocks, kind of like barbers. We transitioned while I was there to the more fire department-like shirt and pants. Yeah, white pants and white smocks with snaps on the shoulder, like surgeons in old movies. I had a focus on medical and fire and I was always trying to get more experience.

I wasn't academically oriented in high school, so I ended up in community college, Merritt College, which turned out to be great. I wasn't thinking about getting a degree, so I just took the classes that had the best field trips. I went there for four years but never got the AA. I had the requisite 70 units, but I was missing a few key classes. I took geology, geography, desert studies, mountain studies, and forest plants, which helped me learn the basic trees and plants, and their scientific names. I did a number of trips with one of the instructors, Ron Felsner, to the Southwest, and we went backpacking in the Canyonlands and the Escalante River. We went twice to Mexico, to Baja, once all the way down to the tip, over Christmas break.

In the summer of 1977, I applied for a job with East Bay Regional Parks and I was hired as a beach ranger, which was like a non-swimming lifeguard. I would walk around Lake Anza in Tilden Park telling people that they had to stay in the designated swimming area. Nowadays they swim everywhere. There was a rock where they would sit and drink beer and then jump off. I remember I suggested that we put a garbage can over on the far side of the lake, which we did. But then it would instantly fill up and then somebody would have to drive over there and empty it. So later when I went to Midpeninsula, I thought one of their best ideas was to have no garbage cans. Pack it in. Pack it out. It saves tax dollars.

~~~

The following summer I applied for a job with the National Parks Service and was hired as a summer seasonal in Sequoia National Park. I had done several hundred miles of backpacking in the Sierra by then, including hiking the John Muir Trail when I was 19, my "Coming of Age Hike." That was partially with my friend Peter Johnson. I was one of the few seasonals hired who already had a lot of knowledge and experience in the backcountry. Many seasonals were from other parts of the country. My job was issuing wilderness permits at the trailhead of the High Sierra Trail at Crescent Meadow. There used to be a little kiosk there, but now they do it centrally out of the Lodgepole Visitor Center. I wasn't trained in law enforcement. The National Park Service was just starting a program in Santa Rosa for law enforcement for seasonal employees. I gleaned as much from that seasonal job as I could.

I went on every fire and every rescue that they would let me. They knew I was interested, so the permanent employees would pull me off my regular job, "You're going to a fire for a few days." "We need you for this search and rescue. Meet at the helicopter pad in an hour." I got to ride in the helicopter several times. It was a heavy snow year so there weren't a lot of fires, just lightning strikes. At the end of the season, I got to stay two more months on the fire crew. They would fly a couple of us in to monitor the lightning strike fires. The "Let It Burn" policy had recently started, but there was one fire that was close to Forest Service land that we needed to contain. It was small, just one tree, but if it had escaped into the Forest Service land, the Forest Service would have put it out and then billed the Park Service for their work. There were also some big campaign fires with hundreds of firefighters, the Hockett Fire, and the Potwisha Fire. The Potwisha Fire started down near Three Rivers and burned up to the ridgeline through the hard chaparral. Three days of rain put that one out. I got some good fire experience.

At this point I was 23 and I knew I wanted to be a ranger and so I signed myself up for the Santa Rosa academy. I was in Class 3, the third class ever run there. This was the fall of 1978. I had worked at Sequoia until Thanksgiving. Back then Santa Rosa was only 200 hours. Now it's like 600 hours. I already had my PC 832, which I'd taken through the Alameda County Sheriff's Office, and I already had my EMT and my minimal Red Card series for firefighting, so I could go on the fires in Sequoia. I took those Red Card classes at Sequoia. They are supposed to be 8-hour classes, but I think I did all three in four hours. Class started at eight o'clock in the morning and I was in the helicopter on my way to the fire by two o'clock that same afternoon.

The Santa Rosa campus was still at Los Guilicos, the old girls' school, before they built the new campus at Windsor. It was right next to the San Michael Winery. There were two rangers from Midpeninsula in my class, Dave Camp and Judy Frosh. I was still living in Oakland, where I had girlfriend, so I went home on the weekends. I could drive from Oakland to Santa Rosa in 70 minutes. I knew about Midpeninsula because I had been checking the job boards at East Bay Regional Parks, and I had seen and applied for a job with the District in the spring of '78, and hadn't gotten it. That probably worked out for the best, because if I'd gotten it, I wouldn't have gone to Sequoia.

~~~

I applied to Midpeninsula again in the spring of '79, now with the Santa Rosa academy under my belt. My interview must have been January or February. I remember distinctly this other candidate, the one interviewing right ahead of me. He had a black mustache, black hair, and was wearing kind of a Madras shirt. It was John Escobar. John ended up first on the list and I ended up second. He was hired right away and I started three months later in June. Eric Mart was the one who interviewed and hired us. He had come from the National Park Service, from Point Reyes. I had already been offered a job back in Sequoia as the seasonal supervisor, and I really wanted to go back, so I asked Eric if he would delay my start until September, but he said no. I can see why. They needed rangers. One of the other rangers, Wendy Lieber, was out with an injury from a car accident. She was living in the adobe at Fremont Older at the time.

I had already been to Santa Rosa, and John still had to go, but he still had seniority on me. He was also much more driven toward management, whereas I preferred being out in the field. I did later become a supervisor, which I liked a lot. I wasn't into administration, or the financial stuff or running projects. Later on, as a supervisor, I was always late getting in my performance evaluations. I was notorious for that. I liked directing emergency situations on the ground, being in the moment. I think when things were at their worst, I was at my best.

I think there were only six rangers and 5,000 acres when I started. I feel like my career of 35 years really spanned the land acquisition phase of the District. We had low pay, and no retirement medical. It was unconscionable that they didn't have things better set up. We felt like we were doing it for the cause. Some of the District Board members felt like everyone should be a volunteer. My field training consisted of riding around with Dave Camp for a week. The other rangers were Wendy Lieber, John Escobar, Jim Bolan, and Sherwin Smith. Judy Frosh resigned right after the Santa Rosa academy. She realized that law enforcement wasn't for her, so I sort of got her spot. Sango and David Topley were both hired a year after I was. They were hired together, on the same day, which they always said was a mistake because it was a problem about who had seniority. They were the ones who got that changed for the future so hirings would always be staggered.

A big part of my enjoyment of the job early on was all the land acquisition. I followed acquisitions really closely. It was fun to be the first boots on the ground on a new piece of property, not truly the first, of course, because the acquisition people had all been there. I remember that one of the only pieces of what is now Sierra Azul that we owned was the Pennington property, which we called Manzanita Ridge. This was the land in off Kennedy Road at Gate SA01, at Top of the Hill Road in Los Gatos. I installed the first sign there. The first District signs were wood, 12" X 24" and they said, "Wildland Area." I think it was John Escobar, Dave Camp, me, and maybe by then Sango and Topley who came up with that term "Wildland Area." We didn't feel like we could use the word "wilderness" because we thought that was a federal designation and meant something different, so we called it wildland. Those signs had four little pictures on them:

No Dogs, No Bikes, No fires, No Camping. Something like that. That was the early regulation sign. I'm not sure the names of the preserves were even on the signs early on. They were generic. There were no public maps, of course. I drew my own patrol maps. This was before computers. The main office had topographical maps with the land boundaries on them, and I bought my own set of topos and, using a light table, traced the property boundaries and wrote in names.

The maps we were given were terrible. They were made on a mimeograph machine and were so blurry that you couldn't even tell where the contour lines were. They were black and white. I remember driving up to what I thought was the top boundary of Manzanita Ridge only to realize some time later that the actual boundary was much higher, all the way at the top of the ridge. I had been stopping and turning around at what we later called "the campground," where there was a big oak tree in the middle of the road. We were also told that, "Over the top of the ridge there are marijuana growers with Uzis," so we were scared to go beyond the campground.

~~~

We all worked out of Rancho. There were no maintenance people at all. The job title was, "Patrol Ranger and Maintenance." It was kind of a unique thing to have that blend. When we got up to nine rangers, we would rotate three at a time into full-time maintenance, for three months at a time. The way it worked out, it was always a different season of the year when you'd hit your maintenance rotation, which was good because you'd have weekends off during different seasons of the year.

When I first got hired, I was technically still living in Oakland, and I actually commuted a few times, but Jim Bolan was living at Picchetti in the big house, which is now where the winery people live, and he let me stay there so I wouldn't have to drive all the way home. I also would sleep in the office in my sleeping bag on the floor. I liked going from late to early shift, and would switch with people to get it, because I wanted that early shift before my weekend.

In January of 1980 I moved into the cabin at Monte Bello, where Loro later lived. I always joked that it was the only real ranger residence because it was a log cabin and the only heat was a wood-burning stove. The bathroom was a little attachment in the back, which was added after the District bought it. There was a loft accessed by a ladder where I stored my skis and camping stuff. I did a bunch of work on that cabin. I re-did the cabinets in the kitchen area. Nothing was to code. I remember there was a rigid copper pipe for the gas, not a flexible line, mostly because I didn't know better. I lived there for five years.

I joined the South Skyline Volunteer Fire Department during that time. My name is on a brass plaque on the building at Saratoga Summit Station. I would go out on calls with them. The lines are kind of blurred in my memory between what was a fire call and what was a ranger call. I think Pat Congdon joined after I left. I moved to Purisima about the time he was hired. He started living at the Saratoga Gap house down Charcoal Road. He was much more involved. I think he was the chief, and a Volunteer of the Year, but we didn't overlap.

~~~

Before Santa Clara County bought the land in 1981, there was no Rancho San Antonio County Park, and so there was no parking lot. People would park under the 280 freeway overpass at the end of St. Joseph's Avenue. The first, and for a long time the only, parking lot the District had was at Los Trancos. We didn't yet own all of Monte Bello. Lorrie's Stables was still operating there. People would later say, "Oh look how green it is." Well, the green was all star thistle because the horses had ripped up the ground.

~~~

There was a doughnut shop that opened in Cupertino called George's. I would stop there and get a couple of doughnuts and a cup of coffee and drive to Manzanita Ridge to a viewpoint. In the summertime, in the morning, the Santa Clara Valley would be fogged in, but you could see the Hamilton Range across the valley. It was so cool because you couldn't even tell that there was a city down there. You were on one wooded Wildland Area looking across at another. I'd sit up there and enjoy my two doughnuts and my coffee. Later we bought more properties along the ridgeline in Sierra Azul. Schwabacher was one where they had done a lot of recreational bulldozing which has now completely overgrown so you can't even tell anymore. I remember driving through the new properties, across El Sombroso and along the PG&E tower corridor.

~~~

Although we acquired a lot of land along Skyline Boulevard, we didn't yet own the top of Black Mountain, which was the Winship property. We did own where the campground is now which had been Stanford land. There was a little cabin there and two barns where Al and Julie Lind lived with their two kids, Briana and Quentin. The kids were just babies when I started. We ended up taking over the cabin to make it a field office, which just had a desk and a phone in it, which we never much used. The Linds lived in what we called the bunkhouse, which was a three-tiered structure with a cow stall on one end, and then a composting toilet, and then the living space. There was a big barn with a pitched roof on both sides, but a huge windstorm blew half of it down. Al kind of put it back together which was a hell of a lot of work. Al used to go down to the Kramer's who lived on Monte Bello Road to study for his PhD. I think he was already working at USGS. He was Mr. Earthquake, studying seismic stuff. Max Kramer had been a math professor at San Jose State and Dorothy had been an author of books about Southwestern art. Dorothy developed Alzheimer's and now and then we'd get the call, "Dorothy went out for a walk and hasn't come back," so we'd go out and search for Dorothy. We knew her usual route was out to Adobe Meadow, so we'd go drive the Adobe Creek Loop. Sure enough, we'd find her out amongst the wildflowers. She'd probably just lost track of time.

~~~

This was also the time of The List. I think Craig Britton and Herb Grench were trying to avoid having to give public notice of what properties they were negotiating for, so they had this brilliant idea of listing every property within the District boundaries for which they could negotiate. Well, that freaked everybody out because there were hundreds of names on that list. They were trying to comply with the Brown Act. That's like the Sunshine Act, which says that you are required to give public notice. I think there were about 300 parcels listed. So they could just say, "Well, it's on our list, so, yeah, we gave public notice." That's the period when we'd be getting the finger as we drove down Skyline Boulevard. Everybody hated the Open Space District up there, and The List had a lot to do with it, and the use of eminent domain. They used eminent domain to buy Rancho, at least the Perham property. The Perham house now functions as the Annex to the Foothills Field Office. The Perhams were still living there at the upper house, which is now staff housing, and the mother was at the lower house, the Annex. There was a little bungalow next to the lower house that we tore down. They also owned the farm buildings at what is now Deer Hollow Farm, and the construction yard where the FFO is now. They had a construction business running out of there. The front area, of course, was part of St. Joseph's Seminary and Santa Clara County bought that.

~~~

One acquisition that struck me as being very thoughtful was Purisima, the first Purisima property, which we bought from Wilkins. He still has the right to drive around in Purisima, and he still has his Life Estate out there. He had a Toyota sedan he'd drive around in. He used to keep some lawn furniture chained to a tree up by his place. He was from Texas and had a southern drawl. He was a good guy. He did logging but he'd select trees that he wanted to save, like all those big trees down by the creek at the west end of Purisima. He was harvesting second growth and trying to save the bigger trees. Purisima was a number separate of acquisitions. One of the first was Grabtown Gulch. Graham Nash (of Crosby, Stills, Nash and Young) was going to buy it at one point. Young, of course, had his property further down Bear Creek Road. There were lots of hippies all hanging around the Santa Cruz Mountains.

I was assigned to drive some District Board members around to look at both Corte Madera, which was owned by Hosking, and Purisima, on the same day. We had offers to buy both but we couldn't afford to buy both. I guess I must have had three of the Board members with me. You couldn't have four, because you couldn't have a quorum of the Board without calling a public meeting. Nanette Hanko was one. My job was to show off these two properties, as best I could. I can't remember where we went. I guess we went down the main haul road. We had the ranch manager from Hosking with us, but he was kind of unsure about the roads. I remember we were driving into Corte Madera along the creek on this logging road. They were still logging after we bought the property because there were existing contracts we had to honor, and there was active logging at the time we were driving down this road. We came nose to nose with this big logging truck coming uphill. We had to figure out a way for them to get past us. I remember having to park my vehicle and climb up on the running boards of this big logging truck to talk to the driver. I just wish I had a picture of that: this District vehicle with its logos and the logging truck loaded with logs, nose to nose. To me, that speaks to all of what the District has done. It was the transition, the change from private resource extraction to conservation. I guess I probably backed up to a point where he could pass me. Then we headed over to Purisima. The Board had to make this decision about which property to buy. They chose Purisima, rightfully so. Wilkins was also a friendlier seller. Eventually we did buy Corte Madera, but it took about five acquisitions from Hosking. He would retain ridgetops where he could build some houses. It was always a compromise.

~~~

About the time of the 10-year reunion, in 1982, when we were looking at the Purisima and Corte Madera purchases, the Hassler property purchase was also going on in what's now Pulgas Ridge Preserve. That had been a City of San Francisco tuberculosis sanitarium. (My mom contracted tuberculosis in the Navy during WWII at Pearl Harbor, so I feel this sense of connection.) It had four 2-story wings with a hospital and doctors' quarters. There was a real nice house there that John Escobar was hoping to move into, but there were problems with the plumbing so they tore it down. There was a big fight with this group that wanted to convert the buildings at the site into artists' studios, like the Allied Arts Center, in Menlo Park. Something similar had been done in the Marin Headlands with some of the old military buildings there, repurposing them. There was some sort of deal where if we did all this remodeling, we would get to keep some of the buildings. It would have been millions of dollars, even back then. But the Board said, "That isn't what we're about, and we don't have the money." Some of the Board members were sympathetic and didn't want to say no. In the early years there was not as much staff, so the Board got more directly involved in some ways. Those buildings were probably all full of lead and asbestos anyway.

We were going back and forth on the restraining order on the District's plans to demo the TB hospital buildings. The wrecking equipment, the Grade-All, one of those things for knocking down buildings, was already up there waiting. Then this judge overruled the restraining order, and Herb Grench, the GM, called the ranger office and said, "I want somebody up there right now! Tell that equipment operator to start the demo." He called back five minutes later, "Has that ranger left yet?" It was Joan Ferguson that was supposed to go and she was still in the office yacking. "I want them out the door right now, with the lights and sirens." Well, she didn't do lights and sirens, but she did go and get them started.

It might not have been at the 10-year reunion party, but it was at some sort of staff party that Dan Wendan, one of the early Board members, stood up and said, "We had this choice. We could either fix up those buildings, or we could buy Purisima. We're in the business of buying places like this." The buildings all got knocked down, but the controversy lingered for a while because some people didn't get their way.

~~~

In 1975, before I started, when they were still doling out Land and Water Conservation Fund monies to buy land, the District used some of that money to pay for half of Edgewood County Park. They wanted to leverage their money for buying land if some other agency would manage it, or share costs, and San Mateo County said they would. The District said, "We're not going to tell you what to do with this property." The Board never came right out and said, "No," to the County's golf course plan, even though they all were opposed to it. They held to their agreement to not tell the County what to do. The fight between San Mateo County and the Native Plant Society people and the golf course people went on for a number of years. Of course the reason there was even that big chunk of land sitting there in the first place was because it was supposed to become the site of a California State University college, CSU Edgewood, the counterpart to CSU Hayward.

Used by permission of MROSD
Dennis Danielson talking to staff member

I remember a few incidents in Devils Canyon. They were almost always at night and involved kids drinking beer. They would fall while climbing around the waterfall. I remember this one girl whose group had scrambled down to the middle falls, not the very top one, and she had fallen and broken her femur. It was a serious injury and time was of the essence. San Mateo County Fire was on scene and probably the Sheriff. Half the time those guys would show up in cowboy boots and literally had six-shooters with white handles and bullets in their belts. Whenever the Sheriff showed up, I would always check to see what shoes they were wearing. Often they were cowboy boots or slick-soled pavement shoes. I can't remember whether I was there as a District ranger or as a volunteer firefighter because I was living at the Monte Bello cabin at that time. Highway incidents I'd go as a volunteer. For Devils Canyon, I was probably there as a ranger.

We got this girl packaged into a litter, but it was going to be a rope haul up the waterfalls. They had done a call-out for BAMRU, the Bay Area Mountain Rescue Unit, which is under the umbrella of the San Mateo County Sheriff's office. BAMRU is skilled in all the rope rescue stuff. We had gotten her up the first set of falls, and BAMRU set up the next pitch. I had scouted a easier, alternate way up the south side of the falls, so I felt like I made a real contribution toward getting this girl out of there.

These Devils Canyon rescues were always at night for drunk people, and going up the north side of the falls was so steep. We may have had the newer orange plastic litters by then rather than the old Stokes Litter metal baskets, but they still didn't have wheels, I'm sure. Once you got the patient up above the falls, you still had a half-mile of rough, informal trail to carry them out.

What happened, how this ongoing problem in Devils Canyon was largely resolved, was the following: you used to be able to park right at the Portola Heights gate, in that turnout. The rangers and supervisors lobbied San Mateo County and Caltrans to put in No Parking signs at that spot. Unbelievably, that worked to perfection. The kids had to walk just that little bit farther from the Grizzly Flat parking, carrying their coolers, of course. I don't know if kid traffic dropped off completely, but it made a difference. I wanted to plaster "No Parking Dusk to Dawn" signs all along Skyline Boulevard, at least in all the big turnouts and the areas where there were problems. The Clouds Rest Vista Point got a lot worse in recent times. I could hear cars racing up and down Skyline Boulevard while lying in bed at my Skyline Ridge residence. The tuner Cars doing spins certainly got worse. They are those little Japanese cars that kids lower and put special engines in, and they follow each other tightly in a little line at high speed. Brendan told me it had gotten really bad to where rangers were going to a lot of accidents and doing a lot of traffic control.

~~~

I admit I was a bit of an ambulance chaser. I liked going to the emergencies. You never knew until you got there what the real story was. You'd hear, "Motorcycle down," and it would turn out to be a fallen bicyclist a mile down the trail. Or they'd say the patient was on Skyline Boulevard, but they were actually in one of the preserves because we owned so much land. Plus, nearly all the LZs were on Open Space District land. I would usually go, especially when the fire stations were down-staffed. In the wintertime they would have just one engine with two or three firefighters on it. They needed the extra hands on these accidents. But rangers would complain about being stuck directing traffic for 40 minutes or whatever. The supervisors were all directed to go to the BC (Battalion Chief) and tell them to get CHP up there because doing traffic control was pulling the rangers out of our preserves. The BC might try and get someone to come, but they were often way extended. My argument was that if we expected the sheriff or Cal Fire to come out and help us all the time in our preserves, because we needed a medic or an armed officer or whatever, then we should also expect to help them in return. If you respond to a highway accident, you might be there for a half an hour or so. If you go on a parks rescue, it could be four or five hours. The District's police and fire capabilities were questionable.

There is a lot of District land that is SRA, (State Responsibility Area) that is not a part of any fire district or municipality. East Bay Regional Parks has an actual fire department, with wildland engines and a specialized crew. Patrick Congdon and I were talking about this 20 years ago, saying how we could buy old CDF engines that were being retired out, even though they were still good, although not maybe for driving to L.A. We might staff those engines on Red Flag days. Something like that. I always wanted the District rangers to be POST certified and armed. I know not everyone felt that way. Part of being an independent special district is that you are taking those lands off the tax rolls, and one of the primary roles of property tax is to pay for basic services like public safety.

~~~

Certainly the bread and butter of the job was trail use management, mostly bikes and dogs and some after-hours violations. I don't think anybody likes writing tickets, and I can't say that I did. I didn't mind the rule enforcement, because I believe in rule enforcement to get people's behavior to change. I think it's a necessary part of the job because it gets the word out. If all you ever do is give warnings, then visitors learn, "Oh, you'll just get a warning." That's what happened up in Marin Open Space, which is totally within the Marin County so their sheriffs are their real law enforcement. Their rangers didn't issue tickets. I talked to one ranger who worked up there, (Suzanna, who later worked for us) who said, "Yeah, I'd talk to the same person every single day for a year. 'You can't have your dog here.'" "Oh, okay. Thank you." This would just go on because they knew they wouldn't get a ticket.

~~~

I remember this marijuana grow incident just off the side of the road, just a small, personal grow. It was near Skyline Boulevard, across from the tree farm, south of the Monte Bello cabin. Two sheriff's deputies from San Mateo County found a car parked on the side of Skyline Boulevard. The guy was maybe out taking a leak. I guess there must have been something suspicious about the vehicle. There was a water tank in the back, actually an oversized cooler with a submersible pump run by a 12-volt battery. From there a skinny little hose ran over into the bushes. The Sheriff cuffed this guy, put him in the back of their patrol car, and went to investigate. Sure enough, there were these planters with marijuana plants, not very many, like maybe six plants, and rubber snakes to protect the site. Miles Standish, the state parks ranger came by and pointed out that it was on Open Space land so I got a call-out. I remember it was the third of July.

The SO were like, "It's in Santa Clara County." I'm like, "It's actually in the City of Palo Alto." They wanted to arrest this guy but they had such poor radio communications that the SO had to drive up to the Clouds Rest Vista Point to get out on their radio to ask if it was okay to arrest this guy out of their jurisdiction. They called Palo Alto and the Palo Alto dispatcher told them, "We don't own any land on Skyline," and they wouldn't send anybody. I was telling the San Mateo deputies, "The Palo Alto city limit sign is right here." We could practically see it. Finally this very experienced Santa Clara County deputy showed up who knew the rule that says, basically, if it's within 800' of the county line, you can do it. I was showing them my maps because they didn't have a clue. Then the San Mateo guys had to drive back up to the Vista Point to tell their supervisors what the decision was.

The reason I remember that this was July 3rd is because the next day, July 4th, I couldn't find my flashlight. I had left it on the roof of the sheriff's car. I got it back later, but John Maciel, the operations manager, was riding with me that night and now I didn't have my flashlight on the Fourth of July.

~~~

I never served as a medical trainer for the District. As much as I liked to talk, I had some insecurity about organizing, and feeling confident that I'd done a good job. I'd probably have been better than I gave myself credit for. But I did always feel like I was at my best when things were at their worst. When there was total chaos, I was the one to be there. You train, train, train, but it never goes that way. You have to be ready to adapt. I felt like stopping at the fire stations and getting to know the firefighters a little bit was worthwhile. When you got on an emergency scene, they might not know your name, but they at least recognized your face, and you recognized them.

324

~~~

At the District's 10-year reunion, which was at De Anza College, the keynote speaker was Wallace Stegner. He started off by joking, "I didn't know that I was going to be the turkey at this Thanksgiving." He talked about various things, but one thing I remember he said, because I really believed it was true, was, "In 100 years they will be laying wreaths on your graves for what you have done here."

Thank you, Dennis

Some comments on Dennis' interview:

By my day, rangers would have enjoyed no such say-so in the design of the regulation signs such as Dennis describes, and even no opportunity to give the planning department our input on their designs. In the early days of Dennis' career, patrol rangers' voices could still be heard downtown. However, by my day we did have vastly better mapbooks.

Compare Dennis' recollection of the Board's restraint in telling San Mateo County what to do at Edgewood with Alice Cummings' story of doing rare plant surveys of the property with the objective of stopping the golf course development.

Ranger Frances:
Four Medicals with the Kings Mountain Volunteer Fire Department

Dennis freely admits to being an "ambulance chaser." He liked going to medical incidents, being first on scene, and being the incident commander. One of the perks he certainly enjoyed as a supervisor was getting to be the IC, at least until fire got there. Given his aptitude and predilection for emergency medicine, I do wonder how he dealt with the Kings Mountain Fire Volunteers' captain featured in the following stories. Somehow I just can't quite imagine the two of them being all buddy-buddy. Indeed not.

Journal entry 11/17/2013: Yesterday I went to my first big medical since coming to Skyline. Ellen, who is the District's Volunteer Program Lead, had a volunteer project at the Galloway Property, a new addition to Corte Madera OSP, down off of Native Sons Road. She and about 15 volunteers were pulling slender false brome, an invasive grass of wet, shady places. I had never been out to the Galloway Property as it was a new acquisition and still closed to the public, so I figured this was a good opportunity to check it out, and stop by the volunteer project at the same time.

From Skyline Boulevard, I made my way down Tunitas Creek Road, to Starr Hill Road, to Native Sons Road, and located a District pipe gate, Oxford brown, with a 2C10 lock in the chain, but no gate numbers. This had to be it. I was cautiously driving around inside this gate when I heard Ellen on the radio, with a tense voice, asking for any ranger near the Galloway Property. I answered that I was in the Galloway Property, but couldn't see them anywhere. Where were they? Ellen explained that there was a second gate, farther down Native Sons Road, also un-numbered, and they were working just inside this other gate. She had a volunteer with a badly injured knee. Could I respond? I called for San Mateo County Fire and medics to respond, plus any other rangers in the area to help with navigating, as this place was not easy to find. I got the truck turned around and headed down to the lower gate.

My patient wasn't far inside the lower gate. It was Lucy, a 50-something-year-old female with a leg injury and clearly in a lot of pain. Lucy was a longtime volunteer, veteran of many projects, and someone I had worked with before. She was fully conscious and oriented and had no other injuries. She had been following Ellen and some other volunteers up to the gate, carrying equipment back to the truck, when she tripped over a root and fell awkwardly. Everyone reported hearing a loud "pop." I sent Ellen back to my truck for some blankets as it was cold and damp under the redwoods, and Lucy was already shivering. I hate chopping up expensive clothing, but there would be no wiggling her clothes off today, not given her level of pain, so I sliced open both pant legs. Her left knee was so obviously deformed and swollen that a comparison with the right knee was hardly necessary. There was a large, baseball-sized lump on the outside of her left lower leg, just below the knee. While the skin color still looked okay in her left foot, and she said she could still feel me touching her leg and foot, she couldn't move her toes at all, or was unwilling to try for fear of pain. I couldn't find a pedal pulse, but that's not unusual; they are hard to find.

We bundled her up in blankets and I was just starting to splint her leg when the Kings Mountain Volunteer Fire Department showed up. The lead guy came sprinting in the gate, hollering directions to his crew behind him as he ran. I think he may have said something like, "I'll take over here," before pushing me away from my patient. I was happy to see these guys; I'm always relieved when fire gets on scene and I am off the hook for responsibility, but this guy's behavior seemed erratic and rude. Who was he?

This was my introduction to Kings Mountain Fire. This all-volunteer department operates under the auspices of the San Mateo County Fire Department and responds to emergency calls in the northern Skyline Boulevard area. When District rangers respond to fires, medicals, and lost persons in Corte Madera and Purisima preserves, we can expect to be dealing with the Kings Mountain Volunteers and their adrenaline- and testosterone-laden captain, Val.

Ellen and the weed-pulling crew and I all stood around and watched while Val's minions repeated the patient history and secondary exam and re-took vitals and asked poor Lucy, multiple times, "How is your pain on a scale of one to 10, with 10 being the worst pain you have ever experienced?" What difference does it make? You're not giving her any pain meds anyway. I felt like they were using her as a training dummy for new recruits. The ambulance finally got there and whisked her away. Ellen and I, aided by some of our helpful District volunteers, shuttled her car from Skyline back to her home in Redwood City, as she had no family available to help.

After a prolonged stay in the hospital, Lucy ended up having to stay at a rehab place for many months because her apartment was on the second floor of a building without an elevator, and she was stuck using a wheelchair. She didn't have the upper body strength necessary to keep all weight off her leg while walking with crutches. I imagine it was a long recovery, but I never heard her complain, and she even returned to volunteering a year or two later, although only in the main office.

~~~

I missed out on the next medical adventure with Kings Mountain Volunteer Fire. I was out of position (taking a very good optional wildlife tracking training at Russian Ridge) and got stuck covering the patrol of Skyline, while all other rangers were working this evacuation. My frustration is clear in the following journal entry:

Journal entry 3/3/14: The medical call I wasn't on illustrates perfectly my point that we need to name and sign the trails at Teague Hill OSP. The reporting party couldn't even tell us what trail the patient was on, because none of the trails in there even have names! (This has since been partially rectified with the placement of numbered signs at trail junctions, so lost persons can at least say, "I'm just past a sign with a 3 on it.")

The patient with a broken leg was somewhere on an unofficial side trail from the "Power Line Trail," the service trail that runs under the PG&E high tension power lines. The Power Line Trail intersects the Bay Area Ridge Trail about half a mile south of Kings Mountain Road. The stupid Kings Mountain Fire captain, (the same egomaniac from the Galloway call) insisted on taking the patient out the other way, south on the Bay Area Ridge Trail, which is a couple of miles uphill to Skyline Boulevard, instead of north, which is one mile downhill to Kings Mountain Road. Why the rangers on scene—three District rangers and two District supervising rangers—didn't stand up to Val is beyond me. But then, hadn't I also let myself literally be pushed around by this guy?

~~~

During incident number three below, which I was definitely on, things got way out of hand between Val and me.

Journal entry 9/10/14: Both Ranger Andrew and I were all the way south at Saratoga Gap, investigating a report of wood smoke in the area, when a call came in for, "any ranger in the area of Purisima Creek Redwoods." Saratoga Gap is absolutely as far away as you can get from Purisima on Skyline Boulevard. Dispatch had a report of a 16-year-old female runner with a broken ankle, unable to walk, on the Purisima Creek Trail. I took the call and headed north. Probably Andrew should have gone, as I am renowned as the pokiest driver in the District. At some point, Kings Mountain Fire came up on the San Mateo County Fire channel telling the Half Moon Bay engine to meet them down at PC05, off Higgins-Purisima Road, outside of Half Moon Bay. I had been headed for the Northridge parking lot on Skyline Boulevard, but now turned down Highway 84, then up Highway 1 and up Higgins-Purisima Road to Purisima Creek's west entrance. My total time from Saratoga Gap was just under one hour, record time for me.

I arrived at Gate PC05 just in time to see Kings Mountain Fire's lime green engine pulling through the gate. Wait a minute! How could they be driving out of the preserve? They must have driven through from Skyline, all the way down the Purisima Creek Trail, including crossing the bridge halfway down that is clearly posted as no longer safe for emergency vehicles, due to its age and decrepitude. There are signs on barricades on both sides of the bridge telling vehicles not to cross, and even a sign at the top of the Purisima Creek Trail where it leaves Skyline Boulevard, warning emergency vehicles that this bridge is out of commission, and they cannot drive through. But, quite clearly, the engine in front of me had done just that.

I was ticked, but had to wait for patient care to wrap up before confronting Val. They had found the injured runner, who had the reported sprained ankle, en route while driving down the trail, and had brought her with them in their truck cab. She was 16 years old, meaning that, as a minor, she could neither give nor decline consent for medical treatment. Further complicating matters, she could only be released to a parent or guardian, and her high school cross-country coach, who might have qualified as a temporary guardian, had forgotten the medical permission forms. There is no cell phone coverage from Gate PC05, so our patient waited with us while the coach drove to Half Moon Bay and collected one of her parents to come out and sign the release form.

I'm not sure if I waited for all of this to happen before confronting the Kings Mountain Fire guys. I asked them who was in charge, and who had been driving. Val answered, defiantly, to both questions, "I am," and "I was." I asked whether he had authorized driving through the preserve, and over the unsafe bridge, to which he responded, "Oh, I didn't see the signs." Right. I said that I would have been in a lot of trouble had I just done the same thing, and told him I would be reporting his misbehavior to my supervisors. Now he got furious, absolutely livid, saying, "Since when does Midpen tell me what to do?" and "I can look out for my own safety!"

I suppose I should have expected his angry and defiant reaction. Val is not the sort to simply admit to his bad decision and sheepishly express remorse. Those were an awkward and uncomfortable few minutes, which left my blood pressure soaring. I hate such confrontations. Again, no big surprise that, when I reported this incident to my supervisor, he laughed grimly and let me know that mine was not the first such run-in with Val. As a result of this incident, however, we did physically barricade the unsafe bridge, making it impossible to drive across.

~~~

My most recent run-in with Val and company had a different bad guy: me. Once again I was in Purisima, in the Northridge lot, parked just inside of Gate PC01, stocking maps and toilet paper, checking the restrooms, and monitoring the jam-packed parking lot on a beautiful, sunny, Sunday afternoon. The lot was full and visitors were parked all up and down Skyline Boulevard. There was no place left for me to park anywhere else near the restroom, and, as long as I was near-by, it didn't matter that my truck was blocking the gate into the preserve.

Photo by Emma Shelton
Long tailed weasel

Then my friend Emma unexpectedly showed up and wanted to take me down the Northridge Trail a little way and show me the spot where, a month or two before, she had seen a dead long-tailed weasel. These tiny animals, about 10-to-12 inches long including the tail, are a rare and endangered species. She said she had hidden the corpse in some ferns near the trail and we were eager to see if we could find the skeleton. But what was I to do about my truck?

This was the end of February of the wettest winter in California in 120 years, and the roads and trails were just drying out from weeks of rain. We hadn't been able to drive a regular patrol truck out of the parking lot and down the Northridge Trail for months. Since sometime the previous November, motorized transport into the preserve had required an ATV. I reasoned that, if I snugged my truck into the bushes enough such that an ATV could squeeze between it and the trail sign, it wouldn't matter if I were technically blocking the gate, in clear violation of the posted sign.

Twenty minutes later, Emma and I were happily poking around in the ferns looking for a tiny, fragile skeleton, without success, when a call came in for "any ranger near Purisima Creek Redwoods, Northridge Trail." Oh dear. Now what should I do? Should I continue on down the Northridge Trail on foot looking for the patient, or hurry back up and get my truck? The patient was reported to be an 18-year-old male suffering from heat exhaustion on the Northridge Trail. This patient was most likely simply going to need a ride out, I thought. It was a warm day, but not hot. This guy was probably just tired and dehydrated. I better go get my truck.

So, I started speeding back up the hill (sorry, Emma) only to hear on the radio, that Kings Mountain Fire was stuck at the gate, which was blocked by a Midpen patrol truck. Damn it! Now the whole world would know of my transgression. I was sweating bullets now, moving as fast as I could, when suddenly Kings Mountain Fire's lime green engine came swerving around the corner toward me. What? I thought they were stuck at the gate. I couldn't understand how they'd gotten past Dumbo, but here they were, and then they actually stopped, and let me pile in the cab with Val.

Val must have enjoyed watching me squirm as he chewed me out for blocking the gate. I was so clearly in the wrong that it didn't seem appropriate to attempt to explain or justify my actions. I didn't even venture to ask how they had managed to get around my truck; obviously they had squeezed past. The trail turned out to be completely drivable, not muddy at all, so that defense was gone. We found our guy, a pudgy, out-of-shape-looking teenage boy who was feeling fine by this point and just wanted a ride out, which we provided. San Mateo County Fire paramedics met us back up at the parking lot and had the patient sign an AMA (Against Medical Advice) form.

I was expecting Val might want to get in another couple digs at me, so I was startled when he climbed into their rig's driver's seat and started to drive away. Then, as he came past where I was still standing in the parking lot, he paused, leaned out the window, and said to me, "So, we're even now, right?" He might be human after all.

Photo by Jessica Lucas
Me at Skyline Field Office, My Last Day, 12/17/2018

Final Ranger Frances:
Out the Door, 10-7 O.D.

Journal entry 2/23/16: I went over to Big Dipper Ranch, Russian Ridge, thinking I'd go check out the pond on the edge of the Gunther Life Estate, more or less straight up the hill from Cindy's house. Turned out she was home, and she accompanied me. It was raining lightly the whole time and the roads were a muddy mess from the cows, but it was fun seeing the little pond, which has a ramshackle old pool house and a funny little pier. Mostly I enjoyed talking to Cindy. She and I are the same age, started at the District at the same time, have sons the same age, and share a lot of interests and activities. It was good to hear her thoughts about retirement. She pointed out that you shouldn't give away your intentions too soon because from that point on, you're seen as a lame duck. Good point. Hadn't thought of that. She wants to work part time, but wants to retain her housing. Hmmm…

Journal entry 10/22/16: I think I have decided to retire and I don't want to talk to anyone about it yet, so maybe just write about it. Strangely enough, I'm already in mourning for my job, already bemoaning how much I'm so going to miss saying, "I'm a ranger." That rings of competence, fitness, and excitement, versus saying, "I'm retired," which rings of incompetence, age, and futility. So, am I reluctant to retire because I am proud and vain? Probably. This job, like most jobs, confers a degree of status, and I'd be lying if I said I wasn't going to miss that. I need something respectable and empowering to do when I retire. David, my husband, hiked the PCT (Pacific Crest Trail) when he retired and could no longer say, "I work for USGS." As my old friend and District volunteer Ulf Stauber once said, "Being a volunteer carries no status. You get no respect. You are 'just' a volunteer."

Journal entry 11/12/16: I turned in a "pre-retirement" 457 pre-tax adjustment form that will increase the amount coming out of each paycheck by $1,000. Having done this, I must retire by 4/2/19, but can retire earlier. Am I feeling sad and lonely because I am discouraged about my job and the District, or is it my thoughts of leaving that depress me?

Journal entry 8/9/17: I just let the cat out of the bag. I was doing the cite run, one of my least favorite tasks, and happened to be just outside Tom's office door down at AO2. Chris and he were there chatting with the door open, and I thought, "What the heck, let's get this over with," so I waited for their attention, then announced my retirement. It was gratifying to immediately get a warm hug from Tom, and Chris reportedly put out a complementary email to the whole District, but I haven't seen it yet. I'm still in shock. I mostly feel sad, so sad. Why did I do that? And yet, I do not at all want to retract my decision.

I've been thinking about retiring at the end of this year since the end of last year, but now it is suddenly all too real. I wasn't going to tell everyone quite so soon, but then I got an email from Cindy a couple days ago saying she was about to announce her retirement, with a date of December 18th. Did I want to go out together? I had had the 20th in mind, but the 18th seemed just as good. Cindy's companionship helped nudge me out of my inertia. I guess I needed that little bit of help to temper the pain of this first little cut in my bond with the District. One great thing about retiring with Cindy is that we can plan the party together, a domain in which she excels and I suck.

As ever, when attempting to answer the "why" question to myself, I was struggling for answers. I could certainly have kept working. No one was forcing me out. I still mostly enjoyed my job. I didn't have anything else I was longing to do with my life, and no big plans. And yet, this seemed the right thing to do. I definitely wanted to get out while I was still enjoying the job, not wait until I was sick of it. Would that ever happen? I wanted to leave before my co-workers came to see me as a worthless old fuddy-duddy, hopelessly inept and useless. I think I have escaped that fate as well.

Maybe it was the fire at INE the previous month that had made me honestly question my fitness for the job. As much as I felt like a fifth wheel stuck guarding the Chestnut Trail I realized that I was dreading the possibility of having to help with actual firefighting, doing hose lays and digging line. I was physically incapable of doing it, of doing my job. I didn't like feeling that way.

Of course some co-workers joked that they had known I wouldn't last long once the computers went into the patrol trucks. The computers were just the tip of the iceberg of technology-driven change. I felt so disconnected from the direction the District was heading (bigger, fancier, more hierarchical, with a less concise mission) and even somewhat disconnected from co-workers, having lost touch with people at FFO and AO as the District ballooned outward. I suppose everyone occasionally feels overlooked and unimportant, like their observations and opinions are completely disregarded, but I'd started to feel that way a lot.

~~~

Retirement Speech: given at Picchetti Winery 12/12/2017. Cindy Roessler, Sue Scheckman, (the District's general counsel) and I had a joint retirement party. It's not every ranger who has the District Board of Directors show up for her retirement party—thank you to Sue.

I've had a great time as a Midpen ranger, and I would stay on if my body wasn't starting to object to the physical parts of the job. Some friends tell me that I am too young to retire. I respond, "It's not that I'm leaving too soon, it's that I got here too late." I would certainly have been here for 30 years, like Sango, Tom, Kerry, Michael or Dennis, had I only landed this job 15 years earlier. Furthermore, I'm not leaving. No, don't panic. I'm turning in my badge, but I'm not going anywhere. You're not getting rid of me that easily! I'll be moving to the volunteer department, seeing what trouble I can stir up for Paul and Renee.

By far the best part of this job was the time I spent off trail on foot, exploring the backcountry, both alone and with other rangers. I loved poking around out there, running into remnants of long-ago people's activities, and maybe a few not-so-long-ago and not-so-legal activities. Some adversity like rain, steep hillsides, poison oak, and a dash of uncertainty about whether I ought to be there at all, only added to the fun. If it was totally safe, it wasn't really an adventure, was it?

A ranger leaves nothing behind to show for her efforts. The visitors and violators I have contacted over the years will not remember me in any personal way. It's a Leave No Trace job, and I'm okay with that. I leave only footprints and take only memories. I leave nothing behind to show that I was ever here, just some old Rangerchick stories. I leave the job of protecting this land to the eager, young rangers of the future, and trust that they will come to love the job and the land as much as I have.

There are some aspects of my work that I did take some pride in, such as my role as a CPR and EMR instructor, where I always favored ditching the PowerPoint and inserting skills practices and scenarios. I've also prided myself on a thorough knowledge of "what's out there," of knowing both the human and natural history of the land I patrolled. I contend that rangers should work to protect the land, not just to serve the visitors. My curiosity about the areas I explored, and the chance to share that wonder with like-minded co-workers has added immeasurably to my ranger experience. I also always enjoyed giving "ranger talks," whether to Deer Hollow Farm campers, at District outreach events, or to casual visitors. I am an enthusiastic proponent of the District's mission.

I look forward to being a District preserve partner and docent, pulling weeds and leading hikes, two of my favorite things. I hope to spend more time hiking, camping, and backpacking with my husband and others.

When I retire, I will not miss being on top of Windy Hill or Hunters Point on freezing cold evenings in the fog and wind citing afterhours violators, or dealing with fake "service animals," and "mobility devices." I will not miss PowerPoint presentations, on-line forms and trainings, the cite run, the weekly update, the twice-annual evaluations and all the other activities that took me away from where I truly wanted to be: out on patrol.

I will miss being on top of Windy Hill or Hunters Point on warm, sultry evenings walking in the moonlight pretending to look for afterhours violators, but actually just out strolling along in the moonlight. I will miss having access to the closed areas, and nailing naughty neighbors encroaching onto public lands or bad boy bikers riding on illegal trails. I'll miss helping confused, angry, injured, lost and hurting people. Most of all I'll miss being an integral part of something bigger and longer lasting than myself.

~~~

How is retirement? (Email sent to former co-workers)

It's now the end of January 2018, and I've been retired for five weeks. I'm still uncomfortable with the idea that I am done working, and not just between jobs. I enjoyed working and, if I were to find some truly wonderful form of part-time employment, I might just take it. I'm sure that part of my discomfort is due to my reluctance to see myself as an "old retired person."

All my pre-existing extra-curricular activities have expanded to fill the additional time. Hidden Villa now appears on the schedule every week, rather than every other. Getting to swimming and yoga is no longer a problem. There's the book group and the writing group. I've signed up for another volunteer job with Sierra Club National Outings, and am due to meet my first twice-a-week student through Project Read at the Menlo Park Library. Docent training for MROSD doesn't start until April, but I've signed up for a bunch of preserve partner volunteer projects in the meantime. There are still some blank days on my calendar, but I'm sure I can take care of that. What with housework, yard work, and even trying to do something with my husband now and then, I don't think too much free time will be a problem.

Do I miss being an MROSD ranger? Well, of course. Absolutely. I loved that job. It was one of the highlights of my life, and I am proud of my service record, and of my reputation.

It was a great time, and I'm sad it's over, but it was time to go. As much as I can't say, "I'm a ranger," I can always say, "I was a ranger." I tell friends that I would have stayed with the District for 30 years if I had just gotten there sooner. But the job really isn't cut out for 60-year-olds, and I'm almost there. As Mary Poppins once said, "All good things must come to an end."

Although I have been out on many hikes in the last month, I do miss being out on the land all day every day. That was one of the greatest benefits of the job, seeing all the sunrises and sunsets, watching the days pass, the mornings, noontimes, and evenings, day after day. Now I can't imagine wasting the gasoline to drive up to Skyline or down to Umunhum every day. When I was working, I had to, and that made it okay. Yes, I miss the daily intimate contact with nature, the landscape, the weather, and the wild inhabitants.

I also miss all of you guys, my former co-workers. I got such a nice send-off between the retirement party, the Board proclamation, the farewell hike down Harrington Creek, and, finally, everyone hopping on the radio to wish me well when I logged off for the last time. I had tears in my eyes. It was very moving. It means a lot to me to know that I left in your good graces. Some of you I may never see again. Some of you I surely will. Time hurries on and our time together will slowly recede into memory. Years from now, when I find myself thinking of you and our by-gone days together, I can imagine you will also be remembering me with similar fondness and nostalgia.

Photo by Frances Reneau
Off trail in Harrington Creek, La Honda OSP, with co-workers during my final week.

Proclamation of the

MIDPENINSULA REGIONAL OPEN SPACE DISTRICT

GIVEN TO HONOR THE RETIREMENT OF

Frances Reneau

WHEREAS, Frances Reneau has been an employee of the Midpeninsula Regional Open Space District for over 24 years and is retiring; and

WHEREAS, Frances fulfilled a number of roles with the District including Seasonal Open Space Technician, Docent Coordinator, Farm Maintenance Worker, and District Ranger; and

WHEREAS, Frances has shown tremendous honesty and professional integrity as well as demonstrating a deep caring for open space and the people with whom she works; and

WHEREAS, Frances has a passion for patrolling and exploring District lands especially on foot and in areas where there is poison oak; and

WHEREAS, Frances has demonstrated the ability to remain calm and in control at numerous emergency and law enforcement incidents; and

WHEREAS, Frances has personally trained many of the District's staff in CPR and emergency medical care, and has raised the standards and professionalism of the instruction provided to staff, resulting in lives being saved and injuries being minimized; and

WHEREAS, Frances is a trusted colleague who is well appreciated and respected among her co-workers, supervisors, and managers; and

WHEREAS, Frances has shared her passion for open space lands, wildlife, and natural wonders through excellent interpretive work with visitors of all ages; and

WHEREAS, Frances has maintained the highest levels of personal fitness and been an example to staff; and

WHEREAS, Frances has reflected the true essence of being a generalist ranger by continuously developing her maintenance, interpretive, emergency response, and law enforcement skills; and

WHEREAS, Frances will be greatly missed by her colleagues and friends at the District;

NOW THEREFORE, I, Larry Hassett, President of the Board of Directors of the Midpeninsula Regional Open Space District, along with my colleagues on the Board of Directors, unanimously and enthusiastically congratulate Frances on a well-deserved retirement, look back on her accomplishments with gratitude and awe, and wish her all the very best for the future.

Larry Hassett

LARRY HASSETT, BOARD PRESIDENT

Made in the USA
Middletown, DE
17 July 2021